“C[illegible] the art's greatest teachers together, both past and present, into one compelling ‘dialogue’, Kallas delivers an excellent insight into our craft with bogglingly useful exercises and the warmth and passion of a truly gifted writer and teacher. Of the many fine books on screenwriting one might have in their library ... this is among the best.”

David N. Weiss, co-writer, *Shrek 2* and Vice President of the Writers Guild of America, West

Creative Screenwriting

Understanding Emotional Structure

Christina Kallas

Translated by John William Howard

palgrave
macmillan

First published 2010 by
PALGRAVE MACMILLAN

Palgrave Macmillan in the UK is an imprint of Macmillan Publishers Limited, registered in England, company number 785998, of Houndmills, Basingstoke, Hampshire RG21 6XS.

Palgrave Macmillan in the US is a division of St Martin's Press LLC, 175 Fifth Avenue, New York, NY 10010.

Palgrave Macmillan is the global academic imprint of the above companies and has companies and representatives throughout the world.

Palgrave® and Macmillan® are registered trademarks in the United States, the United Kingdom, Europe and other countries

ISBN 978–0–230–22140–6 hardback
ISBN 978–0–230–22141–3 paperback

This book is printed on paper suitable for recycling and made from fully managed and sustained forest sources. Logging, pulping and manufacturing processes are expected to conform to the environmental regulations of the country of origin.

A catalogue record for this book is available from the British Library.

Library of Congress Cataloging-in-Publication Data

Kallas, Christina.
[Kreatives Drehbuchschreiben. English]
Creative screenwriting : understanding emotional structure / Christina Kallas ; translated by John William Howard.
p. cm.
Includes bibliographical references.
ISBN 978–0–230–22141–3 (pbk.)
1. Motion picture authorship. I. Title.
PN1996.K21513 2010
808.2'3—dc22

2010010810

10 9 8 7 6 5 4 3 2 1
19 18 17 16 15 14 13 12 11 10

Printed in China

to Alex

Contents

THE MIDDLE: TECHNIQUES OF CREATIVE SCREENWRITING 75

THE END: APPLICATION OF CREATIVE SCREENWRITING AND EMOTIONAL STRUCTURE TO THE COMPLETE SCREENPLAY 151

Acknowledgements

This book, like any book I guess, is a work in progress. It is, also like any other book, based on the work of others. I therefore wish to thank my teachers, especially Frank Daniel and Linda Seger, for their deep insight into the art and craft of screenwriting – much of this is based on what I have learned from them. I then want to thank all those who drove me to the brink of despair over the years as a screenwriter, who caused me to rethink my ideas and my stories, and who occasionally made me rewrite until I did not know what I had ever started out to do. In so doing, they helped me discover what was important to me and what was not.

A teacher learns most of all from her students; so many thanks are owed to all of my students in the German Film and Television Academy in Berlin and in the Cinema Department of the Aristotle University of Thessaloniki. I especially want to thank the following for their permission to use their ideas and papers in conjunction with this book: Ana-Felicia Scutelnicu for the text of "Every Ending tells a Story," Chris Roth for "The Story of a Sound," and Ariane Pollo for "A Scene Seeks the Reason for its Existence" – which was based on one of the wonderful short stories of Wolfgang Kohlhaase. I thank him for his permission to my student to use his short story as an inspiration – and for an unbelievably hilarious dialogue we had in that context. Craft is surely there to help us take certain steps into uncertainty!

This book started as an excellent translation by John Howard of my German book *Kreatives Drehbuchschreiben*. Apart from thanking him for the wonderful work, I thank him for the process and for making me think about the importance of words, the fine nuances between translating to the writer or to the reader, about the art and the challenges of translating, the evolution of language and about the soul each of the different languages expresses. Being a writer who constantly struggles with her many languages, I treasure what I have learned; and I was grateful for the opportunity to revisit my text in the most naked of all languages, which to me is English. Thank you also to Craig Batty for his insightful and careful reading of the first draft of this manuscript and to Betty Kaklamanidou for the meticulous preparation of the book's index.

The German language book took a step beyond my Greek book, *Screenplay, the Art of Invention and Narration for the Cinema,* just as the English language book has taken a step further in thought than the German book. In essence, they are three different books, each going a bit further and deeper than its predecessor, but basically all three presenting the theory of emotional structure and the method of creative screenwriting. The creative screenwriting method is based on my experience working with other methods over the years, as a screenwriter and on my testing creative writing techniques in class, while constantly adapting and adjusting them to the requirements of screenwriting. The emotional structure theory is basically unprecedented, and I would not have felt confident enough to develop it further if it were not for the help of a few daring and supportive minds with whom I have shared inspiring conversations, some over time and some while revisiting the material during translation. I particularly wish to thank Dagmar Benke, whose memory I will always cherish, Nikos Panayotopoulos, Razvan Radulescu, Christina Lazaridi, Guillermo Arriaga and, most of all, Milcho Manchevski.

Anyone who has children knows that they never stop teaching us to tell stories. I thank my son Alex, who was the first to "play a part" in every exercise in the book, for the wisdom of his early years and for having all that insatiable curiosity, which never lets me lose focus.

Prologue

Why creative screenwriting?

In order to break the rules, one must know them – but what if the best way to learn the rules were to break them?

We in Europe have had to wait a long time for the renaissance of screenwriting. Most of the educational institutions, whether film schools or cinema departments and courses at universities, completed the transition to the inclusion of the screenwriting faculty in their curriculum as late as the 1990s. The same is true for the financing of screenplay development, which is so important as a foundation to the existence of cinema screenwriters, at least in Europe.

But why is that? In order to understand this, one should address the difference in attitude towards film culture in general. What we could call the international cultural order was long dominated by Europe, in the eyes of both the Europeans themselves and others. This order, nonetheless, was disrupted at the start of the twentieth century, and since the early 1950s, America has replaced Europe as the dominant force. Furthermore, whereas culture in Europe is supervised by the state, there is no ministry of culture in the United States. This difference is more than symbolic; in fact, it reveals two models: the American one and the European one. American culture continues to exert a growing force of attraction on the world, from which the Europeans are not excluded: to put it provocatively, one could say that every European has two cultures; her/his own national culture, and an American not European culture. Cultural funding and film funding in particular is thus part of the European model, perhaps with the aim in mind of supporting or even creating the idea of a European culture – but mainly in order to protect the individual culture of each European state.

Having said that, whatever form European or American inspiration takes, the economics of culture today pose a threat to creativity, with screenwriting being at the heart of such endangered creativity, both in

American motion pictures and in European films. So as soon as European filmmakers and producers realized (again) the importance of screenwriting, almost all of the film funds – an institution so important to the European film industry because of the fragmented nature of its markets (whether public or private, national or international) began to allocate part of their budgets to so-called development funding.[2]

At the same time, a series of seminars and continuing education measures were initiated at the national as well as the international level. The weekend screenwriting seminar, and the flood of published screenwriting literature associated with it, made up the third wave of the writing fever after the success of Goldman in the 1970s and the spec boom in the 1980s. For Europe, that had just reinforced the idea of coproduction as the answer to American film dominance in the cinemas, the third wave was also the decisive one. Europe discovered screenwriting anew and the professional training that went with it. American screenwriters and screenwriting professors acted as tutors – they brought Aristotle back to Europe. They supported the European screenwriters, the novices as well as the established writers who finally wanted to know if they were doing something wrong,[3] because they had lost their audience to the American motion picture industry. The flood of seminars, or the "seminarization," the ironic way one describes this former trend today, had positive as well as negative consequences: perhaps a positive result is that the profession of the screenwriter has been rediscovered – accompanied by some long overdue respect and by more influence by the screenwriter on film politics as well as on legal questions concerning rights. The negative result was the setting up of rules that govern successful screenwriting that were disseminated through seminars and books. At the same time, new professions sprang up around screenplay development, beginning with specialized dramaturges and script consultants all the way to producers and story editors. European producers discovered the art of firing and hiring a writer and of commissioning re-writes by different writers; but what's more, powerful normative rules began to be employed, often as a tool against writers and later as an argument against understanding screenwriting as an autonomous literary form. Writing by numbers came into play, even in Europe.

What does writing by numbers mean? What are the rules and who set them up? The dominant (and the majority of) screenplay theories were and still are based on Aristotle's *Poetics*, even if some of them utilize a different terminology and present different approaches. It is time to put these terms next to each other and compare them. The comparative investigation of diverse structural models and of their suitability for the screenwriter (and not the analytical writer, for example) and their adaptation to current practice is just one of the goals in this book.

Why creative screenwriting? It probably sounds like an aphorism, but inspiration can get lost in the shuffle of so much know-how. Knowledge is necessary; but unfortunately the more we know and the more we learn, the more we begin to control and tame our imagination. It is Einstein who said, "imagination is more important than knowledge" – and this is doubly so with writing. Can one teach imagination, artistic sensibility and ideas? I think so.

This book is based on more than ten years' experience teaching a method that has slowly developed into a "method of creative screenwriting." The catalyst for this was provided during teaching at the German Film and Television Academy in Berlin, when I was teaching a group of students in their third year, which I had been in charge of two years earlier at the beginning of their studies at the Academy. The difference was alarming. It was instantly clear to me that the same students I had gotten to know two years earlier and who back then were full of ideas and stories they absolutely wanted to tell, were now "dried up" after only a few semesters of professional training. They did not have anything left to tell (or so they believed) and their imagination and enthusiasm had vanished. They had lost their "innocence," an innocence that is essential for artistic creativity. "Critical thinking destroyed their creative thinking," as Frank Daniel used to say.[4] Anyone who writes knows the name for this condition, "writer's block" – a creative inhibition. I decided to work against this loss of inspiration and to treat my students as though they were suffering from writer's block – a condition I had experienced myself.

I began to formulate and to teach my belief that we all have imagination, a unique artistic sensibility and an inexhaustible well of ideas; and that there are ways to awaken and activate them. I devoted myself to the research and development of a method with exactly this in mind – designed for the special needs of the highly specialized field of screenwriting that was mostly taught from the vantage point of film analysis and not of inspiration. My ambition was to develop a method that would help my students regain their original state of inspiration. My conviction was and is that teaching a good technique of screenwriting should be accompanied from the beginning with the development of inspiration and ideas along with activating the imagination and the artistic sensibility. This book, then, began initially as a collection of notes and exercises for students. The techniques and the exercises that I describe stem in part from completely different scientific and artistic departments and are the result of experimenting over several years.

"Great scripts do not spring from a vacuum. They come from writers who are willing to explore darkness, rough roads, and confrontations in their journey towards transformation. This is where drama resides," writes Linda Seger.[5] Writing is just as hard and deserves just as much respect as open-heart surgery or sending a probe to Mars or splitting the atom, says Linda. The novelist and screenwriter John Irving once stated that screenwriting is the most difficult form of writing to master. The great theoretician of the theater, Gustav Freytag, said something similar about drama in general, which he viewed as the art form that places the greatest demands on the poet.[6] Despite this, opinions are divided about whether the screenplay is an autonomous literary form.[7] The *auteur* theory posits that the screenplay has only one single reason for being: to be made into a film.[8] Conversely, others – predominately in television – see directing as a purely technical process of filming the screenplay, the film being a creation of the writer and not the director.

The truth probably lies somewhere in the middle, since "one can certainly make a bad film from a good screenplay but never a good film from a bad screenplay."[9] That quote is ascribed to Billy Wilder, just as is his classic observation, that "there are three important things in a movie: the screenplay, the screenplay and the screenplay." The director Jean-Pierre Melville once said that the success of a film is determined as follows: 50% by the choice of the story, 50% the screenplay, and 50% the actors, 50% the score, 50% the director of photography and so on. When there is a mistake with one of these things, you risk 50% of the film. Perhaps Frank Daniel said it best, "Scriptwriting ... is filmmaking on paper"[10] – and as such, an autonomous art form.

While working the method, I simultaneously set out to seek, approach, find and examine the qualities and the characteristics of a screenplay that make it succeed in moving us, that is, succeed as a work of art; and this even when the screenplay refuses to follow traditional rules of the narrative and comply with the usual formats. For that task, the approach to screenwriting structure from an emotional/thematic standpoint rather than the classical plot structure model and the presentation of new ways that screenwriters have used and are using to transcend classical structure so that they can liberate themselves from the stifling one-size-fits-all model, was important. I realized that screenwriting is a living literary form, a living work of art and – what is more – a work of art still in progress. As a matter of fact, screenwriting is the literary form that corresponds most to how we perceive the world today and as such is persistently experimenting with different perspectives, chronological order and narrative concepts. Complex narratives create films, which upon repeated viewings can provide the viewer – each individual viewer – with a different experience. Screenwriting becomes more and more the creation of a conversation with the viewer and at the same time the audience.

To honor this I needed different tools than the ones I used until then. Slowly, a new structural theory emerged that seemed to be the pendant to a creative screenwriting method, the "emotional structure theory" – strangely enough based among others on a chapter from Aristotle's *Poetics*, and in particular a chapter which has been ignored until now by screenwriting scholars. I would like to consider the emotional structure theory as a first step to something new, something that needs more thought and contributions from different writers and sources. What's more, this book is not here to guarantee success if instructions are followed properly. It is the narrative that must find its form and not the other way around, so each story needs to be approached on its own merit.

It is not a secret that one may learn theories better if one puts them into practice parallel to learning them. Therefore, this book has become a mixture of theory, examples of analysis and creative writing exercises. Like a screenplay, it is intended to guide the reader/writer on his or her journey. Add that screenwriting consists of more than the first draft, and that it is a literary form that lives from revisions. Writing means rewriting – and in order to rewrite one first needs to understand what one has written and how one can improve it. The creative screenwriting method is suitable for the first draft of the screenplay – for the idea, the inspiration, the discovery of the story, for thematic riches and emotional depth. Schiller once wrote to Goethe,[11] "The more I think about what I am doing and about the way the Greeks treated their tragedies, the more I realize that the *cardo rei*, the most important thing, in art is the discovery of the poetic idea." Goethe answered, "Everything stands or falls with how good the idea is." Screenwriting theory and the ability to analyze are, on the other hand, necessary to acquire the correct assessment of the idea and to approach the revisions. As Linda Seger says, chaos is the beginning of all creative work – but not necessarily its end.

The art of creative writing

Creative writing was taught long before it came to be called by that name. Predecessors have published their writing secrets in manifestos: Schiller in his program of the distinction between naive and sentimental art, Edgar Alan Poe in his art of combination, Emile Zola in his naturalistic novels, Ludwig Boerne in "How to Become an Original Artist in Three Days," André Breton in his first "Surrealist Manifesto," Novalis in his romantic technique, Marinetti in his "Futurist Manifesto" and Raymond Queneau in his "Exercises in Style."[12]

However, in its modern form it is wrongly thought to be an American invention. Creative writing had indeed become part of the curriculum in American universities first, as early as 1949. Currently around 400 American universities and colleges offer a Master of Fine Arts Degree in Creative Writing. Many successful authors have an MFA. Raymond Carver (the first big "success story" of creative writing programs) graduated in the 1960s from the Iowa Writer's Workshop, still considered by most to be the most renowned writing program. The dissertation required to complete these programs is called a "creative thesis" and must constitute a "substantial manuscript" such as a novel, a book of poetry or a short story collection – but never a screenplay.

Corresponding courses of study in European universities remain, if they exist at all, in an early stage of development. The technique of creative writing is commonly treated with benign neglect, often with scorn. As it once was in America, writing is seen as a process that is inherently creative and cannot be taught; either one has it or one does not. This view is no longer in step with the times – there is enough scientific research available and enough experience gathered from creative writing studies to lead to a contrary conclusion. If painting and music can be taught, why not writing?

Since the beginning of the 1970s, a number of papers have been published that present the interpretations and teaching methods of creative writing concurrently at odds with each other. One of them stresses the discovery and development of a personal style and as a rule utilizes the "free writing" method.[13] The other one represents the Aristotelian approach (see the Chapter: "The old Struggle between Poetics and Philosophy: It All goes Back to Aristotle) or What we owe Plato and Aristotle," and highlights the methodology of writing, that is, the gathering of ideas, concept building and structure – beginning with the various genres and their influence on the reader.[14] That indeed is closer to the way screenwriting is being taught, a discipline which strangely enough is usually not included in creative writing courses but which is mostly incorporated in film schools. Since the mid-1980s, some representatives who merge both interpretations have finally surfaced – an approach clearly best suited to the creative screenwriting method.[15]

The goal of creative writing is to activate a greater percentage of the potential of the brain than we normally use by stimulating our creativity.[16] "Creativity" will be defined as a synonym for "aberrant thinking," which enables us to break the forms and patterns of experience continuously. To be "creative" means to be at work constantly, to ask questions incessantly, to discover connections and meanings and doubt simple answers, to be in a position to judge autonomously and independently; and last to employ objects and concepts in new ways, to combine existing elements and bring them a step forward.[17]

Research and experience have demonstrated that creativity increases in proportion to the increased use of diverse writing techniques. The technique of creative writing employs all of the usual writing techniques and incessantly experiments with new ones, while it also communicates and assimilates different styles. Automatic writing, for instance, springs from the unconscious, employing both cognitive as well as emotional elements and processes, and these need to be worked at to succeed.

What is most important is quantity – namely as a general goal and as a tool for creative writing.[18] If nothing else, the secret of writing is writing itself. As mentioned before, while the teaching of writing in America can look back at a 100-year-old tradition and although the origins of creative writing can be traced back to European literary tradition, creative writing in Europe, unlike music or the fine arts, is not taught at school – and this happens even though writing is an inseparable part of the development of the human personality; even though the educational and academic system is based on writing. The closest one gets to learning writing in schools is through text interpretation and analysis – along with grammar and spelling – but not through synthesis (ideation, structure, composition) and certainly not through creative writing.

Another element of great importance in creative writing is the idea of the group. The "Berlin Romantics" and their collective novels, the "Storm Circle" of expressionism with their collective myths along with the famous evening meetings at André Breton's in Marseille, were notable forerunners who have used that idea of the group and turned it into a useful tool for individual creativity.[19] Besides, all modern literary currents seem to have formed schools of writing (see the section on

"The Methods of Creative Screenwriting: Technique and Rules of the Game").

The history of creative writing is not to be separated from Sigmund Freud's dream interpretation, and may have even begun with it. The use of childhood complexes as a source of ideas and emotions and the principle of interpreting dreams (that was decisively developed and thrust in a new direction, primarily by Carl Gustav Jung), have changed the content as well as craft of writing. Expressionism with its technique of mythological imagination, surrealism with automatic writing; Dadaism with "cut up" writing and the various schools of art, have developed production techniques that go beyond free association, surmounted text interpretation and opened the way to word games and experimentation with language and through language with thought and emotion.[20] They were important harbingers of the evolution of the art of creative writing that in the end may be defined in simple words as "playing and experimenting with writing." The word "playing" is more important than it may at first seem.

Our educational system – which is based on the triad of preparation, learning and competition – predominantly stresses criticism and logical thinking.[21] The holy trinity of education, moreover, while useful in many fields of science, is perhaps the greatest enemy of art, because in the end it restricts art. The artist seeks ways to return to the wellspring of inspiration. The artist strives to remain "pure" and "innocent," apart from how many skills or how much knowledge he or she has acquired. What is the right way of looking at this, asks Keith Johnstone.[22] Are children immature adults or are adults repressed children?[23]

Creative thinking is childhood thinking, the thinking of a child that loves to explore, to discover and to have fun. In that sense, the triad of creativity would be exploration, discovery[24] and entertainment – in place of preparation, learning and competition. For art, filmmaking and screenwriting, the return to the world of childhood fantasy is not merely something devoutly to be wished, it is essential.

The idiosyncrasies of audiovisual storytelling

Seen historically, the "mutual enlightenment of the arts,"[25] or the "symbiosis of the arts,"[26] is a topic that was being discussed at length long before the new art form of the cinema raised anew the correlations between the narrative arts, literature and the other arts in both theory and practice.[27] Audiovisual narration exhibits some distinctive features that arise due to the possibilities of using images, sound and music, as well as editing them in different ways to create different meanings. These distinctive features, that is, the fundamental principles of audiovisual narration, comprise the difference between creative writing in general and creative screenwriting in particular. Since we will attend to these fundamental principles in detail in the course of this book (in terms of the theory primarily in the section on "Creative Screenwriting in the Context of Prevailing Theories of Drama and of Screenwriting – a Little Review"), I will limit myself here to a more general context.

First of all, the distinctive features of audiovisual narration entail that the screenwriter cannot or may not write anything that could be transferred to the screen as either image or sound. The use of the word in the context of a voice-over as a somewhat different use of sound is perhaps the only exception possible, one which we will speak of later in more detail (see the section on "The Trick of Failure: The Courage to Fail and the Law of Quantity"). Here it is sufficient to point out that even this way of using language involves a relationship between the image and the sound, since the voice-over is more effective if image and sound provide a contrast. For example, the image can be amusing but the sound or the voice-over can relate something dissimilar to the image being shown – and another, new meaning may arise from the resulting synthesis.

There are different views about how far the screenwriter can go, in describing image and sound; views regarding the amount of instructions to the director and the actors or, for instance, whether and to what extent referring to certain music pieces is "permitted." The more highly detailed the description and the more concrete the vision of the screenwriter, the less room remains for the creative and interpretive contributions of the remaining collaborators, including the director. Regardless of the discussion about whether the screenplay is an autonomous literary genre, it is a valid opinion that in the moment in which it appears on the screen, it becomes an indivisible part of a new work of art – the work of a pair of creators or perhaps even a group of creators. Thus, one may conclude that the screenwriter should indeed leave room for further creative interpretation. The descriptions of image, sound and ways and means of interpretation are significant only if they affect the dramaturgy – and the better the screenplay, the more evident this effect becomes.

On this point, the power of the image and the sound provides a second important clue. The well-known phrase "less is more" is assuredly a generalized bit of wisdom that we will come back to later. Writing means making decisions. And one of the most important decisions a screenwriter faces over and again is what to put on the screen and what to leave off – beginning with the scenes he will select that deal with the time and chronology he will use in his narration up to the moment he decides to start or end a scene.[28] Which details he uses to describe something is also crucial, exactly what to stress and what he wants to say through the dialogue. Some of the most important exercises of creative screenwriting concern the visualization of events and emotions. The classical principle behind it is to remove everything that you will not miss in order to tell the story you really want to tell – and that, as is well known, is no simple thing.

"Less is more" also relates to the dialogue. The formula D – 1/3 = 3D is not only to be understood as a joke: The dialogue, less one-third, becomes three-dimensional. While improvising the scenes in the improvisation exercises, we will learn much about dialogue. It is, for instance, impressive how Spartan and clear the use of the word is in an improvised scene, if the screenwriter clearly states the goal and the status depiction of the characters (see more in the following chapter).

The main topic of all arguments among the creative community of the filmmakers, including almost all of the manifestos in cinema history, was and is the use of image and sound in audiovisual narration. The operative example today is still the Dogma Manifesto, written and distributed by a group of filmmakers close to the ingenious Danish filmmaker Lars von Trier that forbids, among other things, the use of artificial light and music. The goal is to concentrate on the significant part, that is, on the story and the characters. In the case of the Dogma films, the paradoxical phrase "less is more" has once again shown its validity.

The methods of creative screenwriting: Technique and rules of the game

The techniques and exercises presented here are, as already said, the result of experimenting with the research and experience of different scientific and artistic disciplines. Poets and writers in general, scientists and philosophers, psychologists and therapists, journalists and managers have all developed their own tools for creative writing. The selection in this book is limited to those techniques and exercises that are useful for the special art of the screenwriter. The method of creative screenwriting, as with creative writing in general, does not necessarily presuppose the founding of a group. Most of the exercises and techniques suggested here can be used singly without recourse to a group.

Where possible, however, and at any rate in the context of a course, group work is desirable.

The participants of the well-known Group 47, for instance, met regularly in order to read manuscripts to each other and criticize them.[29] Group 47 required that the writer read from his or her own script. This is slightly different with creative screenwriting. One often works on scenes, and when these are presented, the respective writer will hand out the parts to other participants and will pick someone to read the action segments. Alternatively, he decides who will read the narrator's voice if the manuscript is written as prose. This kind of presentation is particularly effective, since the writer can gain some distance to his writing, at the same time hear, and see whether the passage being read actually works: The "actors" may trip over unnatural, badly structured or interminable sentences that are unsuitable for spoken dialogue.

Another technique that presupposes a group is improvisation. In discussing how to write a scene, improvisation becomes more and more important. But what exactly are we talking about, especially in this context?

Aristotle explained (*Poetics* 1455a, 32) that:

> two types of people share the prolific imagination suitable to poetic creation: The intelligent ones who are adaptable and possess by their nature the rare ability to slip into another person's situation and are therefore in a position to show the tragic case quite plainly, as well as the manic ones that, because they lose control of their consciousness, intuitively communicate with the situation of the other, and in fact of their ecstasy (this surely is the source of the Platonic attitude towards poetic creation).[30]

"Those who by their nature have this special inclination have created poetry out of improvisation by developing this (meaning: the improvisation) gradually." (*Poetics* 1448b, 21–23.) "Those with this special inclination" are for Aristotle the "intelligent ones," that is, they belong to the first type described. At the same time, Aristotle considers improvisation as the loss of logical control. Although it is clear that his statements partly contradict themselves, Aristotle suggests that art is as learnable as any other craft and introduces the term "improvisation" as a kind of genesis of poetry.

Improvisation – a particularly constructive way to increase the riches of creativity – has played an important role in music and dance plus the performing arts for a long time: from *Commedia dell' Arte* to the

"Happenings" of the Living Theatre. Improvisation plays a particularly important role in the method of the Russian Theater reformer Stanislavski, which also became the basis of Lee Strasberg's method,[31] as well as for Keith Johnstone, who in the 1960s elevated improvisation to high art as a member of the English Writers' Group and later with the theater ensemble "The Theater Machine;" and, among other things, discovered how to use it as a way to write.

Using the method of creative screenwriting as introduced here, the participants improvise a specific scene, in the way the writer must have imagined it before he wrote it down. In the following chapters, some improvisation scenes from my seminars are provided to demonstrate how this works. The screenwriter will select the "actors" and describe the most important character traits as well as the goal of the scene (if he is not able to articulate a goal, then this is important information). He will specify the status of the characters at the beginning and at the end of the scene, in addition to the premise of the scene. This means that before we start we will have answered the questions regarding the status of the character and the action.[32]

Improvisation is, as Johnstone says, like walking backwards. You know who you are and what has happened, but you cannot see where you are going. If one of the "actors" does not know something (because the actor, for instance, is intended to receive this information in the course of the scene), then he or she may leave the room while this information is given to the other actors. From this moment on only one thing remains: enjoy. The result, in any case, will be impressive and often surprising, even for the screenwriter who has provided us with the characters and the premise. The characters and their respective relationships, as well as other elements of the narrative, will often evolve into something different from what the writer had in mind and from what he will subsequently read out loud. For this to work it is important that nobody but the writer knows what has actually been written down beforehand.

Another set of rules concerns what I have come to call the "Game of Aporia" or the game of wondering – this technique corresponds in turn to what I call the system of two questions, with which I will deal in detail later. The dialectic questioning of a scene or a text (a technique that is particularly effective when used for the climax of a story) is based on the familiar Socratic Method. As in that method, if the game of wondering is played out properly, the screenwriter will discover the answer within himself. This procedure is certainly time intensive and assumes a certain amount of experience on the part of the person who co-ordinates the questioning or actually does the questioning. When Plato referred to the "long way" that signified a "great effort," he was talking about the "way" or "journey" (*Poetics* 532e, 3) of verbal dialectic.

The dialectic partner in these talks produces his arguments in the course of personal discussions with the writer, but at the same time, he uses them according to the expertise he possesses concerning the soul and the subject. For the dialectician there is just one obligation he observes that is as indispensable and binding as a religious oath: to convey "the things of value to him, only if the cognitive and moral conditions for their reception are present."[33] Even though the dialectic partner may recognize the solution to a problem relatively soon, sometimes even right at the beginning of the conversation, the explanation and presentation of this solution will often be ineffective, if the writer does not "discover" such a solution on his own.

In the course of the dialectic convergence with a text while in a group, the participants will ask the writer questions about the psychology and motivations of the characters and, as a consequence, any gaps or uncertainties in the story, the scene or screenplay will surface. Before we come to the questions, I mostly want to know from the listeners how they would sum up the story in one sentence. Such a request is usually asked from the writer and every writer will know how difficult an exercise it is. In this case, the writer gets to experience how his initial audience would sum up his story. This frequently comes as a shock. The emphasis and interpretation of the things heard and read is often very dissimilar to what the writer intended. Often it is impossible to relate the story in a sentence, or holes appear in the plot and the motivation. Certainly, the problems become evident and easily understandable. The goal of this kind of summarization, as well as the questioning that follows, is for the writer to determine, that is to the extent he has committed to paper what he has had in his mind and soul. Generally, the answer is "very little," especially if it is the first draft of a story or scene. Not least, the method helps us to find out what has touched our first audience's heart and mind, and why.

Transposing our thoughts and emotions to paper is difficult in any form of writing, even more so in writing screenplays where the power of the image and of the editing is so crucial and often leads to results that at times are the exact opposite of those intended. Reading, improvising and discussing a key scene or a text written for an audiovisual narration makes it possible to test it in a phase in which our most important goal has to be to find the heart, that is, the substance of the story. Close co-operation is of the greatest importance during this kind of process. In creative work, we need each other. The art of cinema clearly resembles soccer: Whoever kicks the goal, it is the team that wins. Here it does not matter who is better than the other, who learns fastest or is better prepared. The winner is the one who brings out the best in his teammates in order for the team to win the game.

The creative process does not license theoretical discourse or criticism, because criticism creates angst and angst creates tension. Tension in turn hamstrings creativity.[34] "When fantasy arrives, leave all doors open," said Schiller. However, criticism (negative as well as ostensible constructive criticism, which is a somewhat paradoxical concept) shuts all the doors again.

That does not mean a screenwriter will not experience criticism or that he should not learn to deal with criticism and to accept those elements that could be useful to him. The screenwriter is the one who, among all writers, draws the most critical fire from various directions. To add to the confusion, analysis of the narrative and dramaturgical "problems" or "issues" of a screenplay do not lead all interpreters to the same solutions. If you were to put ten experienced screenwriters or dramaturges in one room, they would probably agree about what and where the problem was, but there would be as many solutions offered as the number of people in the room.[35] One of the most important and helpful pieces of advice I ever got came from Frank Daniel, who was teaching that what is important about criticism is not necessarily the proposed solution but the place in the story where the criticism is focused. Linda Seger, like Frank Daniel, preached that there is only one correct solution for each screenwriter. The dialectic encounter with the text I am proposing here has exactly this in view: to identify the problematic places and to find the right solution, the one and only which applies to the specific writer and which the writer himself will figure out.

Sometimes, a producer, director, dramaturge or a writing partner who concerns himself with script development will find himself defending a text he did not write. An effective game played in creative screenwriting consists of defending an unfamiliar text and responding to questions asked off the top of your head or following your instincts; to a certain extent this is like playing the part of the writer's lawyer and leads to interesting suggestions.[36]

In the course of this book, we will encounter dramaturgical terms from time to time, which I will analyze systematically and in so doing reference various contemporary theories of screenwriting. Reading screenplays or studying movies or parts from screenplays and movies will prove very useful during these parts. While doing so we will focus on the emotional reactions and information we receive as members of an audience, as it is my firm conviction that we "see movies as we write them," that is by utilizing both the right- and left-brain hemispheres.

Before we proceed, it is important to present the theoretical basis of creative screenwriting and of emotional structure: especially the latter's position within the framework of the predominating theories of drama and screenwriting, as well as through the presentation of the ancient struggle between poetry and philosophy that began with Plato and Aristotle. Since this particular segment, in contrast to the main body of the book, is very theoretical, I chose to see it as a kind of pre-credit sequence.[37]

The examples of analysis mentioned above, as with the theoretical information, work like subplots in the three-act structure of this book. The three acts, or rather sections, are called the beginning, the middle and the end: The first section has to do with the tricks and the second with the techniques of creative screenwriting. The third section deals with the application of the method of creative screenwriting to the whole screenplay of a feature length film and its relationship to the technique of revision. There is a slow development of the emotional structure theory throughout the entire book that finds its climax in this third part.

The term "trick" refers mainly to a certain mental attitude, which we need to assume in order for the appropriate exercises to function properly, even when our logical "I" provokes us to be skeptical. An example of this would be the trick of reducing responsibility by declaring we have no responsibility whatsoever for the content of our fantasy.

We should not forget that the stories we tell in this phase are nothing more than "copy." The method of creative screenwriting presupposes that we deal directly with the audiovisual narrative and with scenic writing, while our primary goal by no means will be to keep revising it up to and through the final draft. The first point of departure for further revision often occurs in discussion. The goal is that we obtain the tools for the requisite revisions systematically, that we will learn the rules by breaking them, and that we will then discuss the technique of revision in the third segment of the book.

Every one of us has his own creative identity. It is certainly unrealistic to expect to discover and to develop it in a short time within the framework of a course or through completing a set of exercises – but it is, however, possible to make a beginning. Therefore, it is important that we take notes while we contend with the suggested exercises. In this way, we can recognize which exercises are easy for us, which ones are difficult, which ones have entertained us, which ones have held our attention and why they have done so. This way we can eventually discuss and discover our own personal themes and artistic forms.

Finally, I want to stress that for me one of the most important components of the occupation with creative screenwriting is play and through play, entertainment; and this in the classical meaning of the word. Creating a playful atmosphere or a playful mood is not always easy, even more so because the idea that the education of the brain must be a somewhat melancholic affair is the most difficult one to fight.[38] Yet, wrote Friedrich Schiller, "The mensch only plays when he is a mensch in the actual sense of the word and is only a mensch in the actual sense of the word when he plays."[39]

Pre-Credit Sequence: Theoretical Rules of Creative Screenwriting

Creative screenwriting in the context of the prevailing theories of drama and screenwriting – a little review

Aristotle was the first to make drama an exclusive subject by dedicating an entire disquisition to it, the *Poetics*. For him, drama and especially tragedy, held not just one but the most important position among the poetic forms. So the theory of the *Poetics*, which is primarily a theory of the drama and especially of the fundamental category of the "mimesis" (imitation), became the rule and the source from which sprang the theory of the poetic arts and literature (see the following section on Plato and Aristotle) after the Renaissance.[1] All of the ensuing theories of drama, such as the one by Goethe, who in 1819 designated the drama, the epic and the lyric as the three "natural forms of the poetic arts;" and the *Technique of the Drama* by Gustav Freytag written in 1863, reference without exception Aristotle's *Poetics*. They constitute the first systematic disquisition of Greek Antiquity, and in so doing, they are seen as the beginning of not just European thought in literary criticism. The peculiarity of this partially descriptive and partially regimented opus would be that it examines the poetic phenomenon, and indeed not in the context of a philosophical disquisition such as the Platonic texts *Politeia* or *Ion*; or a rhetorical play that involves human intellectual activities such as Gorgia's *In Praise of Helen*; but rather treats it as if it were an autonomous domain of human intellectual activity. It elevates it to an exclusive research object, encompasses it; formulates its synthetic principles and its particular characteristics.[2] The text of the *Poetics* retains its meaning, even after the introduction of the "non-Aristotelian" dramaturgical theory and practice of Bertolt Brecht (to which we will return later, especially in the section on "Working with the psychology of the audience").

So it is not surprising that perhaps the most well-known author of screenwriting literature, the American Syd Field, also based his model (Field's paradigm) on the *Poetics*, and first and foremost on the thesis that every narrative must have a beginning, a middle and an end, which he called the three act structure.[3] He presented his model in his first book, published in 1979, and it immediately whipped up a firestorm of controversy. Many were and are of the opinion that writers have to pour their constructed stories into his mold and this, of course, produces a restrictive, stifling sameness.

The American Robert McKee, who published his book, *Story*, 20 years later, after he had trained many screenwriters in his seminars all around the globe, accused Syd Field of minimalism. McKee designated his own model as a fusion of the three-act structure with the five-part story structure, which consists of an introductory event followed by complications, a crisis, a high point and the denouement. Furthermore, he accuses European filmmakers and the avant-garde of filmmakers in general of lacking structure in their film screenplays and argues that American movies outperform European films, because Hollywood respects the rules of storytelling that moviegoers secretly crave.

John Truby has also found fault with the theory of the three-act structure – his version of classical storytelling structure presents seven main steps or main elements: problem/need, desire, opponent, plan, battle, self-revelation, and new equilibrium. He adds 22 additional steps to these 7 main steps, with the intention of creating a tight person-centered action to advance each scene towards the goal of the hero (the want).

In contrast, the mythical story-structure consists of 12 steps and 8 archetypes based in turn on the much-admired book, *The Hero's Journey*,[4] by the ethnologist Joseph Campbell, adapted by Christopher Vogler to screenwriting in his 1992 book *The Writer's Journey*.

Not least, mention should be made of the fans of the five-act structure, such as Kasache Rachid Nougmanov, who was one of the most famous representatives of the Soviet New Wave and who described the five acts as follows: organization, intrigue, learning, difficulty and confrontation. This breaks down to organization and intrigue belonging to the first and second half of the first act, learning and difficulty to the first and second half of the second act and confrontation to the entire third act. Five act structural theorists base their ideas primarily on the work of Gustav Freytag. In his book, *Technique of the Drama*, Freytag confers the following designations to the five acts: introduction, intensification, climax, return and catastrophe. These five acts contain the three most important dramatic moments, the stimulating moment, the tragic moment and the moment of final tension – in other words, the beginning of the battle, the climax and the catastrophe.[5] These moments generally correspond to the first turning point, the mid-point and the second turning point:[6] In a way Freytag stresses that if these three moments are very intensive, it is best to write the plot in three acts – and in this fashion, he returns to Aristotle's "Beginning – Middle – End."

By no means does Freytag regard ancient tragedy as the ultimate model, since the characters often change due to events that occur unexpectedly, that is, the plot changes the character while ideally the plot should grow out of an inner need of the character. This inner need of the character, as well as his fate, may not deviate from the flow of things that in turn spring from their personalities and that should seem plausible and logical at all times to the audience, even if they are surprised by unexpected turns in the plot.[7]

The division of a story into three parts is not only a Western idea. Storytelling also falls into three parts in the tradition of the Japanese No Theater. The three parts always follow the same chronological progression: the Jo (introduction), the Ja (development) and the Kyu (end).[8]

The structural models, which consist of numerous analytic steps, are impressive tools to apply to film and screenplay analysis; but scarcely permit any room for innovation and in the end prevent the creative process from unfolding or even make it more difficult. There is too much cognitive work involved in trying to keep up with complicated models. Therefore, despite their dissociation from Syd Field, the two most important screenplay gurus, Linda Seger and Frank Daniel, remain faithful advocates of the simple three-act structure.

The Czech Frank Daniel, Dean of the School of Cinematic Arts at the University of Southern California in Los Angeles as well as first Artistic Director of the Sundance Film Institute, was certainly one of the greatest teachers of screenwriting – and in fact of some of today's most successful screenwriters of independent American and European cinema.[9] In Frank Daniel's system one works mainly with the eight sequences of a film screenplay as well as with a "theme," but also with a "conscious want" (a desire, a goal), and the "unconscious need." In this way one concentrates not on the statics of a story, but on its emotional center, the heart and soul of a screenplay. Associated with this is Daniel's thesis that the author must find the story in himself and tell it "truthfully."

Similarly, Linda Seger stresses the emotional center of a screenplay. She has not only created the profession of "script consultant"[10] but has even written some of the most important and most useful books about screenwriting. Linda Seger primarily highlights the elasticity required in screenplay structure: it is not the story that must fit into the specific form, rather the form that must adapt to the needs of the story. From there, her method aims at working out the organic form the story needs.

Some few screenplay theoreticians, such as the Frenchman Jean-Claude Carrière and the Germans Peter Rabenalt und Dagmar Benke,[11] studied the alternative narrative forms and in doing so focused on the so-called epic[12]/episodic or non-Aristotelian form of the narrative, aka the oriental story form: convoluted, endless, uninterruptedly enhanced, uninterruptedly transformed.[13] Benke differentiates between the epic, the dramatic and the lyric cinema narrative and presents evidence that most alternative narrative structures belong to the category of the epic narrative but do not eschew using elements of the dramatic structure; and that the majority are experiments that blend both kinds of narrative. It is important to stress that Dagmar Benke, like Peter Rabenalt before her, references the Brechtian theory of the epic theater. Brecht himself, moreover, felt the concept of the "epic theater" was deficient and too formalistic – he also admitted that in reality his theater utilized a large number of dramatic and scenic modes of expression and techniques, also when the epicenter and goal was alienation and audience estrangement (as opposed to identification through compassion).[14] Seen this way, the screenplay theorists Benke and Rabenalt ascertain that in most cases screenwriters who use alternative narratives, in fact use a blend of alternative or epic and dramatic elements. In this context, the theme – as Frank Daniel first pointed out – is more important than for classical drama.

Still, which structure provides the basis for the screenplays of the *Nouvelle Vague* films, the philosophical parables or the *films d'auteurs*, or even the non-European films of other artistic origins, the postmodern, the alternative or postclassical films?[15] Previously evident in the methods of Frank Daniel and Linda Seger, we can approximate to a surprising degree the idea of the narrative system behind these alternative forms of narration as opposed to classic drama narration. Although these two theoretical thinkers offer the greatest creative freedom to develop a screenplay, writing its first draft is not their primary goal; their efforts are directed towards being able to analyze a finished screenplay and this in terms of the thorny development process. In addition, books on screenwriting mostly deal with structure and plot but almost completely ignore story creation. Taking an opposite tact, brainstorming – concerning both classical and alternative narration – is the exclusive topic of the first level of the creative screenwriting method presented here, while analysis is introduced only on a second level. The analysis in turn has the express goal of letting the revision happen in the spirit of the original idea.

The creative screenwriting method rests to a significant degree on the work of Daniel and Seger (despite the frequent referencing of various other theories of structure), but at the same time it rests on techniques and theories from theater, such as those of Lajos Egri[16] and Keith Johnstone. Certainly, some of the most effective methods of the "king of improvisation," Keith Johnstone, go back – at least in relation to their approach – to the work of one of the greatest thinkers of the twentieth century, Carl Gustav Jung, whom we have to thank for the term "archetype" as well as for the creative investigation of dreams. The most important aspect of psychological thinking by Jung, at least as far as the creative process is concerned, is the concept of the collective unconscious, which in comparison to the Freudian concept of the individual subconscious (the place where suppressed desires are kept) creates a whole new world "... a real and fundamental part of our personal lives, like the conscious, thinking world of the 'I,' only far more comprehensive. The language and persons of the collective unconscious are symbols connected to us by our dreams."[17] According to Jung, the collective unconscious is the best friend, helper and advisor of our conscious mind.

The collective unconscious at the same time is also the best friend, helper and advisor of every artist and is indispensable in the creative process – on the other hand, artistic endeavor and art in general do nothing else but stimulate the collective unconscious of their audiences and provide them with "satisfaction and joy."[18] It follows, therefore, that even if the rules of screenwriting are internalized or learned by heart, the creative process will remain difficult or occasionally impossible to use as long as one is uncertain how one can "open" his or her own unconscious. Using this thought as their springboard, the surrealists developed a series of techniques, like automatic writing, that are unsurprisingly of great importance to creative screenwriting.

At any rate, it is important to say that Jung's thesis does not posit the collective unconscious as the sole source of artistic inspiration. Such "psychoanalytical" thesis rightfully provoked Adorno's reaction, because "unconscious stimulation is only one impulse among many in the artistic creative process."[19] On the contrary, Jung's philosophy includes the insight that the conscious and the unconscious have to co-operate and compliment each other. This, precisely, is the goal of creative screenwriting.

Writing the Natural Way by the American professor of linguistics, Gabriel Rico, has been especially important towards developing a method to reach this goal *vis-à-vis* audiovisual narrative. Rico has been experimenting for 30 years with different techniques to awaken the creative potential when writing, by stimulating a part of the brain that is rarely used – techniques like "clustering," "recurrence," "improvisation," "creative tension" and "constellating" have found their place here and are being developed further in order to master the special challenges of screenwriting. The same is true of especially effective techniques that have been discovered in brain research and that have been developed by doctors and psychologists such as Jean Houston, the director of the Foundation for Mind Research in New York and author of the books, *Mind Games* and *Psychedelic Art*, as well as Tony Buzan, the creator of the revolutionary Mind Maps.

Contemporary intellectual discourse about the nature of human consciousness, which has resulted in old philosophical questions being "freshened up" by new scientific insights, is enriching both creative writing and screenplay theory. It has also made consciousness a topical and important subject of study in the natural sciences. The newly aroused interest in the field of the study of consciousness yields new insights almost daily. Two developments of particular interest to us are as follows:

1) A large part of the current scientific research stresses the essentially narrative nature of consciousness. The neurophysiologist Antonio Damasio, in his book *The Feeling of What Happens: Body, Emotion and the Making of Consciousness,* stresses that "telling stories is probably a brain obsession."[20] Daniel Dennett writes in his book *Consciousness Explained* something similar, "Our fundamental tactic of self-protection, self control and self-definition is not spinning webs or building dams, but telling stories, and more particularly connecting and controlling the story we tell others – and ourselves – about who we are."[21] "As spiders weave webs and beavers build dams, so we tell stories"[22], concludes David Lodge in his book *Consciousness and the Novel,* where he gives us a glimpse of the mysterious workings of the creative mind.
2) The statement that logic does not solve all problems, which ultimately leads to the "emotional turn" of analytic philosophy, emotional psychology[23] and in the motion picture sciences.[24]

David Bordwell's thesis from the 1980s – that one can also understand a film without an emotional reaction and that therefore it is methodically better to actually exclude the emotional portions in the analysis of a movie – is legendary.[25] Even though repeated claims are made that no other art form produces as intense and varied a set of emotions as cinema does, the emotional reactions of the audience have only recently become a central theme in the evolution of film theory. The discussions over the past few years have produced a whole host of theoretical modeling of the relationship of emotional interplay – here understood as field, perception, affect and emotion – to film. This means a pronounced turn, perhaps even a paradigm shift that inevitably will even lead to avoiding other avenues of investigation. The new interest in emotions puts psychoanalytical film theory in the background, particularly the Lacanian School of Critical Theory.[26] A specific context for the emotional pivot is easy to determine. While semiotic theory generally sees motion pictures as discourse or text, the emotionally oriented approach assumes film is predominately an event.[27]

Two main threads of the debate are discernable: a more philosophical-aesthetical one from which the psychoanalytic tendency of the 1970s has also largely rematerialized, and the more psychological cognitive thread, which developed from the cognitive film theory of the 1980s.[28] For film theoreticians of the first thread,[29] dealing with emotion means sniffing out the modeling of the film experience while avoiding the dictum of reason, whereby emotion is not to be understood as the opposite of reason; rather as something else, a precursor to reason. For cognitive theoreticians such as Noel Carroll, Murray Smith or Ed Tan, rationality and emotion are inviolably tied together[30] – an insight which was formulated by Antonio Damasio along with psychologists such as Nico Frida and Joseph Ledoux, or philosophers such as Ronald de Sousa. Theoreticians of the second thread assume that reason without emotion is blind. Common to the two threads is that they explode the narrow framework of previous film theory to expand the horizon of emotion.

Nevertheless, what is emotion? We owe the clearest definition – and the one that appears most suitable to me for cinema experience – to Michel Foucault's attempt to describe the effect of Duane Michals' photo series;[31] to show how these suggest "thought emotions" to the reader-spectator: "Emotion is that movement which sets the soul in motion and spontaneously spreads from soul to soul."

The method I present here is and remains a "work in progress," just as creative writing in general is constantly in development – on the one hand, because of the continual technological developments in the audiovisual field, and on the other hand, because of the creative, i.e., narrative experiments of screenwriters.[32] While developing the method of creative screenwriting – as well as the theory of emotional structure, that is the corresponding method of analysis – I focused my attention mostly on how the screenplay reflects consciousness and emotion, how the conscious and the unconscious minds of the creative screenwriter function, and how the analysis of the emotional structure can describe the nature of these processes. The theory and the method presented here can be seen as children of their time and certainly also as a suggestion to synchronize the theory and practice of screenwriting with the "emotional turn" of the arts and sciences.

The old struggle between poetics and philosophy: It all goes back to Aristotle or what we owe Plato and Aristotle

Most screenplay theoreticians refer, as previously stated, to the *Poetics* of Aristotle and to the thesis that each film story has a beginning, middle and an end, which we have come to call the classic or three-act structure. In the recent past one has often faulted the Europeans for writing screenplays that suffer from having little or no structure and claimed that American mainstream movies have a larger audience because they respect the rules of the dramatic narrative as Aristotle first formulated them: a complete, closed whole that has an uninterrupted unity and a thought-out architectural plan as well as an entertaining (even if often superficial) and ethical (even if often moral) approach. The most frequent statement one can hear in this framework is that "it all goes back to Aristotle." Accordingly, the proclaimed rules are correct and stand undisputed.

The Aristotelian closed form, however, has also led to similar reactions in the sphere of cinema just as it has in the theater of Bertolt Brecht, leading to his supposed non-Aristotelian dramaturgical theory and practice. The theories based on the *Poetics*, says the tenor of these reactions, often introduce restrictions and "moulds;" and a series of similar "products" in place of unique artistic works. Many find that the classic Hollywood cinema of mass consumption is in a creative as well as commercial crisis comparable to the theater crisis of the nineteen century. Back then, they incessantly repeated the same sure formulas, constellations of characters and situations with only slight alterations.[33]

Why hold Aristotle responsible for this development? One thing is certain: the study of the *Poetics* is and remains a work in progress. One can assume there are many different ways to interpret the writings of Aristotle. This in turn means that Aristotle still has much more to teach us – but it also means one can reinterpret contemporary conventions fashioned in his name by most screenplay theoreticians. Cézanne said that for an artist "the return to nature" (i.e. creation) should go through the Louvre – by which he probably meant that the character of an artistic work depends on its significance and has to be seen in relation to the history of art.[34] If we analyze the origin and the reason for the existence of certain rules of classical dramatic cinema narrative together with the history of the dramatic avant-garde, we can place our own work within a general framework and in doing so better understand what we write today and why.

The goal of this chapter is to provide a brief overview of what Aristotle actually wrote and to suggest a new possibility of interpretation for screenplay theory. What were the motives behind the theory? Why do his writings continue to exert influence even today, not just on the discourse of cinema narration, but also on cinema narration itself? We will examine passages from Aristotle that have been completely ignored; but that, in my opinion, are more interconnected to narrative structure (and, most importantly, not only to classic narrative structure) than the so-called rules that the strict conventions promote in most screenplay theories. In this chapter, as well as throughout the book, I will try to answer various related questions. If a whole with an unbroken unity is desirable – what exactly produces this unity? Is it the plot, the character development or perhaps something completely different? What does Aristotle's entertainment oriented and ethical approach actually mean?

I mean that such an overview becomes more significant if it happens in combination and confrontation with Aristotle's teacher, Plato, a comparison that script theoreticians have ignored to date. Aristotle's *Poetics* is not only a fundamental work about the nature and development of artistic creation, but also a cool, scientific and aggressive answer to Plato's views about art. Here again, in order for us to better understand the consequences and staying power of Aristotle with regard to certain important passages, we first must become acquainted with Plato's views.

As in any good drama, this is about a daisy chain of actions and reactions that continues right up until today: The "mental terrorism" that Plato allegedly exercised in the time Aristotle created his *Poetics* in a tragic-ironical way is not dissimilar to the mental terrorism exercised by modern screenplay theoreticians in the name of Aristotle. The response of the other side, however, is often just as absolute, categorical and laden with ideology as it formerly had been in Aristotle's method of argumentation.

Aristotle wrote his *Poetics* with a dual goal in mind – on the one hand, to interpret the phenomenon of poetry, that is of drama; and on the other hand, to disprove the views of Plato. In this sense, the *Poetics* is a courageous book. But to what exactly was Aristotle reacting? Opinions about Plato diverge widely. He is loved as much as he is despised. It is valid to acknowledge that Plato's view of the correct method of philosophical communication can be irritating, even though this irritation can be corrected by reading Plato's works, says Thomas A. Szlezák, one of the contemporary researchers and representatives of the Platonic interpretative school, which has become renowned as the "Tübingen School." In his much-read book, *Reading Plato*, Szlezák analyzes and disproves the most important points of criticism against Plato: "This is the only way to prevent the temporary irritation from becoming a lasting obstacle to the adoption of Platonic thought"[35] – and concomitantly for the adoption of everything he has to teach us regarding the creative process and dramaturgy.[36]

What, then, do we owe Plato and Aristotle – we screenwriters and screenplay theoreticians? The two giants of Western philosophy, according to the commonly held view, symbolize two diametrically opposed standpoints and ways of thinking. Raphael impressively presents this difference in his mural, "The School of Athens." Plato points his finger towards heaven, Aristotle at the Earth. From this perspective, Plato and Aristotle seem to embody the two different poles of intellectual life. The former is a utopian, the latter a realist. Ideals enchant the former; the latter is open to field research. The difference is clear-cut: Theoretician versus pragmatist, a deliberate spirit versus an encyclopedic researcher, a dreamer versus a scientist. Plato seemed to wish to escape the terrestrial, in order to reconnect with the source, with divine perfection. Aristotle methodically noted everything we hold in our hands, everything we see in front of our eyes and have in our heads.

This key difference persists: Aristotle teaches; Plato investigates. The former constructs foundations and systems, the latter wonders, points out pathways and examines a thousand assumptions; far too often, he does not reach just one conclusion, and he most obviously distrusts rigid terminologies.[37] Aristotle seems to submit to the rules of language, of the words and of the drama. What he tries to teach everyone who wants to understand the world, above all, is the need for a method, for a technique. Plato, on the other hand, demonstrates an ability to adapt continuously as new thought results emerge prior to sketching out a theory. His goal is to make clear, to enlighten the spirit and to shake up rigid certainties. He brings us the art of asking the right question and the game of doubt. His goal is and remains to find the truth – a truth that pre-exists.

Yet the distance of art from truth, that is, the distance from the considerable goal of Platonic philosophy, is allegedly so vast for Plato that the work of art immediately becomes suspicious.[38] Poetry is unnecessary, he says, since from an ontological point of view, it is the copy of a copy;[39] and from an epistemological viewpoint, it is beyond the pale of conscious creation. At the same time, it also endangers politically organized society and its interests.[40]

It is important to understand and keep in mind that this was the ideological climate when Aristotle wrote his *Poetics*. The Aristotelian *Poetics* is nothing less than the first systematic theoretical text about poetry that attempts to define the best – that is, the most effective – poetry using descriptive analysis and governing regulations.[41] Let us remember that when he says poetry, Aristotle means drama. What, then, is the most effective drama – and in what way is it effective?

In order to answer this question, we should have a look at the three most important arguments Aristotle used to evade or disprove Plato's above-mentioned theses. These are, interestingly enough, also the three fundamental arguments – arguments that recur repeatedly, as we will see later – that were employed against the Aristotelian approach and for the creation of alternative narrative forms.

The first argument revolves around the degree of truth found in a work of art. Aristotle's *Poetics* contributes to the rehabilitation of a poetry threatened with banishment – a rehabilitation that happens due to abandoning Plato's theory of ideas as well as to the rebuttal of his most important arguments dealing with the concept of mimesis and mimicry. The main difference between the pupil and the teacher is that the first believes that art is a reproduction of the sense world; and that the second insists that it is a deceitful image, since the sense world has for him a low standing. To Aristotle, the artist copies reality directly, not indirectly, as Plato maintains. Moreover, Aristotle expressly rejects the theory of the direct and true reproduction of the senses in the world of art and reclassifies the term mimesis higher by maintaining that the writer can freely invent the story of a tragedy.[42]

Plato places the fable, that is, the myth (τον μύθον) in clear opposition to logos, to the word (τον λόγον) and thus the narration in opposition to the argument. In the dialogue named after him, Protagoras lets the listener choose between the analysis of his perspective or of his argument, either through a fable or through logos (*Protagoras*, 320c). The choice will be left to him in the end, so he begins with the "more graceful" form of the fable. In *Phaidros* (274c–275b), Socrates has not quite concluded the story of the invention of writing by Theuth when Phaidros scolds him for having invented that story. It is further on proved that Phaidros has stripped off the elements of fable in the story and captured the logos of the myth in light of the transparent message – a procedure Socrates implicitly endorses by stressing that it depends solely on whether the intended factual content has been rendered (*Phaidros* 275bc).[43] In plain words, Socrates concludes that it does not matter whether the truth is conveyed through logical arguments or through an invented story.

Undoubtedly, the dialectic penetration to reality that is reached by using logos to argue is Plato's most ambitious goal.[44] All the same, he cannot ignore the entertaining power of the fable. The ability of the images and the narratives to present a theme in its entirety and intuitively is for Plato the necessary add-on of intellectual analysis. According to his view, the fable constitutes a second way to get to know reality, which cannot be independent of logos as to content; yet at the same time has an advantage nothing can replace. This sounds paradoxical, but it shows that Plato recognized the power of the drama – however, a power he regarded as dangerous and harmful, above all if it fell into the wrong hands. The controversial discourse about the improper exercise of power of the drama continues to this day, particularly in the context of motion pictures.[45]

Plato did not only notice the influence of the image and the narrative – his remarks remind us in this context even of Aristotle's in regard to the "καθόλου" (the universal, the general and/or the general and universal themes), which constitute the foundation of story and which are of great importance for the theory of emotional structure. We will grapple with this issue more thoroughly in the chapter about the emotional theme as well as in the chapter concerning the emotional structure itself. To date, screenplay theory has not dealt with this meaning of unity that was so "important" to Aristotle and that is codified in the deep structure of the dramatic text.[46]

The argument over the seductive power of poetry and its relation to the truth is actually older than Plato and Aristotle: For Pindar (522–443 BC), whatever is decent and moral is genuine. Gorgias (483–375 BC), on the other hand, maintained that one would have to explain the influence of tragedy through deception, and in doing so unburdened the term "deception." Plato loads the burden back on the term by maintaining that poetry is the representation of a representation and for that reason is very far removed from reality. Aristotle directs our attention to the psychological result produced by the work of art and away from worrying about the truth. In this way, he provides an answer to those who state that the purpose of fiction must be to find the truth. He also includes a knowledge factor together with the psychological one in his attempt to maintain an equal distance from the poetics of the sophists and the philosophy of Plato. "Aristotle (and this means analytical theoretical argumentation) has taken the crucial step from ethics to aesthetics."[47]

Why, then, do we connect Aristotle to an ethical, even moralistic approach to drama and, nowadays, to classic Hollywood motion pictures? We will have to content ourselves first by ascertaining that the formulation of the problematic begun by Plato and Aristotle constitutes the ideological argument right up until today: Can cinema represent reality, or does it serve to seduce and consequently becomes an end in itself?

Mimesis, either as representation or as a creative reproduction of reality, has employed the most diverse schools of cinema narration many times over. It almost looks as though various historical cinema movements, such as Neorealismo, Nouvelle Vague, the Free Cinema, the Junger Deutscher Film (Young German Cinema) and the relative contemporary Danish Dogma movement, harken back to Platonic and later Brechtian argumentation, in that they accuse classical cinema of being seductive and declare their programmatic desire to represent objective reality directly.[48]

After the element of distance from reality, we now come to the second element, which in turn represents a further fundamental argument by use of which Aristotle was able to refute comprehensively Plato's arguments about essence and awareness. This second element refers above all to the scientific and artistic concept of catharsis.[49]

In the ninth chapter of the *Poetics,* Aristotle speaks about the "familiar pleasure" as the most important goal of the tragedy. In the sixth chapter, pity and fear are mentioned as the main emotions that summon the familiar pleasure of tragedy and lead to catharsis. The observer becomes conscious of negative emotions (shamelessness, fearlessness and enraged aggression) because of tragedy. The spectator is afraid that pain and ignoble events could threaten him and his beloved ones and feels compassion because the hero suffers undeservedly. In addition, the viewer knows that what he sees happen is not happening in reality, but that it is a mimesis, that is, a representation of events. This safety zone makes it possible for the audience to think about the human situation, about pain and misfortune as an inseparable component of human existence; and to reject the extreme, high-spirited emotions that, though unconscious, are latent in the human condition.[50] Such is the comforting and educating function of drama.[51]

The safety zone does not seem large enough for the Hollywood drama – so the comprehensive restoration and reconciliation in the form of the so-called Happy Ending adds the punishment of the guilty and the triumph of the good and the true, etcl. We come, then, to the point where we can connect Aristotle with the moralistic approach of cinema drama. The reproach made by various avant-garde filmmakers that commercial cinema is very remote from reality stems largely from this intersection.

A pattern of sin, insight and reconciliation transforms the invigorating three-act structure into a comfort providing form, says the theoretician and screenplay teacher Ken Dancyger. This concerns a strict moral narrative that begins with the premise that good intentions will win out in the end. The world is understandable, consequent and easy to navigate; and it carries the good and the true within. As a result, external events can hardly be random.[52] Quite the reverse, one calls them forth. In the three-act structure, not only is the fate of the hero in his own hands but, assuming he is ready to admit his mistakes, the consequences of his acts will even be set aside. In this way cinema becomes a moral institution that is less about establishing a new concept than strengthening a pre-existing one and that emphasizes a certain view of the world. The criticism of this worldview and the core belief that people can take fate into their own hands has caused some screenwriters to react defensively. Those that refuse to use the three-act structure do this most of all, because they equate it with the moralistic and educational mentality of Hollywood mainstream dramas.

Aristotle's third important argument for screenplay theory has persistently engaged filmmakers and screenwriters: it concerns a "solid structural unity" to which Aristotle lends special weight. One thing is most essential to him. The whole must be well structured and not simply follow a chronology, because otherwise it will represent a chronological design and not a poetic composition. In one move, Aristotle completely avoids and in doing so refutes the epistemological arguments of Plato.[53] The elevated ranking of the so-called "closed form" presupposes an active intervention of the writer in the ever-flowing river and chaos of reality and in the many different events that could occur (*Poetics* 1451a, 16).

The goal is to define a core event, which commands the requisite unity or receives it from the "organizational will" of the writer, so that a unity arises according to the laws of the possible or the necessary. What then steps forward is continuity, consequence and the unity of action; in a way that, in fact, should a part of the composition be transposed or eliminated, the whole structure would collapse, for example, would not make sense: "Then whatever can be there or be absent without any visible consequences is not part of the whole."[54] This led to one of the golden rules of classical screenplay theory and analysis, and to one of the main goals of revision. Any scene or character that does not advance the story must be eliminated. Yet, according to which criteria would we recognize the point in a screenplay at which the structure should threaten to collapse – especially if we assume the basic structure is not determined by the plot?

Aristotle uses the argument of the plot produced by the organizational, structural will of the writer, mainly to prove that drama is first a conscious creation. Why did he feel compelled to do that? After all, Plato also consciously sought out this new large-scale literary form (the prose drama) and, since Schleiermacher's realization[55] that form is not a matter of indifference as to the content of the Platonic dialogues, the task remains to examine dramatic techniques of the dialogues and to investigate them in this particular sense as well as to answer the question with which dramaturgical techniques Plato clarifies what is important to him.[56] It would be meaningful, then, to differentiate between what Plato says about art, and how he applies the art themes and forms. Reference is often made in the literature to certain dramaturgical means, such as the give and take of the interlocutors, but there are elements that have remained unnoticed until recently, even though they are of the greatest importance to understanding Plato's works. One of these elements is that of concealment and the intentional constraint of knowledge in the dialogues,[57] a motive that is closely associated with the cinema narrative element "suspense." Another motive, which is perhaps the harbinger of the well-known term "premise,"[58] is that of the basic underlying situation.[59]

The form Platonic dialogue takes is of crucial importance for content.[60] The dialogues must be read like dramas: like works with continuous action and with a conceptual network of relations among the characters. At any rate, Plato consciously employs all the techniques of a well thought out dramaturgy. He uses dramaturgical means, like the exchange of dialogue among the interlocutors and the inclusion of other stories in the narrative stream, the introduction of framing dialogue, the most diverse kinds of allusions and indirect relationships together with his most famous device, irony. Plato also employs status games among the characters: There is no discourse among equals in Platonic dialogues.

The parallels between Platonic and Aristotelian dramaturgy are obvious, especially since "βοηθεια" (help), as Plato seems to have used the term, in no way refers to a character's intellectual ability but rather to the accuracy of the ontological viewpoint – the wellspring for the development of the character in question. As Plato seeks a key higher "science" or "art," he examines and judges the art of writing (the word-creating art, "η λογοποιητική τέχνη," *Politeia* 289c, 7) in an extremely critical way. He discovers that the art of the word can be neither the highest art form nor the advocate of bliss, whereas we read in *Phaidros* that only the dialectic can secure the prospect of bliss (ευδαιμονίαν) for humanity (277a, 3).

In direct comparison, Aristotle accepts the existence of literature as a positive factor in the life of humans based on the higher ranked meaning of mimesis, on the condition that it expands knowledge and enriches experience. In addition, he recognizes that learning spreads enjoyment and pleasure – in the case of tragedy, the familiar pleasure lies in the fact that it evokes pity (compassion) and fear. Logic and emotion, then, are equally active in the pursuit of the enrichment of our knowledge through art.[61] Learning does not only give philosophers the greatest pleasure, but in a similar way other people too, says Aristotle (*Poetics* 1448a–1448b). The pleasure is doubled and indivisible, creating both awareness and emotion.[62] The most effective drama in the end, then, is the one that increases enjoyment, makes sense in the context of the whole, creates meaning, and enriches experience and knowledge.

It is impossible to understand fully the creative processes or the indirect contribution of Plato and Aristotle to screenwriting, without pointing out an important difference between teacher and student. As mentioned above, Plato clearly distinguishes between the emotional and the logical world – and in so doing refers to the writer as a machine that produces literary works.

In *Ion*,[63] Plato asserts that the poet does not create consciously, but rather is possessed by divine mania and falls into ecstasy during the creation of his work. Plato used this assertion to argue that the work of the poet in no way contributes to the enrichment of knowledge as in other intellectual activities and that in the art of poetry the word is all inclusive and has no association with special knowledge. For the theoreticians and artists, who argue against creative writing and the creative process, the argument about ecstasy became the principle one. Ecstasis, they argue, cannot be taught. Poets and artists in general repeatedly describe their inspiration as a phenomenon whose genesis evidently is separated from their ego and their will. This is the origin of the idea of the "muse," the embodiment of an inner voice that influences the artist from the outside.[64]

Aristotle, in contrast, regards tragedy as a coin with two sides: on one side is the stamp of production and on the other the impress of effectiveness. On one side, it is the duty of the poet to construct the plot, while on the other, the audience is the central focus of attention. Proceeding from the perspective of the audience response, the philosopher shows that the enjoyment of the drama is the predominant and definitive criterion. This is the case, as he defines "fictionality as the main identifying feature at the production stage, provided that the fiction completely goes by the rules of the possible."[65]

In past decades of film history, this inevitably led to a "dictatorship of the audience." The screenwriter has to adapt to what the average member of the audience allegedly would endure or to avoid what the audience member would find too difficult, tiring or disturbing – and for that reason what is unacceptable. The screenwriter, then, has to adapt to the lowest common denominator of public taste. This certainly has to do with the fact that cinema is an unusually expensive medium in comparison with the other arts, in the production stage as well as in distribution. It is not surprising that almost all the various schools of avant-garde filmmaking produce low budget films.

Do mass production motion pictures correspond to the rules of Aristotelian effective drama? Aristotle speaks of the double goal of entertainment and awareness. As stated previously, according to his terminology the drama not only has to increase enjoyment, but also to enrich experience and knowledge. In this context, it follows that knowledge cannot mean it is the result of instruction; it is rather the result of self-discovery. The enjoyment is double: enlightening as well as emotional, each inseparable from the other. Accordingly, Aristotelian "pleasure" by no means signifies superficial entertainment in the sense of scattering attention, escapism, relaxation, temporary distraction or diversion. Quite the contrary, it expresses satisfaction on the rational as well as the emotional level – this presupposes stories that challenge and interest the audience, that shake up our everyday life; that broaden the spectrum of our experience since they intrinsically represent an experience themselves.

Even so, Aristotle treats the creative process as a technical one, as a handicraft that can be taught, whose creation clearly and distinctly concerns the left-brain. It is the enjoyment of the art of poetry and not, for example, the expression of the poet or the search for the truth, which should be elevated to an autonomous basis for artistic production.[66] In the attempt to support his epistemological disquisition, Aristotle does not accept external intervention of a metaphysical nature during the creative process of the art of poetry.[67] Because if the origin of the art of poetry for Aristotle were transcendental, his programmatic explanation in the introduction to the *Poetics* – that the goal of creation is good poetry, that is, effectiveness – would be completely incomprehensible. This suggests that the art of poetry can be learned like any other craft, too, and that it follows certain rules. For Aristotle the art of poetry stems from talent that can be cultivated (*poeta doctus*), and not from enthusiasm, because "where ecstasy rules, poetry languishes."[68] Aristotle gives us the rules by which drama functions. Plato begins at the notion of enthusiasm and assumes that the art of poetry cannot be born before logic has left the poet (*poeta vates*).[69] The two giants of philosophy describe the main conflict that has since always troubled the concept of creativity.[70] Yet despite their differences, Plato, the thinker of antiquity, and Aristotle can never be seen as incompatible. Aside from the ideological charge in their results, the two philosophers even use similar terminology.

The method of creative screenwriting makes use of two avenues of thought: chaos and order. It is based on research and the game of aporia and it employs Socrates' "birthing method,"[71] but it also makes the most of fantasy, the unconscious, emphasis, emotions and creative "ecstasy." At the same time, it uses the structure and technique of dramaturgy to promote further development and revision.

Art, in the final analysis, is doomed to failure if thought surpasses it. Of the three art epochs (symbolic or eastern, classic or Greek, romantic or Christian) only the classical epoch achieved a correspondence of the idea with its expression. In Nietzsche's view, classicism is the assertion of order in the midst of chaos – which is why he prefers classical art.[72] The existence of strict rules with enough room left between the guidelines to permit the development of human creativity – assuming, of course, that art is primarily a craft – is what characterizes "classical" Greek art and culture in Aristotle's time, as well as the imitation of the prototypes of antiquity that began in the sixteenth century.

The fuss about contradictions, the linkage of chaos to order, the opposition of concepts – as in research-mimesis, fantastic-logic, unconscious-planning, ecstasy-communication, emotion-alienation, child-adult – are not unknown in the history of the narrative, nor in cinema art nor in screenwriting. But, until now, the discourse has been limited largely to fundamental theoretical and ideological standpoints and mostly gets lost in accepting or rejecting the rules; rules one thinks, rightly or (partially) wrongly, that Aristotle was the first to introduce and defend.

The Beginning

"Begin at the beginning," the King said, very gravely, "and go on till you come to the end: then stop."

Lewis Carroll

The Tricks of Creative Screenwriting

The trick of the commonplace and of the lack of responsibility

Creativity is defined as aberrant thinking, that is, as thinking able to break open existing forms of experience, ideas and concepts in order to apply them in a new way.[1] In other words, creativity is the ability to fashion something original. Even so, we suppress our fantasy and therefore our originality when we try to be original.[2] The danger lies precisely in this attempt. "What does it mean to be called original?" I ask a group of novice screenwriters and the answer comes back immediately: "To think up something new." Before they had a chance to notice, two obstacles are already in the way and ready to block their creativity: thinking up something and the idea of the new. Conscious thinking often functions as the biggest enemy of the creative process. The effort to invent something new excludes whatever we consider old, stories already told, the predictable, and the commonplace.

The first step towards igniting our creativity is what we will call here the trick of the commonplace and of the lack of responsibility. I use the term "trick," since the techniques indicated refer in the end to a concrete mental attitude we should adopt before the corresponding exercises can work – even if our logical ego resists and raises questions. The logical ego will be tricked until we have understood the function of the creative process and are "strong" enough to get along without the trick.

The logic behind using tricks is relatively simple. The more we try to be original, the more we distance ourselves from what makes us who we are, with the direct consequence that our work becomes mediocre, because it is false and therefore has no substance.

> Switch off the no-saying intellect and welcome the unconscious as a friend: It will lead you to places you never dreamed of, and produce

> results more 'original' than anything you could achieve by aiming at originality,

writes Irving Wardle in his introduction to Keith Johnstone's bible *Impro*.[3] At this stage, we will learn to accept the first idea and avoid, at least for now, reconsidering it and making choices and judgments about what has been written. We will learn to accept the commonplace.

In the end, it is precisely this fear of the banal, of the cliché, that leads us to a true commonplace. The cliché, however, can also be the best place to start. It is better to begin with a cliché than to end there, Hitchcock said – and Antonio Gaudi's credo was "Originality is the return to the origin." We have to move in a world that is emotionally familiar so that we can return to the origin. If not, we enormously limit our ability to make use of our imagination and our unconscious mind.

Good examples of this are the characters, which are the primary material of the screenwriter: We are afraid of the commonplace, the banal, the customary and the unimportant. To avoid all this, we invent the opposite or what we believe is the opposite. Since we are of the opinion that created characters should be less usual and less unimportant, we create marginal characters, with the consequence that we do not know what makes them tick or how they should behave, while at the same time we are completely incapable of evaluating their emotions. How then can we present these characters and their emotions; how can we create an entire story around them? Frank Daniel's advice sounds almost provocative. The characters must be genuine, "normal" people, that is, "sell your friends, your neighbors, and your relatives." Tolstoy's journals are filled with notes that show how the writer combined the characteristics of his friends in order to invent the characters in his story.

The thing that most makes us what we are, is not our personality, rather it is our imagination, maintains Keith Johnstone. We can talk ourselves into believing, even as an experiment, that we are not responsible for the content of our fantasy. The idea of a lack of responsibility may initially frighten us. We have learned that we are our choices: Our choices are what lead to our experiences, and they, in turn, form our fantasy. In other words, we want to be completely responsible. As artists we feel responsible for the material we produce, and as a result want to control and adapt it, because it does not measure up to our principles, or because we do not consider this material original enough. Yet if we do that, once we control and adapt, we will create with mathematical certainty the opposite of what we intended.

The journey to creativity never has a known destination. Our destination, moreover, can only be an encounter with our greatest potential. This will only happen if we, even for a moment, forget what our intentions and our motivations are. The fact is that from the moment we assume that art is an expression of our ego, we are lost – since every criticism will be about us. We try to avoid it and we lose some substance, we take it personally. The result is the interruption of the creative process, if only temporarily.

To invent has an older meaning of "to find." The German word, *erfinden*, and the French word, *inventer*, characteristically have their origins in the Latin verb, *invenire*, which means "to find." "I don't seek, I find," said Picasso. I find something that is already there. Keith Johnstone uses the example of the Eskimos: when they make ice sculptures, they firmly believe that there is only one form in the ice. Many artists from antiquity felt the same. They freed the form imprisoned in the marble, a pre-existing form that was there long before they were. We cannot be held responsible for something that existed before us. The marble and the form we discover in it, the words and the meanings we discover when combining them, are not there to express our egos. We are the medium through which something that pre-exists becomes known.

The following exercise and one which may remind you of a game you played at parties when you were a child, should put us in this frame of mind. It is one of the few exercises in this book exclusive to group work, yet it assumes the group's lack of knowledge about the contents of the exercise. It is important to describe it in more detail than the other exercises in the book, because of the way it is implemented. I will introduce some of the texts, moreover, that have come up in my seminars.

Exercise #1:

The participants divide into groups. Each group is made up of a storyteller and an inventor, aka story owner. The storyteller is asked to leave the room, and the story owner is handed the stories he supposedly needs to learn by heart.[4] The goal of the storytellers is to ask questions which the story owners can only answer with yes, no or maybe. The moment the storytellers have the feeling they know the entire story, they have to ask whether the story is finished. After that, they return to the room and tell us the story they have discovered.

The storytellers leave the room. I distribute the corresponding envelopes, which seemingly contain the stories they need to learn. Instead, they contain a blank sheet of paper. I encourage the story owners to produce a random set of answers: One time "maybe," two times "yes," one time "no." Another trick is to answer all the questions that end in a consonant with a "yes" and all the questions that end in a vowel with a "no." In any case, I instruct them to avoid influencing the story by manipulating it, consciously or unconsciously. If a partner asks whether the story is over, something that happens when he or she has the feeling this is the case, then the story owner must answer with "yes."

This exercise is one of the best I personally know of that shows we all have a functioning narrative instinct and that our brain contains thousands of stories which have an intrinsic beginning, middle and end structure, as stated in the Aristotelian principle: "Ολον δε εστίν το έχον αρχήν και μέσον και τελευτήν"[5] (A whole is that which has a beginning, a middle and an end). At the same time, it is one of the most effective tricks to help us cancel out our internal censor – the censor that has made a nest in our brains. Naturally, it is also the best way to forget our eagerness to be original.[6] The stories that proceed from this outwardly random procedure are not only structurally complete, but rather they cover a very wide spectrum of genres and narrative styles. They are often more daring than our wildest dreams.

The exercise has yielded another insight. One can now better understand and follow the process of creative writing. We write what goes "through" our heads, what we think up, improvise, freely associate; we combine narrative elements, and if we ever run up against difficulties, we look back (i.e. for elements that are already there) and never ahead to completely new elements. We always find alternative ways to go, even if our path is suddenly blocked. If a door closes (if our question is answered with a "no"), we open a window.

Following below are three exemplary stories that were taken from the "ice" of the fantasy of the storytellers. I have kept these stories the way they were recited, above all in relation to the perspective of the characters; but also in relation to the narrative style. The titles are the ones the storytellers provided in response to my question about the story's working title, and they are a good hint at where they themselves see the focal point of the story. It is important that the characters are named from the beginning – this follows a straightforward development, since the storytellers tell their own stories without realizing it, and the characters spring from their own fantasy.

Apart from the main objective of strengthening our trust in our fantasy and in stories that slumber inside us, a further goal is to make some of the main principles of storytelling clear based on "stories that nobody has thought up." Interestingly enough, we see that there are structural points between the beginning and the middle as well as the middle and the end that drive the story and our emotions in another direction and that there is often a protagonist who strives for a definite goal; and that there is always conflict.[7]

Stories that nobody has thought up

THE SECRET *The story begins in a house by the sea; Lars is spending his summer vacation there with his parents. He is bored, until he meets Maria, who – unknown to him – prostitutes herself. Lars slowly falls in love with Maria, who manages to hide her secret from him. One day when they are traveling, someone approaches her. Maria does all she can to avoid him, but she cannot. Lars realizes how involved she is. He tries to save her. He tells the person who is stalking her to leave her alone. There is a quarrel. The person suddenly pulls out a gun and fires at Lars, but Maria jumps between them. She is shot. Lars, who wanted to save Maria, winds up causing her death.* ■

It is characteristic that the storyteller uses words like "until" or "one day." After she finishes her story, when the audience asks questions because there is something they have not understood, she answers with the sentence, "Let me put that in context with ..." since that is exactly what we do when we tell stories: We look back and connect. The story is simple, but complete: We can also talk about the theme and the development of the protagonist, but for the moment it should simply serve as an initial step to introduce a couple of dramaturgical constructs, like the ordinary world or routine (the summer vacation), the catalyst (meeting Maria), turning points (falling in love, being unable to escape the past), the climax (the fight) and the denouement (Maria's death). We will look into these termini in more detail later – for now, what is important is that we realize that they are there as storytelling knots in every story we tell, whether we think or know about their existence or not. We can also point out the potential further development of the story, especially in relation to the story's rhythm. For example, at the moment "someone" disturbs them – that "someone" doesn't have a name because the other two characters are evidently more important – the discovery of Maria's secret and the fight that follows could become three different points in the chronology, so that more possibilities for further story and character development can emerge.

TRUE LIFE *The story begins with a funeral. George is burying his wife, Julia. His grief is overwhelming. At the funeral, he meets Julia's best friend, Charlotte. They share their pain. Without being aware of it, George falls in love and Charlotte is not indifferent; no, she requites his feelings – perhaps she was always a little in love with him – but she also feels guilty because of Julia. She knows how jealous Julia was, how much she was afraid George would immediately replace her when she died; no, she cannot be the one who replaces Julia. The relationship ends before it can begin.* ■

It is truly impressive how each story begins with an image. The house at the sea (the comfortable situation of a family Maria never had) in the previous story is the funeral (death) in this one. In the conversation that follows we note that there are three characters and that the energy of a dead, that is, an absent person in a dramatic story can be very important (see *Three Colors: Blue* by Krzysztof Kieslowsky and Krzysztof Pieseiwicz). We also discuss the ending, which many felt was unsatisfying, since they want to know what happens to these characters when they go their separate ways. Actually, they instinctively did not want them to separate, because they felt that a story that begins with sorrow should not end in sorrow. The emotional framework of the structure did not work for them – and they were probably right.

JUSTLIN *The four-year-old Lydia is lonely: her parents died when she was little, and she is living with her aunt. Even though the aunt takes very good care of her, she cannot replace her mother. In her loneliness, she makes up a fantastic character, whom she calls Justlin. She shares her innermost thoughts with her, her feelings and her experiences. With few words, she lives shut up in her world until she gets older and goes to school. She quickly makes some real girlfriends and at some point, she trusts them enough to tell them her secret. Her girlfriends ridicule her, and Lydia feels sick. She meets Justlin and asks her, "Are you real? The others say you do not exist." Justlin gets mad; she is jealous – maybe she was jealous before, and because she is, she tells Lydia to tell her girlfriends that of course she is real and that only if her friends accept that as the truth can they truly be her friends. Lydia refuses, they fight and Justlin leaves. Lydia tries to forget her. She gets older. The girlfriends disappear; life goes on. One day, Lydia is a mature woman; she decides to look for Justlin. Will she find her?* ■

The narrator of this story confides in us that funny enough he had a similar experience when he was a child. He did have a fantastic friend and what a strange coincidence that his exercise partner would have a story with a fantastic friend! Most have a big problem following the particular story through, since it is not clear whether Justlin exists or how she will be presented on screen. They also want to know why and at what point in time Lydia decided to look for Justlin and whether she will find her. The storyteller has created a fantastic world and they want to know the rules. He wants his story to have an open end, but admits that he believes Lydia will probably find her.

At this point, it is important that we take a closer look at one of the most significant, perhaps even the most important and determining narrative element in dramaturgical structure: character.

The structure of the screenplay: First sequence (the character)

"Thought and character are the two natural causes from which actions spring," Aristotle presumed, "and on actions again all success or failure depends."[8] According to Lajos Egri, the character is the sole dramatic material of vital importance.

The Aristotelian "ethos," which is equated with the intention of the hero, that is, the supposed "προαίρεσιν," the inclination,[9] that determines his behavior, in no way corresponds to the contemporary, mostly psychological template of a character. Still, Aristotle requires that the description of mores and conventions meet four preconditions: "το χρηστόν" (the competent: the character must be moved by good intentions), "το αρμόποντα" (the appropriate: the opposition must fit the hero's gender, age, social position and so on), "το όμοιον" (the similar: despite his superiority, the hero may not be so distant as to lose the sympathy of the audience); and "το ομαλόν" (the constant: the hero's behavior may not flip flop, be erratic or inconsequent).[10] The parallels between the Aristotelian protagonist and the heroes of the classical narrative cinema are already evident.

Aristotle, on whose theses most theories of screenwriting have relied, says that plot and character are interwoven inseparably with each other, and adds that tragedy is not an imitation of human beings, but an imitation of their actions and lives.[11] He seems to pose the question for the first time: What is more important in drama, the character or the plot? He himself probably leans towards plot, since he maintains that a drama could make it without a (strong) character, but that a drama without a plot is inconceivable. He also notices:

> A further proof is that novices in the art attain to finish of diction and precision of portraiture before they can construct the plot. It is the same with almost all the early poets. The plot, then, is the first principle and, as it were, the soul of a tragedy; character holds the second place.[12]

Gustav Freytag argues the thesis that ideally the characters develop the plot out of their inner needs.[13] He cautions, moreover, that with the exception of a few tragedies of Sophocles, the tragedies of antiquity do not fracture the supremacy of the plot over the characters. In his opinion, Aristotle had formulated an ideal that did not exactly correspond to the tragedies of his day, since in these the plot was more important than the characters:

> From outside, an incomprehensible fate penetrates into the plot; prophesies and oracles influence the resolution of the story; random misfortune strikes the heroes; misdeeds of the parents determine the fate of later generations, the personifications of the gods stride into the plot as friend and foe, torn between what enrages them and what punishment they must meet out, there is by human standards not always a correlation, still less a reasonable relationship.[14]

The causal relationship that all drama and screenplay theory that draw on Aristotle have in common, is either nonexistent or constructed (we acknowledge the hand, i.e. the will of the writer to guide the story in a certain direction). Although Freytag has made an important remark here, certainly about the controversial theme of the relationship field of character and plot, it is also important to stress that he has limited himself with this criticism to the manner of thought common to his day. For the Greeks of antiquity, the misdeeds of the parents and their guilt in the face of the gods that finds expression in the turns of fate and the pronouncements of the oracles makes up an indispensable part of the personality of a human being, so also of a character.

When using the method of creative screenwriting, we begin with the characters. The result is obviously more person-centered than in some classical films, which concentrate on plot; but also more so than in films which do not emanate from the plot, but rather from their functional substitutes, such as ideology or any given aesthetic. How many characters are we talking about here? The classical narrative form focuses on a single hero, the so-called protagonist. Freytag points out that the audience has an immediate need to learn which of the characters is going to hold their interest the most:

> Whoever deviates from this rule should do so in the knowledge that they are giving up a great advantage; and if the material makes this sacrifice necessary, should ask if the uncertainties that result are offset by other dramatic advantages.

The only exceptions Freytag accepts are love stories with two protagonists.[15]

While classical film narrative presupposes a single protagonist who, during the course of the story, will meet an antagonist, be accompanied by a group of supporting characters, etc., the rule of the one protagonist is happily broken in the so-called alternative narrative forms – and to great effect.

The thing that counts most though, is not the characters themselves, but rather their relationships and primarily, their conflicts.[16] One of the most important starting points of the classical narrative form concerns the development of the protagonist and his underlying philosophy, that is, worldview. As we have seen in the very simple stories of the storytellers from the first exercise, every protagonist has a goal. The goal of the protagonist is known as "the want:"[17] a concept that is used to describe what a character wants and tries to get against all odds and in the face of his antagonist's opposition and the obstacles encountered on his journey. It describes what the character wants and what he will have to get over the course of the story; because, after all, he maybe does not need what he wants, maybe it was a false goal: the false object of desire, the false girl, the false career and so on.

The screenwriter Waldo Salt[18] has come up with a similar idea. He calls it the mode, which has to do with how the character goes about trying to get things done and is thus at odds with his universal need. The need is the character's destiny. It is what he needs in order to become fully human. The true need that parenthetically describes the conscious or often the unconscious desire or longing of the protagonist stands in conflict with the goal. This is what really drives the character, and it is what the character really needs to become whole and to find his happiness. The character realizes his need as he pursues his goal. The need is often the opposite pole to the goal or it represents opposite values. If a character tries to reach his goal, this automatically creates conflict with his need.

The motion picture *American Beauty*, written by Alan Ball, provides a classic example of this kind of character development. The protagonist, Lester, has a well-defined goal in mind. He wants to sleep with Angela, the under-aged girlfriend of his daughter. At the same time, he has the feeling that his life is over. When he finally is about to reach his goal, he decides against it, since he has won back his self-respect in the meantime; and self-respect is his need.

A character can reach his goal, yet not meet his need (tragic, cynical end) or fulfill his need and not reach his goal (happy end) – very rarely do both occur simultaneously and even more rarely still that neither one occurs. It is characteristic that we are satisfied as a member of an audience and experience the end as a happy end if the character has not reached his false goal, but has fulfilled his true need. In a classic resolution of the conflict between the want and the need, the want will be met, but voluntarily given up because as the character has met his need the goal has lost its meaning. The fact that the character notices that his goal has been false and fulfills his need naturally presumes that the character changes over the course of the story in a way that improves his moral sense. The character does not need to know that he has changed – the audience knows it and that suffices – he must, however, demonstrate this in some way. John Vorhaus says that in the world of comedy, the protagonist mostly needs love, and he needs that independently of what he wants to have or to be.

You might think that the most recent manifesto in cinema history, the previously mentioned Danish Dogma 95,[19] in reality has done nothing less than rediscover the character as well as the role it plays in creating the plot. The Dogma films primarily have strong screenplays since the idea is to forswear special effects or music that may stop up holes in the story or give a scene a different meaning. The Dogma screenplays center on and always begin with the characters. It is the inner life of the characters that drives the plot and not the plot that determines behavior. In this way, the Dogma principle works to make dramatic storytelling less predictable.

Dogma has managed to give expression to something that many screenwriters, both European and American, have been doing for some years now. It is clear that the motion pictures that give more weight to characters – movies such as *Shakespeare in Love* (Screenplay: Marc Norman and Tom Stoppard), *American Beauty* (Screenplay: Alan Ball), *Talk to Her* (Screenplay: Pedro Almodóvar), *Lost in Translation* (Screenplay: Sofia Coppola), *Eternal Sunshine of the Spotless Mind* (Screenplay: Charlie Kaufman), *Crash* (Screenplay: Paul Haggis and Bobby Moresco), *Little Miss Sunshine* (screenplay: Michael Arndt) and

Juno (Screenplay: Diablo Cody), just to name some of the Oscar winners for Best Original Screenplay in recent years – are also attracting larger, ever-growing audiences.

As an example for a story that grows out of a strong and complex character, I have chosen screenplay excerpts from a 1970s film – a decade many see as a golden age of screenwriting, a decade that produced strong, person-centered movies such as *Chinatown* (Screenplay: Robert Towne), *One Flew Over the Cuckoo's Nest* (Screenplay: Lawrence Hauben and Bo Goldman), *Dog Day Afternoon* (Screenplay: Frank Pierson), *All the President's Men* (Screenplay: William Goldman), *Ordinary People* (Screenplay: Alvin Sargent) and so on. Here, we will just concentrate on the way the protagonist is introduced.

Excerpts from a Screenplay Analysis: *Taxi Driver* (Screenplay: Paul Schrader)

A disturbed Viet Nam veteran, who is now working the night shift driving a cab in New York, confronts the dominant social and moral abyss and begins a deadly crusade through the city.

Although the film by Martin Scorsese and Paul Schrader is one of the favorite films of my generation, many students today have never heard of it. In one of my workshops, we watch the beginning of the movie no one has seen before, and I ask the participants to let me know if they have the feeling the routine of the protagonist has been interrupted. They do not do it; and when I stop 20 minutes later, they admit they were too curious to want to stop. The screenwriter and the director[20] have reached their first goal: The audience is hooked.

This is the beginning of the screenplay, where the screenwriter introduces the character:[21]

> Travis Bickle, age 26, lean, hard, the consummate loner. On the surface, he appears good-looking, even handsome; he has a quiet steady look and a disarming smile that appears from nowhere, lighting up his whole face. Behind that smile, around his dark eyes, in his gaunt cheeks, one can see the ominous stains caused by a life of hidden fear, emptiness and loneliness. He seems to have wandered in from a land where it is always cold, a country where the inhabitants seldom speak.

What a character description! The writer continues to inform us that Travis is drifting in and out of the New York City night life, like a dark shadow among darker shadows and even to give us an exact description of what he is wearing. He is not noticed, we are told – no reason to be noticed, as he is one with his surroundings. He is a raw male force, driving forward; and one cannot tell toward what he is driving. But then one looks closer and sees the inevitable: that the clock spring cannot be wound tighter forever. As the earth moves toward the sun, this captivating character moves toward violence.

The image of the character driving his cab, with our attention focused on his so very sad eyes, functions as the "gateway to the film," that is, the first image to introduce the main theme of the story, in this case loneliness and sorrow. This image introduces us to the subjective perspective of the movie as well as to the infinite sorrow of the protagonist.

Before we shift to the introductory event (to an event that announces the beginning of the story), we look at how the lead character is introduced. You do not get a second chance to make a first impression, as the old saying goes. The first real sentence that a man with sad eyes says is, "I can't sleep nights." The manager of a cab company is interviewing him. We see how he drinks and takes pills. A man living on the verge of a nervous breakdown. How long can he last? The first impression could not be clearer.

"What is the name of the main character?" I ask. Everyone knows the answer. "My name is Travis," the young Robert De Niro tells the sales girl in a porno shop in one of the first scenes. The protagonist flirts with the sales clerk, and the way he introduces himself is part of their flirt. Introducing a name, something that can be so difficult and wooden, happens here in the most natural way; and we do not even notice "the hand of the writer."

A final point concerns the introduction of an important narrative element, the "voice-over" of the protagonist. The visual equivalent and explanation is as follows: The protagonist keeps a journal, and what we hear is what he is writing. This takes us irrevocably into his world, a world that becomes our world too, for the next 108 minutes – a world of prostitution, junkies, of pimps and drug dealers. The hero uses words like "sick" or "scum" in his journal and warns us, "I have to clean the cum off the back seat. Some nights I clean off the blood." This is how we know – blood is going to flow in this story.

An angel appears in the midst of this hell who represents the normal world, which provides the routine for the hero. The writer describes how the slender figure of Betsy appears, out of the congested human mass, in slowing motion. "The crowd parts like the Red Sea," and here she is:[22] "Walking all alone, untouched by the crowd, suspended in space and time."

She is beautiful, spotless, dressed in light colors: "She appeared like an angel," says Travis's voice-over – while the slowing motion, clearly the visual equivalent of "suspended in space and time," helps us understand, even emotionally, that the routine of the hero will be disrupted and that the story the narrator wants to tell us begins exactly here. Travis notes down something in his journal, and the camera shows us one word in a close up: HER.

Exercise #2:
Define and describe the want and the need of the main character in Paul Schrader's screenplay, and analyze the way the character develops over the entire movie, keeping it inside the framework of these two constructs.

Joseph Campbell has said that myth is the penultimate language – the ultimate is silence. It is impossible to talk of character development without having a closer look to his model. The Hero's Journey, identified and enunciated by Campbell in *The Hero with a Thousand Faces* is a good basis for understanding further character development from which dramatic form evolves. Campbell expresses the Journey through the image of the circle, the cycle, a mandala unfolding in time. The center is his own essence, the umbilicus that connects him to the eternity of life beyond the human condition. We could see this as identical to the need of the main character, the one thing that will make the hero whole again.

While watching a movie, the soul of the viewer is prepared to be taken back to its grounding. There is a Dionysian impulse to lose ourselves, to dissolve for a time into the energy that created us. In that sense, we follow the hero. The hero, in order to get there, has followed the writer. The writer is making this journey before him. To do that, he has to have the complex ability of the true state of playfulness, which is to be passionately involved and reflectively detached, both at the same time. What we think we comprehend as viewers is often but the shadow of the full experience. Sometimes we comprehend more or comprehend different parts each time we watch. We will get back to this at a later point in time, for now let us just say that there are screenplays that have managed to incorporate the whole experience, just as the writer has experienced it.

The heroes' journeys are initiation stories. Campbell divides his analysis into three parts, Departure, Initiation and Return. The first phase Campbell calls the Separation. We are stuck; the life in us is stuck, in *Star Wars* language we could even say we are not connected to the Force. We will be separated from whom we have been, from our outmoded condition. The urge for change, for departing from our routine is announced either from within, as the self inside is stirring, or as a coincidence (synchronicity) or from the outside, as an assignment. In any case, it is the Call to Adventure. In the *Taxi Driver,* it is the synchronicity of the angel's appearance combined with Travis's self-stirring from within.

In this context, growth is a question of revolution in the deep structure of the psyche, whereas death is required for rebirth. We experience anxiety, resistance and the fear of the unknown. The Refusal of the Call seems like the natural thing to do. Supernatural powers and events open the way for us. We let ourselves go when we reach the threshold, part of a general expansion of consciousness and a lowering of the mental threshold that ultimately opens the floodgates of fantasy. Then the ego disappears – from the writer, the character and ultimately from the audience. For two hours, you live the life of Travis Bickle. "Vicariously, you live life on a higher plane filled with drama and meaning; life distilled and compressed to its essential conflict, its essential gestures."[23]

The Crossing of the First Threshold and the Belly of the Whale inevitably lead us to the next part, which is the Initiation. The Road of Trials, the Meeting with the Goddess, Woman as the Temptress, Atonement with the Father, Apotheosis and the Ultimate Boon are the phases of this part of the journey, which very much resembles the Aristotelian Middle, that is, what we have come to call a second act. What concerns us now, in terms of character, is that for Campbell, initiation is not seen as the end goal in itself but as the middle of the journey for the character, because there is another threshold to cross: coming back into the "world" with the new insight. This is where the revolutionary spirit of the Initiated is to meet the "jury of sober eyes," of those-who-have-not-seen. There is a new set of trials during the Return: Refusal of the Return, The Magic Flight, Rescue from Without, The Crossing of the Return Threshold, Master of the Two Worlds, Freedom to Live. The cycle is closed.

How does this compare to Aristotelian character development? Seen as it is currently interpreted and ignoring what we will later come to call emotional structure, which is also partly inspired by an Aristotelian idea, the dramatic model "looks at the same process of growth from the point of how it feels to those in crisis and transformation."[24] Although Aristotle's analysis of dramatic structure reveals features that are exactly analogous to the stages of the Hero's Journey, the myth of the Aristotelian model supposedly keeps our sensibilities engaged on the level of contemplation. It is a rational process. Although at a later point

I will try to prove that this is not exactly true, for our current discussion we will keep the notion that drama tells us that growth requires death and rebirth. Dramatic form is exactly that which happens in classical form through the hero's journey; while in alternative forms, where there is not only one hero, such death and rebirth is told exclusively on the level of emotional experience and is not focused on the emotional experience of the one hero. Instead, it is focused on the emotional experience of the writer being mirrored by the audience.

Now how does all this connect with the want, that is, the mode and the need of the main character? Growth through crisis confronts the character with his need, helps him identify it and bring the elixir back home. The old issues and the want are dead. It is more than a mere representation of conflict, it is energy evoking and transforming, to use a phrase of Joseph Campbell's. Dramatic form, and this is something we will investigate closer, orchestrates an experience of emotions. Having said that, and with the knowledge that all drama comes from character, we can start looking at structure and form as something more than the hero's journey, and at drama as the big, important thing it really is. Drama wants to break down the walls, the limits, of who we think we are. It does so by challenging both the way we think and the way we feel. When I say "we," I do not mean simply the audience or the hero – I mean primarily the writer.

In *Taxi Driver*, the hero is a walking contradiction. His want, which is – as he says himself – to find a purpose in his life, to clean up the mess, is in opposition to his need for love, for respect, for belonging, for becoming whole again. Travis is a dark knight who is struggling to come to the light, but is ultimately attracting even more darkness. This journey, which is almost a study of hate and loneliness, takes us through an inner cave that is very dark indeed. Travis fights the darkness inside in an attempt to clean up the mess, to flush out the garbage and the trash inside – and he fails. Like the Raskolnikov character in Dostoyevsky's *Crime and Punishment*, Travis goes from alienation to the realization that we are all inexplicably bound up with each other. In order to get there he needs to go through the very hell of absolute detachment and estrangement. In the end he (almost) does not fulfill his want to be different, a chosen one, a superman (in the Nietschian sense), but in a very dark way he (almost) fulfills his need of becoming whole again. Travis's blood bath actually accomplishes very little, and he remains quite far from being redeemed or connecting with others. This little word "almost" is what makes the difference between a classic happy end and an unsettling experience.

Exercise #3:

Explain the story of a movie of your choice in one sentence, beginning with the protagonist and trying to concentrate on the main conflict.

We employ the technique of one-sentence re-narration predominately in film financing – later in the marketing of the film: the "log line" or the "tag line." This technique has a long literary tradition as it has been used to focus on an idea, on the essence of the story. Gustav Freytag writes in 1863, that it is even possible that the writer, as the creator, will better understand his idea, following the rules of his art, if he summarizes the basic thoughts of his writing in one sentence.[25] He also recognizes the difficulty of this undertaking: If it is uncomfortable for the writer, or at times difficult to reduce the idea of the developing material to a formula, he would do well to encourage this "cooling of his warm soul" at the beginning of the work and to rigorously test and judge the "found idea" using the basic rules of drama. Freytag continues by saying it is also illuminating for the stranger to seek the "hidden soul" in the finished work and, however incomplete it may be, put it down in words.

The "log line" can be a one-liner or as many as five lines. The "tag line" is what we find on a film poster (e.g. the tag line of the first *Alien* movie was "In space, no one can hear you scream.") The log line can never directly refer to the emotional theme, for example, a film about love and our need to be together with someone, or a story of betrayal and so on; whatever gives the dramatic or emotional theme its power, that is, its universality, must be seen as a flaw here. On the contrary, it is important to stress what makes the story in question so special, as well as to identify an element that makes it stand out. The description of an idea, the pitch – a term taken from baseball – can be thus employed in screenplay development as well as in the ideation phase, that is, in the phase of the artistic transformation of the material into a unifying idea.[26] This requires practice.

Taxi Driver is not a portrait of alienation and loneliness made manifest as violence. It is a portrait of a taxi driver who has come back from Vietnam a damaged man, who goes on a murderous rampage in order to save the world and by this act save his very soul. Can you save the world and your soul by murdering bad people? This contradiction between his good intentions and his bad choices is the central dramatic conflict.

In the next exercise we will go a step further. It may sound easier than it is in practice.

Exercise #4:
Tell the story of the last movie you saw in one sentence without mentioning the title or any names or characteristic elements, so that others can figure out the title from this one line summary of yours.

If citing Gustav Freytag has not persuaded you yet that trying to summarize a story in one sentence is not just a commercial Hollywood technique, let us try to do the same with a European movie. Let us take the *Decalogue 1: Eden. I am the Lord, thy God,* by Krzysztof Kieslowski and Krzystof Piesewicz, the first episode of the TV series based on the Ten Commandments. So obviously a warning to not worship false gods, this is nothing less than a study of the meaning of life and death, and ultimately of faith. Questions like "Why do people have to die at all?" or "What remains when people die?" and "What is the meaning of life?" are pronounced with such simplicity and simultaneous splendor, that it almost feels sacrilegious to reduce this story to one line that focuses on the protagonist and the main conflict: A mathematics professor discovers that rational thought provides little comfort when his son dies. In Freytag's words, however incomplete the result of our efforts may seem, there is no other way to seek the hidden soul of the story and to see how that idea is structured as a story.

The trick of the status perspective

One of the most helpful tricks of creative screenwriting, as it turned out to be, is viewing human relations as a power game. Keith Johnstone uses the construct "status" in the subterfuge. What he means is the perpetual dealing with power and hierarchy that takes place in every human transaction. Normally, status is perceived and conveyed unconsciously. Events are of secondary importance in the relations between characters, as well as in human relations. What is important is whether someone ranks themselves, consciously or unconsciously, higher or lower than their opposite. What, exactly, does this mean?

There are people who prefer to say "yes" (low status players) and others who prefer to say "no" (high status players). Those who say "yes" are rewarded with adventures they experience due to their attitude, while those who say "no" are rewarded with security, which they create, or better retain, due to their attitude. The so-called "high status player" blocks every action unless he has the feeling he can control it. Blocking action is a form of aggression that we are trained to accept and learn to ignore while being socialized, which at best unconsciously creates a bad mood. Children react differently to such aggression.[27] As do some schizophrenics who are uncannily perceptive. All the rest learn with time to overlook them, and we forget that every action, every word or even sound and every movement has a reason or a motivation and is not innocent of purpose. We need to recover the ability to see and feel as we did when we were children.

The following example of blocking communication by a high status player, as an aggressive act, we owe to Keith Johnstone: A small girl and a woman walk by a park. The small girl sees a flower and, suddenly full of enthusiasm, pulls the woman over to the flower. "Look, how beautiful!" "All flowers are beautiful," answers the woman dryly, without thinking about it any further – and the small girl begins to cry. A simple sentence automatically becomes an attack and at the same time an end to the discussion or any other communication.

We can understand the term "status" perhaps still better if we see it as something unconscious (or sometimes even conscious) and not as description of our position, and definitely not of our social position: A gentleman can place himself, for example, lower than his servant and, quite the opposite, a servant can place himself higher than his master (he can become insubordinate and arrogant, or simply be more intelligent or more talented than his master).[28]

Exercise #5:

Try to say something nice or something rude to the person beside you, and observe their reaction. Did the response give the responder a higher or a lower status?

In this exercise, it will soon become clear that we often obtain the opposite result from the one for which we strive. A character does not necessarily have to reach the status he has set as a goal. It is just as interesting to observe them attempting to strive to reach a higher status which, however, they never achieve. The change in status can take place through dialogue or even through attitudes or actions.

We cannot avoid the status game; it is an inseparable part of human relations. Often it is a game among friends, thus a game friends play gladly and consciously and make fun of each other or banter while they pretend mutual respect. The comic makes us laugh by unrelentingly lowering his status and the status of others as well.[29]

Exercise #6:
Spend a whole day in a "status mode" – observe, listen, watch from a distance, discuss, note dialogue and situations until you begin to grow antennae for the often quiet, hidden status game that surrounds us.

An understanding of the status game is an indispensable precondition for the sensitization of the screenwriter. We can arrange our stories and our dialogues more naturally by being able to understand and change the status of our characters. Primarily, however, it is a good way to relate to and create the field of the relations among the characters, both in concrete scenes and in the complete story. From now on, we will use this approach as it makes it possible to use our instincts while writing – because in doing so we think more on the functional level than on the content level.

Thinking in terms of function is an important aspect of the creative telling of stories. Perhaps it is even the simplest way, at least in the beginning, to set the creative process in motion. A storyteller should forget that he is busy creating stories and begin to think in terms of function, "If I say, 'Make up a story,' then most people are paralyzed. If I say, 'Describe a routine and then interrupt it,' nobody has a problem with it," says Keith Johnstone[30] – but there always are some storytellers who try to work "intelligently." They invent ordinary situations, which seem "original" to them, with the result that the interruption of the ordinary becomes senseless. On the other hand, the interruption of a routine can become such an everyday event, we can hardly experience it as an interruption. If we say, for example, two mountain climbers begin to climb a mountain, then the beginning of their activity can hardly be experienced as the beginning of a story, that is, like the interruption of a routine. Continuing this mental game, we can imagine we are in a new routine and keep going by interrupting it if we are stuck at a certain place or are more or less blocked.

Exercise #7:
Begin a scene with a routine and interrupt that routine in the same scene. The scene may not contain any more than two characters, so one of the two characters will inevitably interrupt the routine of the other, by something the other character will not expect. It is necessary that you remain within the time and place limits of the scene, as well as limit yourself to two characters rather than adding a third character or "bringing in" further assistance from the outside. As the scene unfolds, you will need to select one of the four following alternatives:

1) both characters lower their status;
2) both characters raise their status;
3) one character raises his status while the other one lowers hers;
4) the two characters exchange their status.

The goal is to let the scene flow but not control it while it does.

Since this exercise is the first writing exercise that will result to a complete scene, it is necessary to describe the function of a scene in general and in relation to what we are doing here. A scene usually is defined as a change in the place where the action occurs. A screenplay consists of a relatively large number of scenes and, in general, each scene has a well-defined function in the overall scheme of the screenplay; it either advances the plot or facilitates character development. A good scene, however, has further, less important "tasks" beyond its fundamental function, such as introducing characters or a place, making the audience laugh, etc. We will keep an eye on all of this. What interests us now is the relationship between the two characters (action-reaction), and how and where this relationship changes over the course of the scene.

The significance of dialogue as a dramatic element is beyond doubt.[31] At the beginning of our work with the creative method of screenwriting, scenes crop up that all too often rely on canned dialogue. In order to prevent this, we will introduce an object into the scene. The characters will begin to communicate in a different way and stop using predictable dialogue. Two characters have a dialogue just fine about a pair of shoes or a bicycle. Since this makes no difference, the most important thing is whether they will provoke each other, or lure each other into a trap or want to apologize to each other.

The concept of the status game rests on a narrative element that in most screenplay theories is seen as the most important of all. This is conflict, something we will now look at more closely.

The structure of the screenplay: Second sequence (the conflict)

The substance of drama, as well as the essential precondition for its sheer existence, is conflict or, in the broadest sense of the word, contrast. "Conflict is the heartbeat of all writing,"[32] says Lajos Egri, who continues to define conflict as an unbelievable energy, comparable to the energy that produces a chain of explosions when an initial explosion goes off. A piece that has no conflict creates an atmosphere of despair, of the immediate danger of deconstruction. Without conflict, life is impossible, both on earth and everywhere in the universe. The technique of writing is, plain and simple, the representation of generally valid laws that govern each and every atom or constellation of stars. This means nothing less than that the structural laws that are valid for atoms or galaxies are equally valid for writing.

For Heraclites, conflict was the beginning of everything. Everything that happens takes place due to conflict. The Iliad is the model of conflict, since it builds on an emotion – the rage and desire for revenge which Achilles harbors. Here, the main conflict has to do with the core emotion of the story. In motion pictures, moments of conflict may be seen as the source or cause of emotional reactions in the audience.[33] Throughout the history of psychology, conflict has frequently been seen as the main source of emotions and so it is in film narration too. There the conflict mostly describes the fight of a hero against all kinds of obstacles and adversities that block his way. Conflict is engendered if a need, an intention or a goal encounters an obstacle.

In the end, it is about the establishment of patterns of expectation and attitudes that cannot just be created and satisfied. One can also disturb or provoke expectations by the unexpected, by discrepancies. Modern theories of narration, from thinkers such as Todorov and Greimas, dismiss the concept of conflict, but declare the dynamic of the narrative process as the result of disturbances of equilibrium, that is, as the result of tensions between equilibrium and disequilibrium.[34] According to Hegel, the dramatic collision has "its reason in an injury that cannot remain an injury, but rather must be reversed; it is a change in a condition of harmony which itself must be changed again."[35]

There are two types of dramatic conflict: the inner one, whereby one means the conflict that the hero has with his suppressed or dark side, and the external one that happens between two characters through their defiance of each other.[36] According to some screenplay theoreticians, there are other kinds of conflict, like the conflict between the hero and society, his surroundings or nature. Linda Seger even differentiates among five different kinds of conflicts: the internal one, the one among people, the social, the situational and the cosmic conflict.

However one categorizes them, the basic types of dramatic conflict – man against nature, a supernatural power, a group or a situation, man against men as well as man against himself – the rules are the same for tragedy as for comedy.[37] The best stories arise in a natural way when all three types of conflict are present. Those are the so-called archaic stories.

Conflict may be something else too. It is the tension between two opposing poles. A single electrical pole is not enough to ensure that a light goes on; two poles are required. Introducing his word games to create stories, the Italian children's book author Gianni Rodari describes how a word can only become active if a second word provides a charge, forces it to leave the well-worn trail and to discover new possibilities of meaning. Later on, he states that where there is no struggle, there is no life.[38]

Henri Vallon writes that thoughts occur in pairs.[39] The concept of "soft" does not develop prior to or after the concept of "hard," rather it develops simultaneously in a conflict that at the same time is a genesis. This binary structure is the fundamental element of thought, and not the singular elements. The pair is the precursor of the individual elements. Not least, Sigmund Freud ascribes to the unconscious conflict and to the ascertainment of the difference, that is to contrast, such as the conflict, a central role in the emergence of the comic.[40]

Conflict and contrast are everywhere: between the protagonist and the antagonist; between what the characters want and what they get and what prevents them from getting it; between the good and bad sides of a character; between the text and subtext; between what we say and what we really mean; between comedy and tragedy. There is no strong tragedy without amusing elements and no strong comedy without tragic elements. The biggest advocate of this was Shakespeare, who knew the effect of contrasting very well: In his tragedies, he often inserted amusing scenes and characters. Real comedy is much darker than tragedy – make no mistake about that.

In the film *Taxi Driver*, the scenes of "comic relief" are an indispensable part of an otherwise terribly dark tragedy. Another characteristic example is the film *Terms Of Endearment* by James L. Brooks, where the audience has tears in their eyes from laughing through half the movie, up to the point they learn that one of the characters, the beloved daughter and mother of two children, has cancer. Seeing this movie in a theatre with an audience is an interesting experience, as from this moment on laughter turns into tears. This powerful result is only possible because the audience was "dissolved" in laughter beforehand.

Not least, contrast should occur also between the individual scenes. There are always ways to create contrast or intensify it by using everything in the medium that can be changed: rhythm, time, color, light, sound. As Frank Daniel used to say – if one scene is slow, the next one can be fast. If a scene is quiet, the next can be loud. Staccato, legato, variations in camera position and movement, variations in the editing rhythm – anything goes.

The trick of failure: The courage to fail and the law of quantity

Samuel Beckett once said that to be called a writer is to accept the inevitability of failure.[41] After the lack of responsibility trick and the status game trick, we will now get acquainted with the third important creative screenwriting trick, which is what we will call the failure trick. We all know the feeling: What we fear most of all is failure. Subsequently, what we often lack is the courage to fail – because failure takes courage and because the courage to fail is one of the most important preconditions to be able to work creatively.

"You have to be a very stubborn person to remain an artist in this culture," says Keith Johnstone.[42] "It is easy to play the role of artist, but actually to create something means going against one's education," he continues – which taught us one thing with clarity, that we need to obtain success. The inspiration or creative work must be as natural and easy as the five senses, and thinking about success is often the biggest obstacle. One of the most difficult things we must learn is to stop wanting to control the future, to empty our head and to wait and see what will come – something we can learn through improvisation.

"People aren't thinking about how you look to them. They are far too busy worrying about how they look to you",[43] says John Vorhaus in his attempt to make our conception of success relative – but what does this mean for writing? John Vorhaus suggests the following: Of the ten ideas we can have at any given time, we will expect that nine will be useless. We assume a risk ten times, because we know we will be unsuccessful nine times – an idea that frees us from the expectation to be good. This simple law of quantity trick is used to free up creativity, this time from the pressure to succeed. The exact number is rather unimportant (some think twenty is about right, for others five attempts are enough). What is important is the quantity, which includes our certain failures. The law of quantity has yet another advantage: The things we know well are quickly disposed of and the brain begins to produce something new; it becomes creative.

The goal of the failure trick is to minimize our fear, because if we expect success, if we plan for it,[44] if we put our hopes on it, this also means that we need success – and that we are afraid of failure. That fear blocks us. It is not so terrible to fall after all. At least we will be moving forward!

So concentrate instead on the small steps. Stop thinking about the premiere, or about secretly reading enthusiastic press comments; let us free ourselves from our strong desire to keep the creative process permanently under control and concentrate on what we actually do, put words on paper. Most of them, we should concede, will wind up in the waste paper basket. In reality, we learn to write as though we were assuming that what we write would be put in a drawer and nobody will ever see it. Alternatively, as the screenwriter Anna Hamilton Phelan puts it: "Never surrender to the result. Just write the next word."[45]

The following exercises are designed to help us develop our ability to write that next word without surrendering to the result, while we continue to develop the characters.

Exercise #8:
You have five minutes to note down ten special names for ten characters (if possible include their occupation). Thinking this over should be avoided – but if you do it anyway, do it fast. Accept your first thoughts: Count on most of them winding up in the waste paper basket.

"A character is first and foremost the sound of his name," says the writer William H. Gass; and Roland Barthes says that a character is the result of one or several combinations.

Exercise #9:
Select one of the names chosen in Exercise #8 and describe the character that belongs to that name: for instance, his or her physical characteristics (sex, age as well as any peculiarities in appearance to help visualize the character), social status (occupation and reason for choice of this occupation, social matrix and behavior), family situation and network of relationships (whether the character has a family, children, friends, whether she sees family and friends often, when did she last fall in love and how did this relationship end; how are their relations with their colleagues), psychology (mental level, main impression: distant, sad, etc.), ambition and dreams, suppressed desires, fears, the way he or she sees life.[46]

One character among ten

The first possible combination of character elements is put together by name and occupation. These are the outward elements that define us in this world, and even if they may play no definite role in the story that will emerge from the character, we need to know them to be able to bring the character to life. In order to get the most out of this game, we aim for high-contrast combinations. Among them are often combinations that strive to be amusing but fail. Sometimes the contrast will be between what the character thinks she is and what the actual reality of her life is. The following description of character has been developed, based on a combination derived from just such a list. The writer selected the character, "Hans Niemand, Philosopher," from her list. I ask her to answer my questions without thinking about them, that is, to assume simply that the answers are already in her head, that they pre-exist. Interestingly enough, she does this with ease. In a way, this is what we need to do when we have created a character. Ask the questions in our head and try not to think about them, as if the answers were already there – because they are. Here is the result:

SIXTY YEARS OLD, *bald, wears eyeglasses. Single, and LONELY. He writes books that are never published, lives in a house he inherited from his mother, in a good residential area, lives from the little money that she left him, does not have a television. The only person he has contact with is an old friend from university days. They have endless philosophical discussions. Peter, his friend from university, is the only one who knows about the old story and therefore never asks questions. The old story has to do with her. He fell in love only once in his life. With her. When he was still at the university. She had an accident. The road was slippery. She was at the wheel. He waited for her at an abandoned resort; he had thought out the whole scene and planned it down to the smallest detail; not even the sudden weather reversal would prevent it from happening. He wanted to ask her if she would marry him. He waited two hours and when she did not come, he furiously drove away in the other direction. Anger was an emotion he knew too well – it came naturally to him. She was never reliable. The next day he learned she had died at the site of the accident. The road to the resort was untraveled; she lay three whole hours on the road. By the time she was discovered, it was too late. Too late to fall in love with another woman. His heart had turned to stone. He is devoured by pangs of conscience. Day after day. If only he had not been angry. If he had not chosen that resort. If he had only driven back home. If he had not taken the other direction. If he had changed his plans when it began to snow. Why there? Why on that day? Why her and not him? He never speaks about it anymore now. He does not have ambitions. He does not dream anymore.* ■

What we are getting here is the backstory of a character and perhaps even a story in itself. Should the writer decide that the backstory tells a much more interesting story than the one she chose, that is, the one in the period she chose to meet the character for the first time as a writer?

We are informed that the character is lonely right away. He must have a reason for his isolation. When I ask her when he fell in love the last time, she says it was a very long time ago. Then the old story gradually unfolds. The writer answers the questions so firmly and quickly that it is clear that she has a very exact picture of the character in her head. If she had to describe him in general terms, however, she would not know where to begin. The fact that she must answer simple and very concrete questions simplifies the process – and it helps her look for the conflicts rather than the vague and unfocused stuff that she would have written if she were to sit down to "think of" and to describe the character.

Exercise #10:

Now write an internal monologue for the character you have created – in the first person.

The exercise involving internal monologue has one of the most well-known notions of Italian Neo-realism for its inspiration. The film, *Ladri di Bicicletti* (The Bicycle Thief), from a script by Cesare Zavattini, is based on an internal monologue the Italian writer Luigi Bartolini wrote using the first-person voice of a poor painter, who is looking for a bicycle in the streets of Rome. The screenwriter stressed the despair of the character by making it completely necessary for him to find his stolen bicycle – yes, even a matter of life and death for the main character, because he can only keep his hard won job if he finds it – no bicycle, no job; and no job means he will not survive.

The exercise utilizing internal monologue naturally reminds us of the "voice-over," a narrative tool that is difficult to master and is often used awkwardly by screenwriters. The voice-over is then nothing else but the inner voice of the storyteller, often unnamed, that is heard at the beginning and often accompanies us through the entire movie. The screenwriter can thus tell us the story directly instead of telling it through the structure – which would be obviously much more exciting. Dramatic structure has after all one primary effect, it tells the story.

The voice-over, which we will discuss at greater length below, is a device assigned to the epic genre of narrative film, even though its use does not automatically result in an epic. After a long banishment from the toolbox of screenwriters, the off-screen narrating character has become an object of experimentation and variation – we have seen it used in a more interesting way than described above, in motion pictures (*Sixth Sense, Usual Suspects*), as well as in television shows (*Desperate Housewives*). In these cases, the writers have toyed with the question of the so-called "unreliable narrator" and have used it as a dramaturgical device, a perfectly acceptable use of an established narrative device.

A voice-over tells its story

The following text has emerged from the inner monologue exercise, and it represents the inner voice of an aging judge:

DEVIL TAKE IT, overslept again. I'll be late. If you had been here, you would have woken me up. Why aren't you here? Where the hell are you? You all think things are so simple ... still five months. I don't pay enough attention to her, she said. I don't have any time for her, she said. Another five months and then I'd have had all the time she wants. Another five months, and I'd never oversleep again. If I'd just overslept then. If I hadn't been so hard on him. So ... what's that word? Resolute. How could I be so dumb? So rash? And her? She doesn't understand that because of me ... what the devil does she want? Who the devil does she think she is? ... Five months and it would have all been over. It's not my fault. He said that, too. But the evidence ... he was guilty. Twenty years old. No, it's absolutely impossible that I'm to blame. When you're twenty, you don't give up so fast. Who the devil gave him the cord? ■

A story gradually emerges by way of a text that has evolved without previous thought, with no definition of theme, idea or story; but rather quite clearly through associations that sound like the confused thoughts of a character. It is the story of a judge who is five months from retiring. After an entire life lived without any significant problems, a young man he had only recently found guilty killed himself. As if that were not enough, evidence surfaced during the commotion around his suicide that finally proved his innocence. The judge tries to suppress his guilt feelings, but they become unbearable. When his wife leaves him, he is left staring in the abyss. A judge who is five months from retiring arrives at the lowest point of his life.

Exercise #11:

Spend 24 hours as the character you have created. Note down what you have noticed and correct the description of the character if it seems necessary.

This exercise has further character development as a goal. The writer of the judge's story, for example, gets some additional information from the exercise. The judge is absent-minded. He cannot find his things, his toothbrush or his keys. He becomes ever more obsessed by the idea that he is too old, that his life is over. It sounds logical when one considers that he has guilt feelings, because a young man lost his life as a result of the judge's decision. What will this man in crisis do when the next case arrives on his desk? How much of a challenge will that be? What would be the worst-case scenario for that character? Let us stop here. The direction and the process are clear enough.

It is also clear that logic has little to do with this process. At most, one can talk about emotional reasoning. As will the audience later on, the writer submits less to the illusion of a character, in whose pain he participates and in whose situation he enters. It is rather that he or she assimilates much more to a whole world that is presented as an "inner condition."[47]

Exercise #12:
Look for a character from a newspaper article and develop the idea for a story. While doing so, stay with the character and his main conflict. Can you determine what he wants or really needs?

The following text, inspired by a newspaper article, gives us an impression of the character of an undertaker:

THEO is an ambitious entrepreneur. Because of his excessive ambition, he has quarreled with his business partner and brother. Theo's eyes well up when he attends funerals. He is devoted to his occupation. He never asks for an advance payment, for instance, and he becomes emotional when somebody dies alone – in such cases, he often pays the funeral expenses out of his own pocket. ■

Do we as writers have to identify ourselves with the character absolutely, so that we can understand him? Do we have to imagine that we are these persons? Not necessarily. Instead of understanding the characters as projections of the writer, it would be conceivable that we bind ourselves to them in the way we do with persons of everyday life: by shared emotions, sympathy and affection. This approach is often more productive. It is important that we are emotionally involved and that we do not observe the character from a distance and with scorn.

In the original newspaper article, the entrepreneur mainly burnishes his own image. As a result, he tells us everything the storyteller now conveys as a fact. But the difference between what he really is and the radiant nimbus that surrounds him raises questions – and points to the uncertainty of what in the end is a very human figure. After the game of questions, the storyteller decides that she wants to keep what she took from the article. The fact that the funeral entrepreneur cries at funerals and pays for the funerals of the lonely souls out of his own pocket, naturally makes him a loser and creates conflict with his family. The family business is on the verge of bankruptcy and his family despises him – most of all his little brother, who is watching his birthright gradually disappear. Everybody hates Theo, and the only ones who love him are now in the ground – or soon will be.

Another interesting contrast, which lies hidden in the original text and which finally has emerged in the discussion, is the fact that Theo, the undertaker, whom many might expect to be familiar with death, is terrified of one thing – death. Is this superstitious man, this hypochondriac, an undertaker by profession so he can avoid the unavoidable? This is why he is always focused on the details – on why and how his clients started out on their last journey. This is surely the kernel of a truly human comedy.

The structure of the screenplay: Third sequence (the first dramatic question)

All stories begin with an image, which instantly introduces us to the principle theme of the script. It is like a gateway to the story. At the same time, this gateway opens the way into the space and time of the story.

Most stories first tell us about an ordinary situation or about the *status quo*. It is the unimpaired normal condition of the protagonist. It is his outmoded state which creates the urge for change, for moving out of the routine and which is either announced from within or as a coincidence (synchronicity); or from outside, as in an assignment. A construct often used here is the exposition or the introduction. The introduction should provide all the necessary information to the audience for all story elements: the main characters, the surrounding field (the social and psychological context in which the events take place), the style as well as the dominant mood. One speaks also of the preparation. Here not only the introduction of the character is meant, but also the introduction of the concrete time and place of the story.

Lajos Egri also uses the term exposition, whereby he clarifies that "there is a mistaken idea that exposition is another name for the beginning of a play [...] and (that) we must establish mood, atmosphere, background, before our action begins."[48] The exposition is, however, part of the whole piece and not a detachable component placed at the beginning that plays no further role afterwards. Yet most of the writing guides treat the exposition like a separate element of the dramaturgical structure. Quite the reverse, the introduction must unfold continuously right up to the conclusion of the drama. It remains true that you never get a second chance to make a first impression, but you should also give yourself (and the character) a chance to leave a lasting impression. Perhaps the term "setup" would be more correct – a term, which Linda Seger happily uses: "The goal of the setup is to arrange for us all the important information we need for the story to begin".[49] Frank Daniel often used the term "predicament." The first and most important task is to bring the character step by step into the most difficult situation possible.

The theoreticians who base their screenplay analysis on Joseph Campbell's book use the term "ordinary world." Since in the end most stories are journeys that lead the hero and the audience into "special worlds," most stories, according to Christopher Vogler, begin with the establishment of the ordinary world as a basis for comparison. The special world of a story is only something special if we see it as a contrast to the material, everyday world, the "mundane world," which also signifies the starting point of the hero. The ordinary world is the general framework, the "home base," as well as the hero's backstory.[50] The next narrative step is the "beginning" of the story. "A beginning is that which does not itself follow anything by causal necessity," writes Aristotle, "but after which something naturally is or comes to be."[51] That is, other events may precede the beginning – yet they are not inevitably related to the beginning.

The Aristotelian "beginning" is what many film script analysts call the inciting or initiating incident, which disrupts the *status quo* or the routine of the protagonist and sets the story in motion. One also uses the terms "trigger," "call to adventure," "point of attack" and "hook." The readers and later the audience are somewhat like fish that the screenwriter must catch – and to make this happen needs a good hook. This moment is also called a catalyst. It is the moment when "something happens."[52]

The goal here is to focus the attention of the audience, as well as provoke questions whose answers we will look for ourselves as the story unfolds. In reality, it deals with one important question, and the more clearly we pose this question, the more clearly we will be able to answer it later on. We will call this question the first dramatic question or the key dramatic question of a film story. Usually answered at the climax of the story, it creates an arc of expectation, a story arc, which keeps us hooked throughout the film story.

Most screenplay and film analysts flinch at the thought of indicating page numbers or minutes, but in practice they all put this structural point in the middle of the first act, which is usually 10 to 15 minutes into the film. If we were writing or thinking in dramatic sequences, that sequence would normally be one sequence into the screenplay. This is the very last moment for something to happen that begins the story, when we realize what this is all about when the first structural step is taken. Naturally, there are many films where nothing happens for a much longer stretch but, to put it mildly, that is not necessarily an advantage.

Linda Seger describes three types of events that begin the story. She uses the term catalyst and stresses that it is necessary that this point poses the central question: "The strongest catalysts are concrete events which facilitate a story. In *Witness* a murder is committed and John Book must solve the riddle, that is, he must find the killer. In *Ghostbusters*, someone sees a ghost in the library, and in *Jaws*, a shark kills a swimmer."[53] Generally, she states that the catalyst will be located between the first and the fifteenth page of the screenplay, and until it takes place we cannot know what the story is about. The examples cited here are plot driven – but what happens when the story is not so much about events that happen in the outside world or when the events are not told in a chronological order?

For the moment it will have to suffice to see that even in plot driven screenplays, occasionally the catalyst is some bit of information (or a dream or a vision) the protagonist receives. A woman explains that she has cancer; a man gets the job he wanted or is fired. A couple learns they will never be able to have children. A father answers his son's question of what remains when a person dies with a firm answer, nothing – there is no soul. We fall into a state of sadness, even despair. If there is nothing, what is life about? What is death about?

The catalyst can also be a series of events and in this case, it is called "situational:" This means that there is no definite introductory event. It often is simply the point where the hero runs out of options. Some screenplay analysts confuse this point with the first turning point or define the first turning point as the introductory event – or they designate another point located just before the first turning point as a catalyst. Yet what exactly takes place between the "hook" and the first turning point? Linda Seger describes this phase as "act one development." Here we become better acquainted with the characters and watch them in action before we watch them develop more fully in the second act.[54] In her opinion, the best dramatic moment to introduce the main conflict and the backstory of the protagonist is located here – this is also the time to introduce the antagonists, if this has not already happened when the introductory event took place.

David Mamet is in that sense a true master at setting up status games and intense contrast or conflict among the characters. Let us have a look at how he does this.

Excerpt from a screenplay analysis: *The Verdict* (Screenplay: David Mamet)

An alcoholic lawyer, whose career ended a long time ago, decides against a quick profit when he gets a last chance to win justice for his client and fight to regain his own self-respect.

An image of Frank, the protagonist whose name we will learn later, functions as a gateway to the story: Frank is alone, playing pool and drinking. A steppenwolf. As in Herman Hesse's novel, we are confronted with the archetype of the aggressive, even self-destructive, suffering character who concerns himself with being different, with separating himself from those he is around, with being wronged in the past and expecting to be wronged again.

A sequence of absolute degradation of the character develops. The lawyer, Frank, looks for a client among a funeral party at a funeral home, by pretending to be a friend of the deceased – in the hope that somebody will let him take care of his affairs. We are led to understand that this has become a routine with him. The relatively short sequence ends with the sentence, "Who the hell do you think you are?" The dead man's son eventually throws him out. Frank is finished, alone and disgraced – now more than ever. He has hit rock bottom. How did it come to this? This is not the right time to find out.

The hook appears in the form of a naive, sympathetic couple referred by his only remaining friend and sponsor. The friend warns him that this time he is going to stop supporting him financially if he loses. Frank gets a last chance. Will he seize it? Will he return from the land of the living dead? This is the key dramatic question of the story.

The case seems simple at first. The woman who has come to him with her husband is the sister of a young woman who fell into a coma during a routine operation in a famous city hospital. A renowned doctor has apparently given her the wrong anesthetic. The most important information seems to be that the hospital is a church hospital and that the administration wants to settle.

For the first time we see the lawyers and the bishop who represent the other side, and we learn about Frank's backstory, a story his opponents think has made him predictable and have included in their plans. We get the picture of a brilliant, promising young lawyer who became involved in a dirty case at some point and failed – at first as a lawyer and then in his private life. His fall from grace was followed by an ugly divorce from his partner's daughter. Frank was never able to get back on his feet. In the past few years, he seems to have missed the train altogether – he took only four cases and lost all four. Frank is even afraid to enter the courtroom, the opposing lawyers report – and of course, they feel like the case is going to be a slam-dunk.

We are 30 minutes into the movie when the sequence of the first turning point begins. Frank meets the only witness of the defense, a doctor who more or less assures him that his colleagues, who were attending the patient, murdered her. He claims to have enough evidence for Frank to win the case. Why should he settle with them? When Frank doubts his motives and asks him why he wants to do this, why he is ready to be a witness for the prosecution, the doctor falls silent. "To do the right thing. Isn't that why you're doing it?"

We know – and Frank knows – that "to do the right thing" is not the main motive for Frank. We understand that Frank stopped believing in justice a long time ago, because he feels justice betrayed him in the end. We also know that he used to believe in it, that he used to try to do the right thing and that he used to have the strength and the ability to fight and win. The contrast between the Frank of the past and Frank today increases the tension of the moment and poses the second dramatic question of the story: Will Frank be able to do the right thing? When we talk about a dramatic question, we mean all the related questions as well, so let us ask these three questions: What is the right thing? Will he be able to get back up on his feet? Will he do what his opponents expect?

A remarkable scene about status ensues, a status game: Frank is in the office of the opposing lawyers. The moment arrives he has waited for so long. He is about to take the money they have offered to settle – the amount is the highest amount he realistically expects, an expectation we know about from a previous scene. It is a carefully calculated amount: USD 200,000, of which Frank would get one third. Frank realizes that the opposing counsel is confident, and that they have assumed his share will be the most important aspect of the settlement. "If I take the money I'm lost," he says aloud and ... refuses the offer. This immediately raises his status. Opposing counsel is shocked. Is he crazy? "I can win this case," Frank answers confidently, and then leaves.

The second dramatic question, the one that will keep the tension going in the second act, is reaffirmed. Will Frank win the case? We will get the answer at the beginning of the third act. In the context of Frank's line of development, we hope that Frank has made the right decision (and fear that he has not), but his motivation remains questionable. If he wins the case, as he seems to hope, he will take home a much bigger fee. Since we have come to care about the character, what we truly hope for is atonement – not a fat fee that will buy him more drinks and end up adding to his loneliness.

This is a screenplay that is as elegant as the mechanism of a clock – with an impressive, dramatic use of the backstory of the protagonist and an excellent classical development potential for the protagonist.

In remembrance

As we gradually come to terms with the terminology of dramaturgy – with the different terms for the screenwriter's tools, their etymology and function – we should keep in mind why we actually need it.

Definitions and dramatic effects, the right time and place to use them, the rules; it is completely impossible and hardly worth keeping them in mind while we write. Yet if we analyze a screenplay, this knowledge will help us see what is lacking.

Frank Daniel reminds us, "Scriptwriting is mainly re-writing." Yet in order to rewrite, we first have to write, and the most important thing in writing is to be able to feel the flow and rhythm of the story. We get into an almost feverish condition when the characters we have created lead us, instead of us leading them. When this happens, go with the flow and believe in the characters. Easier said than done, because it is a process requiring discipline and concentration. Building the structure comes later.

Of course, one could also first structure the story and then write, but how predictable will the result be? When you know where you are heading, why bother to make the trip? If the writer should have the same cognitive, emotional and philosophical questions when he embarks on the story, as when he confronts the characters as a member of the audience, he cannot know all the answers beforehand, and he should not. In this sense, the screenplay is first written and then structured. In order to structure, one needs tools. If the narrative instinct is functioning well, the story acquires structure as it is written.

What we do here is become acquainted with the tools and techniques of creative screenwriting, as we systematically learn to use structure terminology. At the same time, in this first part, the four basic components of the creative screenwriting method and emotional structure theory have been introduced: improvisation, the game of aporia, the emotional structural knots and the system of the two dramatic questions. Below, we will gradually delve deeper into each one of these components.

And do not forget the following:

1) Rely on quantity.
2) Do not judge, do not try to anticipate and control, try to take and include.
3) Let your initial ideas and status relationships among the characters, the status game, guide your writing.

Most of all, enjoy the game. Convey the emotion, the information about human experience, act and share, connect, relate. Do not be afraid to make mistakes. Treat mistakes like a badge of honor. "Perfection is terrible, it cannot have children," as Sylvia Plath would say.[55]

The Middle

"The question is," said Alice, "whether you can make words mean so many different things."

Lewis Carroll

Techniques of Creative Screenwriting

Gathering of material and the combination technique

The creative process often begins by connecting memories with new elements that at first glance often seem to have nothing to do with each other. The observation and gathering up of material are among the most important and ongoing tasks of the screenwriter. New elements confront us from all directions, and the roads are literally paved with new material. We only need to gather it up. Our subconscious mind will take care of the lion's share of archiving the new material, but even this procedure must be learned and practiced.

In the literature of screenwriting, screenplay mavens mostly propose using the formal method of working, with index cards to structure and direct the writing process. In doing so, the individual scenes are recorded on the index cards and used by the screenwriter to play out all the variations in the way the plot unfolds.[1] For our purposes, we utilize the method of archiving of elements on index cards, which we can use at any time to jog our fantasy. A writer's journal can perform the same function. This could be a simple notebook where we can write down our impressions we want to use later. Index cards and writer's journals are not only used as a means to inspire our fantasy by combining listed narrative elements with previously existing elements in our story, but also as a possibility to train our ability to observe. In this way, we slowly get used to seeing with a more aware and sharper eye and to listening with a more attentive ear.

The index cards that we play could be put in six or more categories: There are characters, people who we meet in our everyday life who seem interesting, and the same applies to places, objects, situations, activities and themes.

The following exercises should be of help in training our ability to get writing ideas down on index cards or in a writer's journal. Our overall goal should be to write down at least one new narrative element every day. The following exercise should not just help us collect precious material for our stories (and for the remaining exercises in the book), but also to learn to write captivating and precise descriptions of characters, places, etc., in the script.

Exercise #13:
Concentrate for three minutes on something that happens in front of your window and describe a character, an activity or a situation that you have observed.

Exercise #14:
Record a dialogue. Later, jot down the dialogue as you remember it and compare the two. Notice the differences. Transpose the dialogue you have recorded to a scene. What is the main conflict? Describe the characters and the impressions they create by what they do or say.

Exercise #15:
Create a small stack of index cards using the narrative elements you have collected. It is important to pay attention to the way you jot down the descriptions. Be precise, clear and try to use audiovisual language as much as possible.

The description in a screenplay functions according to the rules of audiovisual narrative. We only write what we can see or hear. Feelings or thoughts, as we know them from other forms of writing, are only allowed inasmuch as they are dramatized or can be transmitted in an image or sound (e.g. see the scene from Zhang Yimou's film, *The Red Lantern*, in the section on "Working with music and sound"). Avoid descriptions, unless necessary to the purposes of dramatization. A screenplay looks different from, say, a play, where the dialogue is the most important and largest part. In addition, techniques such as montage and close-ups make screenplays resemble a novel more than a play in the narrative sense, where the emphasis, in contrast to a screenplay, rests on the spoken word. The sound and rhythm of the language engender the atmosphere of a screenplay and this is not without significance for the transformation of the script to film.[2] A purely literary formulation sometimes tells us more in a script than the most careful description of a facial expression. Eisenstein used to say: "A sentence in a literary style can conjure up the dramatic climate needed for a description of a narrative element."[3]

Creating a story by combining narrative elements, sometimes in an arbitrary way, is the next step. The painter Max Ernst declared the concept of the "system of external contextualization" by using the image of a cabinet, and in fact the cabinet that de Chirico painted in the center of a classic landscape that was surrounded by olive trees and Greek churches. The cabinet, he maintained, is so much "out of context" because of the way it seems to have been literally tossed into this setting, that it becomes a mysterious object[4] – and in this way invites us to invent a story so we can explain its existence in the setting.

Exercise #16:
Mix the index cards that you have created and choose two arbitrary characters, a place, a situation, an activity, an object and a topic. Think up a story in 20 minutes that combines the narrative elements that you have randomly put together.

The American novelist, William S. Burroughs, developed a comparable technique that will be used as a basis for the next exercise. He called it the "cut-off-technique," since he mixed up phrases or words from different texts to "kindle" the inspiration for a new story.

Exercise #17:
Combine the characters from two different scenes or write a new scene where two characters from two different contexts meet each other for the first time.

The structure of the screenplay: Fourth sequence (the second dramatic question)

In the cinematographic, three-act, plot driven structure, there are two big turning points. The first turning point is at the beginning of the second act or, even better, carries us from the first to the second act. As with Aristotle, where every story has a beginning, middle and an end, the first turning point is that point where the beginning becomes the middle. That is why Gustav Ferytag called it "the exciting moment."[5]

Many screenplay theoreticians apply the term "major plot point" or even "decisive scene," where they mean the scene that has an unexpected event that finally diverts the flow of the story towards the main theme. Frank Daniel calls this moment the "passage" of Act 1 to Act 2, and in doing so confers a lesser significance on it than most other screenplay theoreticians, while at the same time he calls the decision of the protagonist the "lock" and places it in the second sequence. In any event, the story turns in another direction, new events occur and new decisions are taken. In other words, the event, the decision, the information in this scene turns the plot in a new direction.

Most theoreticians describe the first turning point, for the most part, as a moment of decision. The reaching or not reaching of the hero's goal leads to the denouement of the drama at the end of the story. In order for the hero to pivot to the pursuit of the goal, he first has to make an important decision. This decision or action constitutes the first turning point, the one that signifies the transition from the exposition to the complications and describes the attempt by the hero to reach his objective goal.

The goal of the protagonist is also known as "the want" (see the section on "The structure of the screenplay: first sequence"). In each case, the tension that appears in the effort to reach the goal begins at the latest at this turning point, that is, at the beginning of the second act. At the climax of the story, the release of this tension will be completed or, in classical dramaturgy, where the conflict between the goal and the need lies, that is, at the end of the second act. The actual need of the character expresses in turn the conscious or unconscious wish or the longing of the character, and accompanies the character from the very first moment. In reality, this is what causes the character to develop and what he requires to be completely happy as a mensch. The character realizes his need as he pursues his goal. It is the serendipity effect, that is, the effect by which someone discovers something fortunate, while looking for something else entirely.

In the classical resolution of the conflict between goal and need, the character reaches the goal, which in the meantime is no longer important for the character, primarily from the moment when the character realizes his need. The talk is frequently about the goal being located on the opposite pole from the need, which results in a character automatically being in conflict with his need, while he strives to reach his goal.

Linda Seger presents a list of everything that the first turning point should achieve, which for her will take place about 30 minutes from the start of the film:

- It turns the story in a new direction.
- It posits the central question and permits us to seek the answer.
- It is often the moment when the protagonist makes a decision or obligates himself to do something.
- It raises the stakes.

- It pushes the story into the next act.
- Development.

A powerful turning point meets all of the above-named aspects – most of the time it only meets some of these objectives.

The first turning point using the method based on the theory of mythological analysis, developed by Campbell is called "crossing the threshold."[6] It is about the point in time when the hero finally begins his journey and steps into the special world of the story for the first time. The journey that is dedicated to the second act can begin. There is no going back. Frank Daniel uses the well-known term "the point of no return," that is, the point in time in aviation flight when a plane, due to fuel consumption, is no longer capable of returning to its airfield of origin. After passing the point of no return, the plane has no option but to continue to some other destination. In this sense, the phrase implies an irrevocable commitment.

This point is often linked to the decision taken by the hero, often as a response to a moral dilemma. In the famous western, *High Noon*, it is the scene where the sheriff decides to go back to town to fight the bad guys. If he had decided to leave, there would be no story or at least not the story the screenplay promised in the first act.

We have already discussed the idea introduced here, that the inciting event poises the question that is the central or first dramatic question of the story, a question that will be answered at the climax of the narrative. Analogous to that, the first turning point in the rule repeats the central dramatic question and formulates the second dramatic question, that is, the dramatic question of the second act – which in turn creates the story arc of the second act (see the section on "The structure of the screenplay: seventh sequence").

The next exercise has as its goal making understandable – this time through writing – one of the most important structural points of classical screenplay dramaturgy, that is, the first turning point.

Exercise #18:

Relocate one of the characters you have created in the world of one of the stories we mulled over in the first exercise ("Stories that Nobody has Thought Up").

A reminder:

1) A young man spends his summer vacation at the ocean with his parents and is bored, until he meets a mysterious young woman who awakens his interest.

2) A man who has recently lost his wife and is grieving meets her best friend and falls in love with her.
3) A girl who lives with her aunt following the death of her parents invents a little friend that does not exist.

Write the first turning point of one of the stories as a scene or sequence. You may change the gender of the characters.

Since this is the first writing exercise asking for a sequence, it is necessary to explain the concept of the sequence. Sequence is a dramatic unit that in a definite way creates a story arc for a group of scenes that in turn have a common object/subject/theme (see the sequence analysis of the motion picture *The Apartment* in the section on "Working with the psychology of the audience"). A sequence can have a title. One can also pose a question at the beginning of a sequence that is answered at the end.

The technique of the conditional question

The premise or conditional question, says Novalis, are like nets. One throws out the net and, eventually, one will catch something. Perhaps the most well-known conditional question is "What would happen, if ...?" This question is posed by Franz Kafka, for example, is his story, *The Metamorphosis*. What would happen if a man woke up and discovered he had turned into a cockroach?

Exercise #19:

Pose the question using some well-known films, so that your audience understands which films are meant without revealing the title. What would happen if the director of a movie he just had to make were struck blind on the first day of the shoot? That is the conditional question of the movie *Hollywood Ending* by Woody Allen. Allen answers the question at the end of the film with his typical cynical humor. Due to his blindness, he makes an unusual film – and that in turn makes him a star in Europe! Nobody knows he was blind when he shot the film. In America the audiences saw the film for what it was, a film by a blind man – unintelligible, badly shot, absurd. In Europe, everybody thinks he is a genius. Woody Allen, not for the first time, pulls the leg of the American movie industry and this time, using his threadbare Happy End, European filmmakers as well.

Exercise #20:
Write a short description of a new story based on a conditional question.

The following story is based on the conditional question that came up during an exercise: "What would happen if someone returned to their familiar haunts after a 15-year snooze?"

ALEX, 20, *has returned to spend his vacation in his small town. He meets old friends from high school days – among them is his first big love. At a party there, they finally grow closer. A dream seems to be coming true. Alex takes her home, and they part with a kiss. He is so happy he forgets his childhood fear of the dark woods he has always avoided walking home. A strange man, the village idiot, lives in the woods – a man Alex and his friends both fear and tease. One says of the man that he spends his life experimenting because he wants to discover an elixir that will give him eternal life. Alex encounters him, and the man persuades him to try his new discovery: a drink that will send him on a journey in time. Alex does not take him seriously; but after drinking the elixir, he falls asleep. When he wakes up, he does not notice any changes at first, but before long he realizes that the crazy man was right – he has in fact been asleep for a long time, but for how long. And where is the crazy man? Alex looks for his home, his parents, his friends and for a way to return to the world he knew.* ■

The conditional question this story is based on is not quite enough for a movie. This is evident in the way the story focuses on how someone could behave who is caught up in this comic situation. It is also not clear how Alex lets the man talk him into drinking the elixir, and what he wanted to get by drinking it, but we will not try to solve these problems here. First, we will have to look for the heart of the story.

If I ask the storyteller what Alex finds 15 years later and why is he so desperate to go back, she answers that she does not know. So I ask her listeners to complete the question, "What would happen if Alex woke up 15 years later and discovered that ...? What?" So that we can find the answer to this second, very important part of this question, we will use the first part of the book's quantity trick (law of quantity). The result is a row of interesting premises, each containing a fascinating story. The best suggestions follow:

1) "What if Alex woke up 15 years later and discovered that nobody remembered him?" Even his parents would deny knowing him or that he had ever existed. A truly interesting premise that does

not really need the jump in time to function. It would be enough if Alex woke up one day and discovered that somehow he does not exist for anyone at all.

2) "What if Alex woke up 15 years later and discovered that he had changed into a woman?" Again, the 15-year time jump is not necessary to pull off this story. It would suffice for Alex to wake up the next morning as a woman.
3) "What if Alex woke up 15 years later and discovered that people thought he was a murderer?" This premise would be interesting if, for instance, he had found his girlfriend dead in the woods the same night he fell asleep; and for a concrete reason (principally because he disappeared) everyone thought he murdered her. Now, 15 years later, the murderer returns to the town where the murder took place. The 15-year lapse would have significance in this case if the writer played around with it some, for example, if Alex returned and nobody recognized him at first.
4) "What if Alex woke up 15 years later and discovered that he has been buried alive?" Again, the premise for this story does not require the 15 years. A great suspense movie, *The Vanishing*, written and directed by George Sluizer, in fact made use of exactly this premise.
5) "What if Alex woke up 15 years later and discovered that his girlfriend had married another man in the meantime and had children with him?"

When I asked the storyteller which of the above versions she preferred, she told me, without thinking twice, the last one. It was the first version she had thought of, but she had scratched it because she thought it was too common and banal and did not dare use it. The greatest enemy of creativity, the fear of the banal, had hindered her from writing out her idea for an interesting story that had a completely valid potential for development.

Working with the two hemispheres of the brain

The left-brain is thought to control understanding and logic. This hemisphere is responsible for definitions, logical structures, arguments and facts, while the right hemisphere processes emotions, symbols and metaphors.

Gabriele Rico has demonstrated that when writing creatively, the left and right hemispheres of the brain work together. She characteristically calls them "the sign (right hemisphere) and the design (left hemisphere) minds." Most teachers of creative writing, and certainly all who study the creative process, agree that there are at least two different sides to every creative act that are often in conflict. It is a question of the productive or the generative, that is, the unconscious phase and especially the conscious, critical phase that corrects, edits and rethinks everything that is created:

> We can call the two phases the unconscious and the conscious, the creative and the critical. Whatever name we give them our goal will be to keep these functions exclusively for the appropriate phase and to find ways for them to cooperate effectively and not create dissonance.[7]

Exercise #21:

Look for a text or scene that you have written based on the previous exercise – the goal of this exercise is analysis and revision according to Rico's theorem. Make two columns. In the left column write all the narrative elements of the text that stem from the left hemisphere, while in the right you will list all the narrative elements that arise at the behest of the right hemisphere. If there is no balance between the two, that is, when one of the columns clearly has more narrative elements than the other half, consider how the column that contains fewer elements can be beefed up.

Perhaps one of the most important techniques that Gabriele Rico has developed is the technique of clustering, a non-linear brainstorming effort that Rico calls "a master key to natural writing."[8] The clustering technique rests on the realization that creative work is achieved in stages that require interim decisions and on accepting that one must resist the need for safety as well as the need to visualize and define the final result – that is, the need to anticipate and control. It corresponds to the way visual thinking works, seeing that a key stimulus creates bundles of associations that give rise to new ideas.

Exercise #22:

Write down a word in the middle of a blank sheet of paper. Close your eyes. After a moment, the word will start unleashing associations. Write free associations for about ten minutes. Repeat the exercise using two words.

Tony Buzan's technique of mindmapping used along with clustering is also based on the collaboration of the two brain hemispheres. At the beginning of the "century of the brain," the twenty-first century, we recognize that the creative brain is the whole brain, posits Buzan[9] – and that it functions radially and explosively. A mindmap is a graphic representation of the relationships among different concepts (a dedicated form of taking down notes that uses both halves of the brain) and is understood as a whole brain alternative to linear thinking.

Like the exercises before, the final exercise in this section is intended to activate further the process of association.

Exercise #23:
As with clustering, begin with a blank piece of paper, write in the middle a word, and circle it when done. From the circle outwards, draw a branch that leads to the different aspects of the theme that correspond to the word. From every branch, begin a new branch that leads to further concepts that fit the theme. In this exercise, you may only use the substantive form. A not unimportant detail, use capital letters.

The technique of free association and automatic writing

Predecessors of free association and automatic writing are Fredrich Schiller's "praise of the free idea,"[10] as well as the "Program" of German literature and theater critic Ludwig Börne (1786–1837). In the twentieth century, the surrealists developed this further and even presented automatic writing as the only worthwhile form of writing. The next exercise is taken from André Breton's "Manifest of Surrealism."

Exercise #24:
Put yourself in a passive, receptive frame of mind that enables you to write fast without a thought-out theme so that nothing can hold you back, and you never succumb to the temptation to think about what you are doing. The writing will flow, because one thing is certain: In every corner of your subconscious mind an unfamiliar sentence is lurking that wants to be expressed.

Free association is a technique of creative writing, which has been taken over especially by the psychologists. Today it is systematically employed in psychotherapy – where association is expected to arise in the shallows of consciousness, for reasons that have to do with the intended goal of the method.

What is more important for us is the question: How can we overthrow the censor in our head, who, while we write, tries to murder our initial thoughts, often without our noticing it? The answer appears to be relatively simple: We can either distract it or "overwhelm" it with alternatives. This is exactly what this next exercise intends to achieve.

Exercise #25:

Write freely while you count to one hundred.

Automatic writing needs practicing too. When we write half an hour every day, we will not only develop the ability to silence our inner censor, we will slowly discover we can always delve even deeper.

But automatic writing is a procedure that is difficult enough and does not necessarily work for everyone, and certainly not for those who have not practiced it enough. Keith Johnstone offers an alternative method.[11] He designates it as "automatic reading." "Imagine the following: You take a book from the bookshelf," he begins – and leads the narrator step by step through the exercise while the latter describes not only the book, but also the color of the book cover, the names of the writer, the title and finally its content. In the end, Johnstone coaxes the storyteller to read from the imaginary book and in doing so helps him or her to the birth of what automatic writing would achieve in a different way. It is interesting that the narrators often try to avoid this by claiming the book is written in Russian or that the letters are too small to decipher. Johnstone, if necessary, even offers the slackers, the ones who want to drop out, a reading glass or tells them something is written on the margin – or that something is written in his or her native language.

Like automatic writing, automatic reading helps us develop the ability to silence our inner censor, without having to go to a lot of trouble, as well as to delve deeper in our unconscious. What we finally discover and what matters is most of all in relation to the method of creative screenwriting: the power of the indolence of fantasy. Amazingly enough, through uncontrolled activity what emerges is structure; because, even with the most successful attempts of the surrealists, what we finally discover is that automatism seems to become permanently limited by the exuberant tendency of fantasy to create order out of chaos.[12]

The following exercise is also based on Johnstone's work. He has discovered that exactly the opposite process, that is, the avoidance of every association is even more difficult than free association and, what's more, requires a mind that is both courageous and relaxed.

Exercise #26:
Put together a list of things and ideas that are not associated with each other in any way, by completely avoiding logical connections. Instead of starting with dog, going on with cat and then proceeding to milk, write out the list as fast as you can and avoid looking for a logical connection to the next word. For example – dog, palm, meteorite, soprano, and so on.

Despite the difficulty involved in jumping in at the moment we begin to write, it seems as though someone else's thoughts rain down on us – a process that bears a strong resemblance to hypnosis.

The technique of defining the problem

Solutions mostly come by way of the clear definition of problems. This means that we must be able to define our problems precisely. In order to have this ability, many screenwriters begin with an outline. An effective outline describes each step, a detailed description of each scene (as a step in the story not just in the plot, i.e. also as a step in character development or in the emotional development of the whole), and at the same time includes important narrative elements that make up audiovisual writing when they are important to the dramatic narrative. In the method of creative screenwriting presented here, we primarily use two techniques to define problems and goals: The first technique is improvisation and the second is the dialectical "questioning" or encounter with a scene of a text – a technique, that seems to function extremely well when applied to the climax of a story.

During the dialectic examination of a scene, the members of the group pose questions to the writer. Again, group work makes this kind of technique easier, but it is not absolutely necessary. A writer can step back and question his text himself. The questions primarily have to do with the psychology and the motivation of the characters, but also involve plot holes and other uncertainties that arise with the reading of the text. The first step is to try to relate the story in one sentence. Usually, the problematic parts appear clearly during this first run through – especially when the synopsis is either impossible to understand or incomplete. The goal of the effort to outline the story and the cross examination through questioning is for the screenwriter to figure out to what degree what he had in his head is actually on the page – since this frequently does not happen or happens intermittently in the first draft. In addition, it is important to see exactly what our listeners have experienced and why. They function like a premiere audience. Where possible, some member of the group should pay attention to make sure the issues raised are not questions of taste but of substance.

The transmission of thoughts and emotions on the page, when writing a scene or a screenplay, is not a simple matter. The images and the ways scenes and images are put together, that is, what later will be called the editing of the film and which now happens on paper, contain an unbelievable power and can also lead us to a goal opposite of the one intended. A person in tears can elicit sympathy but it can also prompt laughter – depending on where that presence is located in the story. Reading from a key scene exposes the text to criticism and tests it. A scene is also exposed to criticism when we improvise it beforehand, and in addition compare it with the improvised scene afterwards (see the section on "The method of creative screenplay criticism: technique and the rules of the game"). These techniques help us primarily to define the problematic places and to seek the solutions which for the most part will be found in the text, but which may be now hidden or misplaced.

A scene seeks the reason for its existence

As per the author, who wrote it for one of her group sessions, the following scene is located very close to the climax of the story, that is, just before the final crisis is triggered.[13]

INT. BATTENBACH'S OFFICE – DAY

STRAAT opens the door to Battenbach's office and goes inside. Battenbach is sitting at a table – a plate of sausage is in front of him, a kitchen knife in his hand. He looks up and smiles.

BATTENBACH
(playful, ironic)
Did you finally get up?

Straat stands in front of Battenbach. He knows it is better to keep his mouth shut. He is getting nervous.

BATTENBACH (CONT'D)
Sit down.

Straat sits down on a chair facing him.

BATTENBACH (CONT'D)

Just imagine ...

He cuts a slice of sausage. Straat watches him but doesn't say anything.

BATTENBACH (CONT'D)

They brought me a Persian! A real Persian!

He chews on his piece of sausage, enjoys it. He talks with his mouth full.

BATTENBACH (CONT'D)

I was looking for one for some time now, looked through all the lists.

He cuts another slice of sausage, carefully sizes up Straat, who remains expressionless.

BATTENBACH (CONT'D)

It isn't so simple, you know.

He takes another slice of sausage, chews it and spits it out. He wipes his mouth. Straat's hands grip the chair he's sitting on real tight, as though he's afraid Battenback is about to catapult him out of it. Battenbach observes him for a whole minute that seems to drag out forever. He enjoys watching Straat sweat.

BATTENBACH (CONT'D)

I found one.

Battenbach throws his napkin on the plate and starts to clean his teeth with a toothpick. Another long moment.

BATTENBACH (CONT'D)

He wasn't a Persian.

Battenbach tosses his toothpick in the sausage plate.

BATTENBACH (CONT'D)

He was an Indian. Order and discipline my ass. A shit list!

Straat puts his hands in his lap and tries to stop trembling.

STRAAT

It's just that the Fuehrer hasn't gotten that far. Yet. ■

Questions start raining down in the group. The scene takes place in a concentration camp. Battenbach obviously has a higher status there than Straat. The status game between the two characters works very well. In the discussion with the writer, we learn from the screenwriter that Battenbach is a cook at the concentration camp. His goal is to go to Persia after the war to open a restaurant there.

Straat and Battenbach meet accidentally. When Straat hears about his plans and learns that he does not speak a word Persian, he tells him he can teach him. By doing so, he is trying to escape certain death. Battenbach arranges for Straat to come to the kitchen every day to teach him a language that is anything but Persian. In this scene, Straat is seriously worried. If Battenbach has really found the Persian he is talking about, this would not only make Straat superfluous, it would expose his lie. He is afraid of what he is going to hear, but he does not dare interrupt the sadistic cat and mouse game the cook is playing.

The members of the group now turn their attention to Straat, who seems to be our main character. The screenwriter does not know anything about him, beyond what is revealed in the short story on which her scene was based. She does not even know why he was put in the concentration camp. She does not want him to be a Jew, because that would be too predictable, she says. For the same reason, she rejects all the other reasons he might be in the camp. He is not there because he is a homosexual or because of his politics and was never in the resistance. He is 25 years old, he studies physics; and only cares about his science. He is not interested in politics. Has he ever been in a situation where he had to take a stand and make a decision? The screenwriter does not think so, but concedes that even if he had gotten in a situation like this, he definitely would have lost his courage. He is no hero. His friends were all in some kind of underground movement, she says, but not him. A little "window" opens for the first time. Which friends? Well, from the university. Is there anyone he is especially close to? Sure, his best friend. What is the friend's name? Michael.

I stop the game of questions and ask for a concrete scene improvisation. The scene is seemingly taken from Straat's recent past and tells about Straat's fellow student and best friend, Michael, as he tries to convince him to join him in the underground. There must have been a scene like this. The group members argue about who would play Straat's character, because it seems so clear to them how and why they want to interpret the part.

The improvisation takes a harrowing turn. Regardless of what Michael says – and from a certain point onwards we see him roll out the heavy artillery and explain in detail how Mimi, the girl Straat was secretly in love with, was arrested – Straat does not budge. Politics do not interest him, he says repeatedly. He is just not a courageous man like Michael.

The only thing that interests him personally is mathematics and equations. At some point Michael is indignant: "Do you know what you are? The biggest asshole of all times! You are worse than they are. You deserve to be in Mimi's shoes. You are a living dead, you are a dead man either way!" The "actor" that is improvising Michael is beside himself. The scene ends with Michael enraged. He storms out of the room and Straat picks up the chair his friend knocked over on the way out.

I ask them what Michael would do next. He would put him in Mimi's shoes, somebody suggests derisively. He would "hang him," says someone else. They agree about one thing: Whatever happens to Straat, he deserves it. No, the screenwriter says demurely. The scene has evidently shocked her, even though it has played out exactly the way she described it. Straat will change his mind, she says now. When he reaches the critical moment where he must make a choice, he will prove that he is not what he seems to be. The scene with Michael has changed him.

In line with this information, we discuss the alternative scenarios that could have landed Straat in the concentration camp. The screenwriter decides on two: One is that Michael "sacrifices" him by naming him as his alleged co-conspirator the moment he is cornered. The second one is that Straat is an unwilling accomplice to a scene that forces him finally to take a stand – perhaps even in Michael's presence. Perhaps he wants to show him that he is not all that Michael has reproached him for being. Independently of what he chooses, the perspectives that open up inside the concentration camp, even the ones that concern Straat's character and include the plot that unfolds afterwards, are fascinating.

One could argue that the reason Straat is in the camp does not interest anyone, since the story begins there anyway. Whatever happens in this story springs from the character of the hero – exactly the same way everything results from the character of Fergus in *The Crying Game*, a film we will analyze later. Even when his character and his backstory are not explained to us, and even if the screenwriter does not tell us that backstory, we still sense the integrity and truth of the character. We will have the feeling every step of the way that the screenwriter knows all of this and has simply decided to leave it off screen. That is the point – the writing will flow once we know our character. The writer of Straat's story is not necessarily going to incorporate the scene we have just improvised. It is sufficient if she has "seen" it, so she knows why the character behaves this or that way and so she can give us the feeling the character is real, because in her head he is real. Perhaps we would have arrived at the same conclusion without using the combination of improvisation and dialectic encounter in the scene. The experience would not be so robust and certainly by far not so clear to the writer. So, assuming that there are problems and solutions in every script that only concern the screenwriter, I try to get the writers to use the method I presented to recognize the solutions all by themselves. Working in a group helps, but from a certain moment on you will start being able to stimulate that procedure on your own.

It is often the case that what we are looking for in desperation is like a piece of a puzzle we cannot find. Anyone who has ever done a puzzle knows the feeling. One desperately looks for a particular piece – one knows exactly what it looks like, but even so cannot find it. One despairs and thinks it has been lost. Suddenly, one finds it in a part of the puzzle that is finished; you had just put it in the wrong place! One had trouble fitting it in there, but it sort of fits – so you tricked yourself into thinking it belonged where you put it. You take it out and put the right piece in the right slot – this time you do not have to force it. It really fits well and the image is complete now.

After we have precisely defined what is sought after, we need to learn how to be patient. When we put our brain under too much pressure, then we mostly use the conscious mind, the brain hemisphere that is responsible for logic, to find "sure solutions". Assuming that we define what is sought after, and we preoccupy ourselves with something else, our brain begins to work and try out various, bold combinations and permutations. The story of the Russian chemist, Dmitrij Mendelejew, who "conceived" of the periodic table in a dream after he had "struggled" with the idea all day long, tells us exactly that. The best ideas come under the shower, say experienced writers, joking – or just before we fall asleep or just after we wake up. Scientists, who have begun in recent years to occupy themselves with the mysteries of the human brain, believe this happens because our brain works by itself when we do not put it under a lot of pressure. The synapses that were recently active are reactivated and our new memories will be transposed from our short-term memory, which is like a laboratory for the solution of mental problems, to our long-term memory.

The structure of the screenplay: Fifth sequence (the middle)

The second act in the three-act structure is the biggest and in most cases comprises half the movie. This is the reason it is the hardest act to write.

Ultimately, the art of the thing is to maintain tension over such a long stretch of time.

The cinematographic second act is equivalent to what Aristotle called "Tying and Untying the Knot."[14] "By tying the knot I mean everything that happens at the beginning of the plot right through to the most extreme point, that is, to the moment when the turn to good or bad fortune is taken" – for the story or for the protagonist. The corollary is untying the knot in the second half of the second act and is everything "that happens from the beginning to the end of the change." Gustav Freytag calls tying the knot the "rising action" and untying the knot the "falling action."

Most screenplay theoreticians, especially Syd Field, have located a structural point right in the middle of the second act to make its construction easier. This point, that is theoretically found in the middle of the story and that "breaks" the screenplay into two parts is called the midpoint or the central plot point or even central scene. This point corresponds to Gustav Freytag's "tragic moment' or "turning point"[15] or the Aristotelian "extreme point" and is located in the Aristotelian middle, that "follows something itself as well as pulls something along after it."[16]

Frank Daniel draws a lot of attention to this point by calling it the first culmination, that is, the first peak. Linda Seger, on the contrary, thinks that not every film or every screenplay has a midpoint. Where there is one, it is an uncommonly useful tool with which to structure the second act. She adds that the screenwriter often confuses this with the first turning point. If done this way, it causes the second act to begin very late. Linda Seger also believes that the best midpoints are encountered in the thriller, detective and film noir genres, the reason being that the midpoint gives more structure, a chance to add another clue, or another twist, that is another opportunity. Especially in those kinds of stories, the midpoint can be very effective when it does not take one off the narrative line, but lends to it another dimension.

If we interpret the Aristotelian description of the point "that is the most extreme," we conclude that the second turning point is located on a low point on the wavy line of the story as it plays out in the movie, since this is when the protagonist faces the greatest crisis of his life. The midpoint, on the contrary, must be on a high point, because at this point the protagonist's outlook will be favorable. In this case, the midpoint permits us to catch our breath. One can of course also encounter the opposite (a lower midpoint means a high second turning point), even if this rarely happens, because logically it would lead to a downbeat ending.

According to the theory of Christopher Vogler (which is based on the work of Joseph Campbell), the middle of the script is especially important. One recognizes this in the description of the sequence immediately preceding it ("the approach to the innermost cave"), that leads the hero to the "supreme ordeal," that is to the most important challenge and his greatest crisis. Christopher Vogler defines two types of screenplay structure to explain the phenomenon that Linda Seger describes, that not every film or every screenplay has a midpoint. In the first possible structure, there is a point where there is a crisis in the middle of the story that he calls the central crisis. In the second possible structure, the crisis takes place at the end of the second act (i.e. placed on an equal footing with the second turning point), that he then calls a delayed crisis. In any case, the hero must die so that he may be born again.

The crisis is that moment of the story or the drama where the enemy power launches the greatest conflict. We also use the construct "crisis" in the course of an illness. The condition of the patient is either better or worse after a crisis. The crisis is also an event that divides a story. After overcoming a crisis "that is often the borderland of death, the hero will be born again either in reality or metaphorically, and nothing is as it once was."[17]

For Campbell initiation is not seen as the end goal in itself but as the midpoint of the journey for the character. Now there is another threshold to cross, coming back into the "world" with a new insight. This is when the revolutionary spirit of the Initiated meets the "jury of sober eyes" of those who have not seen. That part of the journey now lies before us.

Working with images

A picture is said to be worth a thousand words. Cinema gives us a chance to penetrate the hearts and minds of characters and to "magnify" their little, private moments. We become witnesses of scenes and moments that show something the characters themselves are often not aware. It is the close-up which Eisenstein regarded as the only and real essence of cinema,[18] the close-up as the embodiment of emotion and therefore as a narrative element of the screenplay. The screenwriter invents these moments: the close-up of a hand that becomes a fist, the beads of sweat on the forehead, a hand that clasps another hand.

According to research, our brain seems able to sustain either visual thinking or conceptual thinking. A picture says more than a thousand words – but not necessarily every picture. We must learn to develop our visual thinking if we want to be able to write the images that really convey something.

Exercise #27:
Visualize an object and then in your mind change its color, set it in movement and so on. Next, imagine a familiar face and describe it. Now describe your room.

"Visualizers" move their eyes in different directions when they, for example, describe a room, as though they see an object while they are describing it. The "conceptualizers," on the other hand, only look in one direction, as though they were reading from a list.[19]

How can we develop our visual thinking and become "visualizers?" If we look at an object and another object enters our field of vision at the same time, in reality our brain constructs that object based on relatively little information, even though we have the feeling we "see" what we have assimilated. We will note the difference and understand in what way we normally "see" (i.e. without looking directly), when we look directly and consciously at the same object.

Since everything in the audiovisual language – even emotions and thoughts – must be transposed to image and sound, we must learn to transform what we sense to image and sound.

Exercise #28:
Write an erotic scene in an unusual place by stressing the sensuous perceptions, but this time concentrate your attention on those senses you use least of all in audiovisual narration. In the same way, describe a scene that instills great fear in you.

In the example of analysis below, we will analyze a complete screenplay for the first time in this book and in doing so review all of the concepts and terms discussed so far.

Screenplay analysis: *The Crying Game* (screenplay by Neil Jordan)

Following an excursion in an amusement park in Northern Ireland, the British soldier Jody is lured into a trap and kidnapped by the IRA. A stirring melodrama begins that is both a love story and a sophisticated thriller all wrapped into one, where nothing is as it seems.

The screenplay by Neil Jordan won the Oscar for Best Original Screenplay in 1993. It continues to occupy a special place among screenplays as "the one with the big secret,"[20] and as one of the first that seriously experiment with the classical rules of screenwriting.

The lead character is Fergus. We have already mentioned that all the scenes in this screenplay flow from this character. We feel the truth of the character, even when the screenwriter does not give us any information about his backstory, even though he toys with our curiosity. Nonetheless, we have the feeling at any given moment that the screenwriter has this information, but has decided to keep it off-screen.

At first glance, the film seems to be divided into two parts. The first part tells us the story of a kidnapping. Fergus is the hero and the focus is on the relationship that develops between him and his hostage, a black English soldier he has personally kidnapped and must execute in three days. In the fortieth minute of the film, we experience the climax of this story, a scene that ends with a dead hostage. Fergus, who did not kill anybody, is the only one who gets away. The other members of his team are killed – a story with a beginning, a middle and a (bad) end.

The second half of the film shows us Fergus in London with a new identity. He experiences a love story, also with a beginning, a middle and an end, that has a special turning point. Perhaps due to the political psycho-thriller we have watched in the first half of the film, the disclosure of the true sex of the woman Fergus has fallen in love with is one of the most powerful and shocking turning points in the screenplay. Neil Jordan manages to mix the genres in a most interesting way, by setting up expectations for another genre and then surprising us by not meeting them.

At about 70 minutes into the film, at a time we normally expect the second turning point and are still in the second story, the past returns even though everything seems to have run its course. Now, at second glance, we realize there are three parts to this narrative, and it is here that the third part of the screenplay begins. We know all the characters, their interests, their goals and needs. The only thing that could still upset us is the ending. We are prepared for a disaster due to the preceding events. This third part also has a beginning, middle and an end. As said, one could analyze this film as three equal episodes (including length of time) that have the same lead character, but it is not just the lead character who connects the three episodes. It is impressive how Jody, the hostage who was murdered in the first episode, maintains an important presence throughout the remainder of the movie.

This screenplay is especially interesting in terms of the narrative – similar, by the way, to *Psycho* from the novel of the same name by Robert Block and adapted by Joseph Stefano, which also begins one story and then tells a different one – similar, in a different way, to *Before the Rain*, written by Milcho Manchevski, which we will analyze at a later point. What is it, though, in *The Crying Game*, that holds our interest over three episodes? It is certainly not the development of the character from bad to good, as in the classic film narrative. Fergus is so vulnerable, true and good from the outset that he can hardly develop any further. So what is it then? The film's title gives us a big hint – the song tells us it is the way the crying game is played, and the music and lyrics that accompany the opening and closing credits support this insight. "Sometimes it's tough to be a woman," we hear, and a short time later we see the kidnapping. The writer toys with us and employs all the means available to the audiovisual narrative.

Our unconscious does not forget the promise of the beginning. What we will see is a love story with more than a surprise and a large dose of existential doubt, that is *The Crying Game*. If we accept this as the true story hidden in the episodic structure of three short films, then we realize that this story is told in a very classical manner. In the first 15 minutes of the movie, when we expect the hook, that is, the initiating event, the hostage Jody asks his kidnapper, Fergus, to take a photograph out of his wallet. The music underlines the potency of the woman in the photograph. Fergus sees the beautiful Dil for the first time along with us. We hear her name for the first time, however, when we expect to reach the first turning point according to the rules of classical dramaturgy. Jody asks Fergus, in case he is killed, to look up Dil and to tell her that he was thinking about her at the end. He asks him to keep the photograph. Again, the music underlines the significance of the scene. Is this the point of no return? Any other character would forget his promise, but not Fergus. That we know.

Jody and Fergus grow closer, so close that Fergus admits to a low self-esteem ("I'm not good for much") and demonstrates a degree of self-awareness ("I put away my childish things long ago"). The lack of self-esteem, of self-love and eventually the ability to love – that has its origins in a loss of identity – is the emotional theme of the screenplay, and we encounter it repeatedly in Dil's face and in her tragic existence. Perhaps this is another reason why we will not learn much more about Fergus, since he is also a face without an identity and remains so. A second theme is entwined around the first one – faith. "Keep the faith" is the motto of the IRA, and the relationship of the two characters is based on what each one wants to believe about the other. At one place Dil asks Fergus to tell her he will never leave her, "[...] even if he knows it's not true." She simply wants to believe, and because she believes, she gets to live what she believes.

The structure game continues throughout the remainder of the movie. Where we expect the midpoint of the film to be (interestingly enough in the 55th minute of a film that has a running time of 107 minutes, in the actual center, then, of the film), Fergus and Dil kiss for the first time. Everything would go swimmingly if everything were as it seems, if Dil were a woman and Fergus a simple worker. We (the audience) know the double identity of Fergus but almost forget it. Agony kicks in when Fergus confesses to Dil that he knew Jody and was responsible for his death. Ten minutes later, at the 65-minute mark, when we expect the second turning point (admittedly somewhat early, but how else could the screenwriter tell us all he still had to tell?), the bomb explodes. Dil, in her sexy dress, is a man! The screenplay ignores the whys and wherefores – our curiosity is never satisfied. The screenwriter prefers to put us in Fergus's shoes. Can a man love a woman who is a man? Can he act as if he loves her – he, who can pretend to be somebody else so easily; he, whose secret is actually much deeper, darker and far deadlier?

Fergus does not have much time to decide. Five minutes after his confession to Dil about his identity, Fergus's old friend, Jude, appears, who was thought dead, another member of the IRA – in fact, the bait for Jody. The organization has located him and is trying to give him another mission. Jude blackmails him by threatening Dil's life. Fergus realizes that he does love Dil, even if she is not a woman. The decision taken by the lead character is part of the second turning point.

The third act, that is the same as the part that we called the third episode in the previous way of looking at it, is structured in a classical manner and even has the rhythm of a third act – short scenes, dead ends, parallel plot lines and an exciting denouement. At about 95 minutes the climax begins that is a sharpening of the drama in the literal sense of the word – violence, despair, tension. The release comes in the last scene when we have the answer to our question about what Fergus has decided to do after he gets Dil out of where the events took place. Dil visits him in prison and she will wait for him until he gets out in ten years – a happy end. Fergus is behind bars, but Dil knows that he has sacrificed himself for her – that he loves her.

As the closing titles run, Fergus tells Aesop's fable about the frog and the scorpion that Jody had told him. "Because it is my nature," says the scorpion to the frog when the frog asks him why he stung him as they were crossing the river, because now both of them will die. Nature is identity is self-esteem is love – the resolution of the theme, and a suitable metaphor for the story.

Let us take a look at this as a whole structure. It is clear that the film cannot be constructed on the plot level, as there is no simple, straightforward plot; instead, three different stories involving the same characters. Even the system of the two dramatic questions, which I introduced earlier on, cannot function on a plot level. Still, the film does not feel like it is broken into fragments. It is clear that it is unified on the emotional level. Here we feel sad about Jody and the injustice in a world that permits human beings to do such unjust things to each other or such unjust things to happen. The photograph of the woman he loves is what moves us. Here is when the first dramatic question is asked and – because it is the emotional structure that keeps the crying game story in place as a whole – the question could be, "Will she ever heal?" The question asks if we will ever heal, we the people, who have put love aside for other darker but easier emotions? The answer to that question comes at the climax and the resolution, and it is a clear yes. There is hope for the human beings who accept love as their driving force. The second dramatic question is raised at the moment we expect the first turning point – if this were a classic dramatic structure. It is when Fergus committed to find Dil. "Can he handle commitment?" is another way of asking, "Can he love?" and – because this is about a human experience – eventually "Can we love?", a question answered in a positive way where the second turning point would have been when he decides to stay with her, even if she is not a woman. The midpoint occurs when Fergus and Dil kiss for the first time.

To what extent can we stand up for how we feel or for love? What degree of difficulty can we endure? Are we prepared to transgress and to change, or will we pretend that nothing has happened and continue as before? This is not just about love or even a love affair. It is about a great leap to another level of self and potential. In a way, it is about a fated, powerful love, in the sense that it has a huge impact on both sides, that it rocks them and their world, with something unknown to either of them, something they (and we) did not even know existed. The impossible is possible. The Promised Land can be reached. It is not too good to be true. Destiny means that something is given, but it does not mean it will be realized if the people involved do not support it. It is given to people (characters) who have the ability to support it. The challenge lies in how we handle what is given; destiny is a magic carpet, and it asks you whether you want to jump on for the magic flight into unknown worlds. You can jump on or be afraid – then your mind will subconsciously create thoughts that underpin your fear. Rationalization will take care of the rest.

This seems to be the existential level of the screenplay and eventually the film. As in every film that has a strong emotional structure, this one challenges the way we think and the way we feel. But what about the way we travel through this story? What is our emotional journey, the emotional journey of the character, and the emotional journey the writer made in the first place?

Emotions seem to come from another area of our sensitivity than, for instance, feelings, which represent fleeting emotions. The difference is that emotions carry knowledge, and whatever carries knowledge, whatever includes information, is a form of communication. Thoughts create feelings but emotions represent something deeper. Feelings are of the heart; emotions go directly or come directly from the soul. This does not mean that feelings are to be scorned. In order to open up our emotional field we need to become unafraid of the fleeting emotions, to let them be, to stand up to them and look them in the eye, to accept them. Most importantly, emotions have something to do with our ability to perceive and the expansion of consciousness; and it is in this area where a powerful film, a film with a powerful emotional structure, can ultimately reach. As Stanford writes in another context, referring to the concept of Aristotelian pity, "You respond to it in the depths of your being, as a harp-string responds by sympathetic resonance to a note from another source."[21]

Working with music and sound

The power of music and sound has long been recognized in the theory of theater. Gustav Freytag wrote in 1863 that the (dramatic) poetics need music and the performing arts to help in its presentation. With the assistance of music and sound, the dramatic arts become more intense and touch the audience, both on the emotional as well as on the cognitive level. In the same way, music and sound can prove indispensable to the audiovisual narrative.

In many cases, music can influence the emotional reaction of the audience directly. A well-known example of this is from the film *Chinatown*, written by Robert Towne and directed by Roman Polanski, whose first preview screening[22] was regarded as a disaster; because the focus group did not know how to react to the ending of the movie. The preview results changed after Gerry Goldsmith's score was added – it transformed the ending into something magical, even though there was no question of it ever becoming a happy end. The score often accommodates the narration. The composers of the classical Hollywood era mostly scattered melodies in short phrases throughout the film and varied them endlessly in terms of tempo and orchestration to accompany the narration precisely. The basis of Hollywood's music vocabulary is the late romantic period, because of its long melodies and the broad spectrum of their orchestral color, which facilitate a narrative punctuation or meet the need of the motion picture narration for variation, shifting and altering of the tempo that flows from the story and the characters.

Theodor Adorno and Hanns Eisler complained in their book, *Composing for the Films* (1947), about the Hollywood practice characterized by the score being subservient to the needs of the narrative, and by the especially obvious use of leitmotivs combined with direct musical mimicry of what was already visible on screen. They confront it by comparing it to their own preferred practice, one that flows from a divergence of the audiovisual from the musical nature of the film and strives for a contrapuntal relationship between film and music.[23]

On this note, we should perceive the use of Samuel Barber's *Adagio for Strings* in *Platoon* and John Ottman's music in *The Usual Suspects*. In both cases, the sensuous and sentimental attitude of that music contrasts strongly with the horrors and bloodbaths in the movie. When it works, it stands for an expanded form of ironic connection that discerns the horror of events, but also for an understanding of their power of attraction. Not quiet in the sense of Adorno and Eisler, other composers – for example, Nino Rota in the context of his work for Fellini, Visconti and Zeffirelli – strived for a score that primarily expressed more the spirit of the film and less the material relevance of a sequence of images.

Music expresses emotions, it transcends all attempts to categorize it in terms of an emotional nomenclature and falls through the net that our threadbare vocabulary of feelings offers. In that sense music should not be used to create aesthetic pleasure or effects, but rather to evoke ideas and emotions of its own. The screenwriter, director and composer, Mike Figgis, explains that at every stage of production and even while writing the script, and even later during the shoot or while editing the film, he tries to remove as much dialogue as possible. That way he creates more room for music and sound that can only enhance the script. Every sound, a step or closing a door, can help the narrative more than any dialogue.

Here is a rule that has been successfully broken often enough: A good screenplay hints at the kind of sound or music that should be used, but does not refer directly to concrete pieces of music. One can find excellent examples of scenes offering the inventive use of sound in the screenplays of Francis Ford Coppola (*Apocalypse Now*, especially the helicopter sequence during the first ten minutes) or of David Lynch. Let us now take a closer look at a scene from Zhang Yimou's film *The Red Lantern*, where the protagonist wants to find out what happened to the adulteress who was arrested and hauled up to the room over a snow-covered roof. The steps of men in the snow are the only sound one can hear. The men go away, and the protagonist goes where she assumes the woman will be – we cannot see her. The sound gets louder and louder and then – absolute silence. After a close-up of the snow-covered roof, a scream is heard from the background and then a sound – a rhythmic pounding that is used throughout the film at certain selected moments of intense sensual importance. Death (and the discovery of corpses) happens off screen – and all of that is in the script.

Music and sound can add a second level of understanding and a point of contrast to what we see. There are many ways to get there. In creative screenwriting, we will even use music and sound as a path that leads us to a wellspring of ideas.[24]

Exercise #29:
Use a song, both lyrics and music, to create a story.

The screenplay for the film *Magnolia* was written largely using a (often random) combination of the stories and various songs from Aimee Mann. Interestingly enough, the screenwriter, Paul Thomas Anderson, has called his story "an adaptation of Aimee Mann songs." It is a slight surprise that in the final analysis, the structure of the movie is based on the music.

Exercise #30:
Think of a sound that has a certain meaning for a certain character. What memories does it elicit? Begin with a sound and let it lead you to the character. Construct a scene by concentrating on this very special relationship.

The following story was developed within the framework of such an exercise.

The story of a sound

THE SHRILL TONE *of a ringing phone. Rosalie can't stand it. The phone rings in the night, again and again. On the phone, when Rosalie picks up the receiver, it is always the same voice – the voice of a child. She tells her that she needs to go to her and help her. At first, Rosalie thinks that somebody is playing a bad joke on her, but she slowly realizes this it no joke. She starts to believe the little girl. Rosalie is studying psychology. In her opinion, everything the girl tells her on the phone can only mean one thing – that her father is molesting her. But how can she help her? The little girl can't even tell her where she lives. Her mother is dead, she says. Her father works and he locks her in because nobody is there to take care of her. The first time she called Rosalie's number was a mistake. Since then she has been pushing the redial button every time she wants to talk to somebody. Her father is a night watchman. The phone always rings at night.* ■

This is how Rosalie and Luise's story begins. The screenwriter has adapted a story a girlfriend told her a long time ago. That friend had felt sorry for the child and had done everything she could to find her, but it was impossible. What would have happened if she had found her? That is the hypothetical question that the writer now asks herself. In the group, we try to get to know Rosalie better by using the now familiar game of questions and by improvising at the critical junctures. We learn that she has a boyfriend, Steffen. They have just broken up. Luise, the girl who moved into the neighboring apartment a few months ago, caused the break-up. Rosalie was friends with her at first. She stopped being friends when she understood that Luise copied everything she did and on top of that even flirted with her boyfriend. Luise's character is so strong that it is easy to forget the girl on the phone. Then the two stories start to converge. The group is doing that job, which would normally be done in the head of the screenwriter. Did Rosalie tell Luise about the little girl? Has Luise ever offered to help her find the child? Would that be possible? The answer to all these questions is yes. An exciting story gradually unfolds. Every day, when Rosalie comes home from the university, Luise has something new to report. Luise waits for her impatiently one day – because now she has the address of the little girl.

Let us remember that for Plato, the oral dialectic process is a "long journey," that requires "great effort" (*Politia* 532e, 3) and that, like the process of dialectic encounter with a text that is presented here, it is time consuming and extremely difficult to reproduce in every detail. The meaning of the story gradually emerges – in the meantime it has taken on fascinating overtones. When Rosalie finally finds the little girl, she discovers that she is a mentally disturbed woman her own age. She has disguised her voice and pretended to be the little girl she was when her father molested her. In this way, the disturbed woman experiences the same story again and again. Rosalie knows this young woman all too well. It is Luise. The complications of this fascinating psycho-thriller now become clear and well defined. The key to this screenplay is apparently the connection of the two stories and the two characters. What was a weakness previously – the existence of two powerful stories, one of which was not even especially original, that were canceling each other out – has been transformed into something new, complex and intriguing. The simple ringing of the phone functions as the initial inspiration of a promising psycho-thriller.

The technique of conflict

Conflict and contrast are universal (see the section on "The structure of the screenplay: second sequence"). They can be everywhere, even in between the different scenes. There are always ways to achieve or accentuate contrast by using rhythm, time, color, light or tone.

We can train our ability to think in terms of contrasts and our ability to develop stories out of these conflicts. One says that Goethe spent his free time "trying out" conflicts in his fantasy between characters of differing temperaments taken from his surroundings. When done, he would incorporate the results of this game of fantasy in his writings.

Comedy is a special field for the game of contrasts. We can place a "normal" character in a contrasting or comic milieu or contrary-wise a comic character in a normal milieu or pit two opposing comic characters against each other. The most important thing to keep in mind is that we need to create an emotional relationship between the characters. This does not mean they have to like each other. In any case, comedy lives from conflict. The following exercise[25] is designed to develop a comic situation in four steps:

Exercise #31:

Select a character that you have previously developed, and write ten comic or exaggerated versions of a milieu in which the character does not fit or belong. Choose one of them. Then think about what kind of person would be an insufferable antagonist to the character you have just developed and note down ten characters to conflict with him or her. Choose one of them. Note down ten possibilities for the inner conflict of this character. Choose one of them. Note down ten places where your character would not fit in or belong. Choose one of them. Combine the four narrative elements in a single story.

In order to develop further the conflict as a mindset, we employ something called the "Janus way of thinking."[26] Janus was a Roman god that had two faces facing in opposite directions. The Janus way of thinking involves two different perspectives and deals with the polarization that occurs with two simultaneously existing, completely opposite viewpoints.

The ability to think by using contrasts is very important and a key to the creative process. Now our goal is to distance ourselves from causal thought – the kind of thinking that seeks reasons, consequences and that uses linear time, which, incidentally, is the mindset we use most. This mindset leads to the need for a causal connection that is in fact an important component of the Aristotelian aesthetic. The Janus way of thinking begins with simple, simultaneous thinking, whereby one focuses on two ideas or two images at the same time and carries on by contrasting two different ideas or images.

Exercise #32:[27]

Place the same character in two completely different situations, for example, in a situation where he is drinking Champagne and in another where he is begging on the street, dressed appropriately for each circumstance. Visualize the two versions of the character and note how you put the combination together:

1) Look at the pictures one after the other.
2) In your imagination, look at the first picture and then tilt it toward the other picture to reveal the contrasting image.
3) Combine the pictures by melting them into a new format and incorporating elements from both of them simultaneously.
4) Look at the pictures as though they are "split screens."
5) Look in the foreground at one picture and in the background at the other one.
6) Place one picture on top of the other. Does one of the pictures dissolve into the other one?

Numbers 4, 5 and 6 are indicative of simultaneous thought. Do the same with two new pictures, this time by consciously practicing simultaneous thinking.

Exercise #33:
Spend a day noticing all the conflicts and contrasts you observe around you as well as how you avoid them, deal with them or resolve them. Select one of the conflicts and instead of avoiding it or resolving it, accentuate it and bring it to the highest possible degree of contention.

Exercise #34:
Remember a moment in your life where you had an especially strong desire for something and someone or something stopped you from getting it. Write a scene about that experience and show how you overcame the resistance or the obstacle, even if this success does not conform to your memory, that is, even if you did not manage to do this in real life.

Working with dreams

The respect of the artists for the world of their dreams is nothing new. Writers such as Rainer Maria Rilke, Jack Kerouac, Ingeborg Bachmann and many others have recorded their dreams in detailed journals. Stephen King writes that all of his stories without exception are based on his dreams. A screenwriter and later a director who had a high opinion of his dreams was Federico Fellini, who was very familiar with the psychoanalytical theories of Carl Gustav Jung, since he was friends with one of his students, Ernst Bernhard, who persuaded Fellini to write down his dreams. The director described how Jung's discoveries helped him trust his fantasy much more than reality.[28] That is why inspiration, memory and unconscious thought are just as important in Fellini's stories as reality.

Exercise #35:
Analyze the various dream aspects in Fellini's film *81/2.*

In that sense, Andrei Tarkovsky's films have a similar fixation. Taking up his childhood memories, that are especially important for his kind of storytelling, Tarkovsky brooded over the difference between the emotional mood of a memory and the alleged facts.[29] He concluded that the disputation about the concrete side of the memories in the end destroyed their poetic character. The same could be said of dreams.

How can we transform a dream into part of a movie story without destroying its emotional mood? The apparently simple connection between dream and cinema is to tell a story as though it were a dream and eventually reveal this fact. Although we find this way of dream reference[30] often enough, the effect on the audience is unsatisfactory.

We will approach dreams in a different way, not so much as a storytelling device, that is, but as a way to find stories or ways of telling stories. The technique presented here is based mainly on the theories of Carl Gustav Jung and his students; it familiarizes us with the way they worked with dreams and the methods they developed, which train our ability to remember our dreams. The method, using stories and themes/emotions born out of dreams, is founded above all on the special thesis that, by the way, Freud's theories diametrically oppose that only those who have dreamed the dream can tell it properly (or interpret it, something that does not interest us here).

Dreams represent the only naturally occurring condition where there is a complete lack of an inner censor. As such, they are a treasure trove for the creative process we rarely make use of, because normally we forget them. Research shows that we have a dream every 90 minutes – so we have between five to six dreams every night. As early as 1844, the neurologist A.L. Wigan wrote that during the dream state our two brain hemispheres function more or less independently and that the right hemisphere is more active than the left hemisphere. His hypothesis has been confirmed in recent times.

Exercise #36:

We all dream but most of us cannot remember our dreams. To change this, you should start a dream journal. Date each day's entry before you go to sleep and put the journal beside the bed. When you do this, you let your unconscious mind know that this time you are going to remember your dreams. When you wake up, stay in bed a few minutes more and try to remember the last dream you dreamed.[31] Write down everything you can recall by retaining the "illogical logic" of the dream. The mood of the dream together with the dominant feeling or emotion you woke up with is of utmost importance. Is it fear, happiness, sorrow, pain or rage? Feelings and emotions have a special clarity in our dreams – try to put this clarity on the page. While you write, try to turn off the control of the conscious mind that tries to change the dream and to create it anew – something that in fact very often happens. Moreover, try to avoid the narrative dimension of "beginning, middle, and end," which is the dimension of real time as we perceive it when awake.

While we work with our dreams, we realize that they are not just full of cinematic images – they also offer endless structural and symbolic possibilities. Dreams are emotionally charged, hardly literary, almost never linear and most definitely visual. They employ narrative elements from the genre of magical realism and are no friends to causal narrative. As is its nature, the usually non-linear dream is in the rule illogical and extremely complex. Still, it focuses on the substance and leaves always behind a little secret by toying with the means of tension and delay (the answer to the dramatic question that has been posed).

In time, especially when we work continually with them, themes, fears and archetypes develop, subsequently dreams are a never-exhausted treasure trove for writers. One must remember one thing especially: dreams often offer up concrete answers – most of all when concrete questions are asked (that arise while writing) – provided we clearly define the problem and have "processed" it in our minds before falling asleep.

Exercise #37:
Write a scene using material from a dream, starting with the dominant emotion. Subsequently, stress the conflict, add a new, clear beginning, then a new, clear ending; change the scene so that your character becomes the driving force and then change it again by putting yourself in the shoes of the "victim."

The model for the cinematographic avant-garde is for many Luis Bunuel's film *The Andalusian Dog* (1928) that originated as a "meeting of two dreams."[32] Bunuel was in love with his dreams, a love that finally leads him to surrealism. He wrote the script together with Salvador Dali, allegedly in less than a week following the dominant principle: do not admit any idea or image that might have a logical, psychological or cultural explanation. In this way, they intended to open the door of the illogical as wide as humanly possible and only admit images that portend to surface without looking for a why or wherefore. This is, indeed, the method we are employing here. The only difference is that we are focusing on capturing the dominant emotion of a dream.

Working with the emotions

The American director, Samuel Fuller, who had a big influence on the directors of the European *nouvelle vague* and was greatly admired by Jean-Louis Godard, Wim Wenders and the Kaurismaki brothers, once answered the question, "What is cinema?" by stating that "a film is like a battlefield. It is love, hate, action, violence, death – in one word, emotion."[33]

The screenwriter thinks in images and sounds. "The air is deadly still," says Pascal Bonitzer. He borrowed that phrase, which conveys emotion via sound or even more via the absence of sound from Eisenstein.[34] Emotion is what the images mainly transfer. Emotions include knowledge of the human experience, that is, information, and because of that they are a means of communication. The famous Italian screenwriter Tonino Guerra calls emotion the "idea of an image." Bonitzer, who worked as a writer with directors like Jacques Rivette, André Téchiné, Chantal Akerman, Barbet Schroeder and Benoît Jacquot, writes that there should not be one image that does not transport an emotion or that does not stand on an emotion. "A scene is unnecessary if it forgoes emotions; because emotion drives the thing forwards and creates movement ..."[35] "Emotions must bring about the action and not the other way around," adds the director Robert Bresson.[36]

Despite this, the dominant tradition in Western thinking regards emotions as a burden of human existence that hinders reason – a viewpoint that finds expression in such different thinkers as Descartes, Kant and Brecht. In the 1960s, artistic movements reacted to the intemperate emotionality of the preceding decades and expressed their disgust with everything based on emotions. Thus, they created an art, which was best described with dry and almost unimaginative phrases, such as "What you see is what you see." The "decriminalization" of emotion by its investigator, the artist, came only at the end of the twentieth century and presented a significant turning point in contemporary art, as it was finally recognized that "being tough is a failure of fantasy," as the British writer Ian McEwan says. Even the film scholars discovered emotion, admittedly relatively late. Most of the studies of emotion in cinema, first and foremost American – from Noel Carroll's various essays to the books of Murray Smith and Ed Tan – were dedicated to the emotive traffic in the course of a narration from a more or less cognitive perspective. Ed Tan claims narration means creating emotions. Narration, according to Tan, is a process through which a fictional event is presented in a regulated manner and is temporally structured to produce a certain effect in the audience.[37] Indeed, that way of looking at emotions (keep the audience excited and satisfied) has been understood by Hollywood on a subconscious level since the beginning of movies. What it means is that writers (and directors and producers) meddle with the structure of the plot, in order to produce certain emotions, that is, in order to manipulate the audience on the emotional level. Even if that observation is correct, pushing all the emotional buttons in the right order has nothing to do with the emotional journey of the audience, which in turn goes back to the emotional journey of the writer. It also has very little to do with emotional structure.

Are emotions universal? The investigation that the ethnologist and psychologist Paul Ekman has been conducting since the 1960s in different cultures has shown that there are a small number of emotions that are acknowledged all over the world and can be seen as universal despite possible cultural vitiations. These emotions are happiness, anger, sorrow, fear, surprise and contempt – the emotional psychologist calls them fundamental emotions, since they are clearly characterized by action tendencies.[38] If we work with dreams, we grasp the power of emotions and their ability to breathe life into both our fantasy and our memory. Memory can also cause an emotion. It is in that context that the French psychologist, Théodule Ribot, introduced and developed the construct "affective memory."[39] We are dealing here with the part of the human memory that registers the emotions as well as the rest of the exciting or less exciting experiences that have been activated in various ways, so that we can later relive them. Stanislawski, who had the collected works of Ribot on his bookshelves, made that theory the basis of his famous method for training actors. Stanislawski further distinguished between "emotional memory" and "sense memory," a separation of concepts, which also played an important role in his method.

Emotions are the key to the theme or rather the emotional theme and structure of a screenplay, and to the search for what we call the "thematic identity" of the artist:

> Whoever has observed the effects of a tragedy on themselves must notice with astonishment how the feeling and agitation caused by the distress of the character grabs his emotional life as it combines with the powerful tension generated by the way they connect to the plot structure. The tears flow much easier than in real life, the lips press together; this pain is, however, simultaneously tied to a powerful feeling of complacency – while the audience empathizes with thoughts, misery and the fate of the hero with such an agility as though they were their own experiences, they also have in the midst of the most powerful excitement the feeling of unlimited freedom which at the same time transports them far beyond the events ...[40]

It is interesting that Gustav Freytag refers to feelings rather than to emotions, a distinction that is important, as feelings and emotions are still often mixed up and discussed differently in different disciplines. Another important aspect that Freytag addresses here is the concept of pity, whereas he seems to think that the audience feels superior to the heroes of a tragedy and that this creates complacency. We will get back to this in a moment. What is important now is to stress that Gustav Freytag in a way describes here what makes up the thematic or emotional structure of a screenplay – a structure that is present in every "successful" motion picture, be it structured in a classical way or not (see the section on "Working with emotional structure"). The concept of being "successful" refers neither to the commercial nor to the artistic success of a film, rather plainly and simply to the ability of the film, as a creation, to reach its audience: in other words, the film narrative can function for purely emotionally reasons, even if the audience fails to notice the code that permitted access to its spiritual content.

Before we get any further into this complex matter, we should stay a bit longer in the emotional field in terms of exercising our sensitivity, that is, of opening up that field for us and for our stories. The following two exercises will attempt exactly that.

Exercise #38:

By using the Trick of Quantity, try to define what must not happen to you no matter what and what you are afraid of more than anything else at this moment in your life. This exercise can and should be applied to the characters, that is, approached with a certain character in mind and address what the character is afraid of most at this moment in his or her life. But the way to reach our personal fears and sensibilities is by the most direct route.[41]

The following exercise is in line with the tradition of the *Cinéma Direct* or *Cinéma Vérité* – a term introduced by the theoreticians of Soviet cinema, Dziga Vertov and Sergej Eisenstein. Vertov felt that cinema did not need either a fable or a story – it was enough if the facts registered and the montage reproduced them, whereby narrative rhythm and emotional package are of great importance. Even if we may not be able to agree with that approach today, as we may have a different, more sophisticated view of the content of truth in the mere facts, the exercise will help us work on the way we perceive and reproduce our emotional experience. It aims at a repetition of the facts, at first on paper. The art of editing, which was so important for Eisenstein, is very much akin to the art of screenwriting. Beyond that, it is also a good way for us to absorb how we transport information by way of the dramatic arts, that is, how we can dramatize it.

Exercise #39:
The goal is to do something that you have never done before. Right after the new experience is over, write five to ten narrative elements down you did not know about before. Next, write a scene exactly the way you experienced it by concentrating on the main conflict. Note above all how you felt while the experience unfolded. When you read the scene, consider whether it is dramatic enough – and if it is not, rewrite it by adding new narrative elements (a new conflict, a new character, a new object and so on) without, however, ever destroying the central emotional experience.

When we try to isolate the central emotional experience, we simultaneously try to identify the emotion that this experience has evoked in us. This is usually connected with the first spark of inspiration in a story. The search for the first moment of inspiration that a story has generated leads us with certainty not only to the emotional theme but also to the dramatic center of the story. This emotion can provide an important hint for the further development of the story, as much for the screenwriter as for anyone who works with the writer when developing the story. It is important to remember, in Chekhov's words, that "[...] every description of a mood should be avoided,"[42] and that, "One should try to convey it by means of the behavior of the characters."

The dramatization, which also and most importantly means the externalization of emotions, is one of the most difficult tasks to pull off in writing the screenplay. Improvisation is certainly one of the best ways to acquire the art of dramatization. Again, we are not talking about manipulation by means of the deliberate creation of emotional reactions. This would mean that the writer feels superior to the audience, which in turns feels superior to the characters. We discussed earlier on how Gustav Freytag seemed to imply that this is inherent in drama and that it even creates complacency. This is not an uncommon view, in fact the effect of ancient Greek tragedy has often been discussed in that context. But how can truth be conveyed if the corresponding parts are not equal on an emotional level, or is the human experience not to be conveyed in a true manner and if yes, how important are emotions in that equation?

Some say that our society is in a crisis, a crisis that is being expressed in different ways: financial, environmental and political – a crisis of principles and faith – and that we are very far from finding the key, the solution to the riddle of civilization. In that sense it is most fascinating to look again at the so-called "poets' solution," a term introduced in the context I will use it here in 1992 by the American professor of government, C. Fred Alford,[43] to depict the tragic poets' vision of pity as man's only reliable civilizing force. Alford's thought is free of an idealization of culture, but he takes the Greek tragic poets seriously in their sole commitment to "truth-telling about the passions," which should be understood as what we here refer to as the emotions. One task of civilization is to denote what is good and what is bad. Interestingly enough, the Greeks, during the period of the tragedies, were in a crisis over just this issue, a crisis Alford refers to as the Dionysian crisis and which reminds us very much of the present situation.

The Greek tragic poets believed that civilization might be rendered more decent and peaceful by cultivating the civilizing emotions based upon love and pity. Greek tragedy was exactly that. It was supposed to provide a *paideia* (an education) in pity, through an emotional journey; it was an effort to educate and channel the civilizing emotions, so that they had to foster civilization.

It seems such an obvious idea to set love, care and concern for others against all those passions that lead us to exploit others. Yet, this solution finds almost no place in modern thought, notes Alford,[44] since they seem to be regarded as more utopian than the rational control of desire. The Greek tragic poets' solution is one long forgotten and finally lost completely with the misinterpretation of Plato and Aristotle (see the section on "The Old Struggle between Poetics and Philosophy: It all Goes Back to Aristotle or What we Owe Plato and Aristotle"). Fear dominated in modern philosophical thought – the fear that civilizing emotions are too weak to quell rage, greed and violence, but too strong, too likely to cause problems of their own. This has led modern political philosophers, beginning with Machiavelli, to the suggestion that the solution to the riddle of civilization is to transform passionate desires into interests, so as to replace the love of pleasure and honor with the love of gain. This has ultimately led to the world we know.

The goal and values of the tragic poets have been totally neglected in modern political theory, as it tried a different way of achieving the same goal – that of setting one uncivilized passion against another. Kant, for instance, distrusts love and compassion in all their guises, as they cannot be commanded. Fear of the uncontrolled nature of the civilizing passions, much like the fear of the uncivilized ones, led to a solution, a construct known as interest:

> Otherwise expressed, love, pity and compassion are not only powerful enough to control greed, lust, ambition and desire: they are so powerful that they themselves become the problem. To set the civilizing passions against the uncivilizing ones is to invite disaster ... Better to channel the uncivilized passions into the activity of acquisition, and so render these passions virtually sacred, almost a calling. This is the strategy of interest.[45]

Inherent in this is the idealization of interest: as though the disruptive, uncivilized passions – greed, unbridled desire, the lust for power and the thrill of domination – are somehow rendered pure, calm and beneficent when transmuted into the pursuit of economic interest! In fact, commerce, money-making and acquisitiveness may lead to hell on Earth. Ultimately, as it seems to have happened now, and has been happening for some time, the condensation of the passions into interest squeezes out both the civilizing and uncivilized passions. Much of the aggression and other craziness present in the world is an acting-out of the pain and terror that stems from the isolation of human existence – as though one could overcome one's own pain and mortality by inflicting pain and poverty and death on others.

So how predictable is the current dead end where everybody is focused on his or her own interests and a culture of love and pity is absent? Would more sympathy and compassion support a stronger community? Can even powerful emotions be educated and refined? What if this were the foundation of civilization: not justice (so difficult to achieve as there are many perspectives and many truths), but the ability to stay connected to others, to share emotions with others and so ease their isolation, their alienation from humanity? In our world, in which so many human hopes have proven to be blind, is it perhaps time to reconsider the poets' solution to the riddle of civilization, and if yes, which are the new works of art that could assume the role of the Greek tragedies? Is it possible that the alternative, non-linear, non-chronological narrative forms, where emotional structure is the defining uniting element, might be the closest thing we have to the poets' solution since Greek tragedy? So has art possibly discovered the way back to a *paideia* in pity, apart from the unsuccessful solution of modern political science?

It is a sign of the times that the Massachusetts Institute of Technology Media Laboratory has just created a new Center for Future Storytelling.[46] The center is envisioned as a "labette," a little laboratory that will examine whether the old way of telling stories – particularly those delivered to the millions on screen with a beginning, middle and an end – is in serious trouble. Its mission is not small. "The idea, as we move forward with twenty-first-century storytelling, is to try to keep meaning alive," said David Kirkpatrick, a founder of the new venture. Starting in 2010, a handful of faculty members – "principal investigators," the university calls them – will join graduate students, undergraduate interns and visitors from the film and book worlds in examining, among other things, how technology, virtual actors and "morphable" projectors might affect a storytelling process that has already been considerably democratized by digital delivery. It will be interesting to see whether the investigation will also touch such issues as *paideia* in pity through emotional structure and non-linear storytelling.

Mind you, pity in Greek tragedy is not identical to Christian pity. The word pity as with the closely related pair, mercy and compassion, have their origins in Latin-based Christian thought. Latin pity (coming from *pietas*), is how men and women share the piety they owe to God with each other in this world. For the Greek, *eleos* and *oiktos*, refer strictly to human relationships. The words stem from inarticulate cries of grief. Aristotle defines tragedy in terms of its ability to evoke pity and fear, using the terms *eleos* and *phobos*. The key to the Greek concept of pity is not the disposition to mercy and compassion but the felt connection to the suffering of others like oneself. Establishing the connection to others, as though to tell us that no matter how great your sorrow, I shall not let you fall out of the world. It is about introducing order into disorderly souls. In Stanford's words:[47] "There is no question here of the pitier being separate from another's agony. You respond to it in the depths of your being, as a harp-string responds by sympathetic resonance to a note from another source." Please note that last sentence, which I have cited earlier on. For me this is a most beautiful description of emotional structure as I present it here: a resonance with a note from another source.

The poets seek to educate the passions that connect men and women to each other in pity and compassion, stresses Alford, advancing Stanford's thought:

> *Mathema*, knowledge, stems from *pathema*, suffering – not merely, I would add, one's own but from the felt connection to that of others. It is this connection that encourages human thoughts, the *sine qua non* of human wisdom.[48]

In suffering we are all rendered potentially asocial: isolated and alone. It is pity that brings us back into the community of others. And not the kind of pity where what we feel for others is ultimately self-pity.[49] Tragedy is born when men and women begin to redefine nobility. It is not only about the shared suffering. It *is* the shared suffering. Greek tragedy is a celebration of the willingness and ability of the people to share each other's pain. Pain sharing is transformed into an act of civic virtue. Such virtue is not tantamount to democracy – it is its very ground. The moderns seem to have found another ground, that of shared interest.

Such compassionate grief was essential to the tragic poets' strategy for civilization, an issue that until now has received almost no attention. The idea is that pity, though fragile, may nonetheless be strengthened through an education (upbringing) in pity. Emotion-cum-reason is susceptible to education. This was the task of tragedy. The heroic ethic, the agonal culture is ultimately about a constant struggle for excellence as an alternative to confronting one's own weakness and mortality. The connections of pity help to contain the aggressive acting-out by which men, women and nations otherwise seek to overcome their pain.[50]

I will end this chapter on that note by stressing the importance of emotions, not only for successful drama but a successful life as a human being or as a society of human beings – as what we do, that is, the vision of what we do could be a new form of *paideia* in pity – and by quoting Orestes in Euripides's *Electra*: "Uneducated men are pitiless, but we who are educated pity much, and we pay a high price for being intelligent. Wisdom hurts" (line 295).[51]

Next, I will analyze a screenplay, which in my view realizes the vision and does exactly that: uses the concept of emotional structure to exercise *paideia* in pity.

Screenplay analysis: *Before the Rain* (screenplay by Milcho Manchevski)

In Macedonia, during the war in Bosnia, Kiril, a young monk who has taken a vow of silence protects an ethnic Albanian girl, Zamira, from Christians who claim she has murdered one of their own. In England, a photographic editor, Anne, meets her lover, a prize-winning Macedonian photographer just back from Bosnia, who has been changed by the violence. Aleksandar asks her to go with him to Macedonia but Anne, knowing she is pregnant, chooses to stay and talk it out with her estranged husband. Back in Macedonia, Aleksandar arrives at his village, which he has not visited in 16 years. There he tries to ignore bitter divisions between his Orthodox brethren and the local Albanians. But for how long?

The screenwriter and director announce the story as "a tale in three parts." The three parts are introduced with three titles, Words, Faces and Pictures.

"Words" deal with silence, the absence of words, and with speaking different languages, the uselessness of words. "The question is, whether you can make words mean so many different things," said Alice in Wonderland. Here, the answer is yes. Kiril breaks his vow of silence for Zamira and still they cannot communicate, as they speak different languages. Yet their communication is so strong that it makes him place this thing, which is so unexpected (or was it possibly expected on another inconceivable level?) and for which there is no language, above anything else in his life. Still, the absence and uselessness of words becomes their downfall. Zamira does not understand him, thinks he is leaving her and dies because of that misunderstanding. Her last gesture to him is to put her finger to her lips, asking him to be silent. The circle of this story closes, and we are devastated because of the loss of love – and the powerlessness of words. Angry, because of the way it happens. Interestingly, it is not enough to speak the same language to be able to understand each other. Zamira and her grandfather have a dialogue where one does not really answer the other – the grandfather upholds his standpoint (which, as we will later find out, might be strategy). He could have spoken Chinese – and, again, we see the uselessness of words.

There is a scene here that opens the next episode, a woman crying under the shower. One could think she is crying about what has just happened.

"Faces" deals with the destruction of faces, and with the surface of things, the misunderstanding of faces. Again, it tells a love story, one that does not work out because of another war, that of everyday life, which entails wrong decisions and commitments. We meet Anne (the woman crying in the shower) and the two men in her life. The comparison is clear – on one hand is life as it comes, with risks and uncertainty of outcome, on the other hand is security and predictability. We ache for Anne to make the right decision, to follow Aleksandar to Macedonia, but she does not go. A wonderful scene follows, one which includes so much humanity, in the sense that it focuses on the main conflict (will Anne go for Nick, will he persuade her?) and at the same time introduces us to all the people around them, through details and little gestures, so that when the big showdown comes, we feel the full impact of life lost. When Anne discovers Nick dead, his face completely destroyed, that is one of the most powerful emotional transitions in film history. "Your face," says Anne in pain and desperation, meaning Nick's face, but now we are traveling over Macedonia and that face is being destroyed through hatred between brothers, hatred that will be written on its face forever; and we are deeply sad, for the impossibility of love, for the victory of hatred, for the weakness of humanity.

"Pictures" deals with the illusions of pictures, the truth and lies of pictures, and the responsibility they entail. At some point Aleksandar writes to Anne and explains what he meant when he said he had killed somebody – and we understand why he has decided to give up his profession. The picture for which he received the Pulitzer Prize, and which was the high point of his career, was taken when somebody shot somebody else in front of his eyes, after telling him to get his camera ready. If Aleksandar were not a photographer, if he were not there at that very moment, if he had not said what he said, that person might be still alive. The picture is true; but by omitting the story behind it, it is also false. There is no truth – because there can be no truth. No picture can include everything, every single perspective, and every single detail, in or out of frame; and because it cannot include everything, it is ultimately a lie. The same applies to story. No story can include everything. The same applies to history, etc.

Aleksandar does not want to use his eyes to see and record what he sees anymore. Macedonia, he says to Anne in the episode "Faces," is the place where the Byzantines caught 40,000 people, poked their eyes out and sent them home – 28,000 eyes. Aleksandar has lost his faith. He has no hope anymore; he does not believe that his pictures can change anything. He has no hope that violence will end, and hope is a dangerous thing to lose.

Aleksandar meets in this episode the love of his youth, Hana, and she begs him to go save her daughter – she asks him "to act as if it were his own daughter." Is she his daughter? We will never find out. Aleksandar dies while saving Hana's daughter – who turns out to be Zamira, the girl of the first story, the girl whom we have already seen dying. We know what he does not know – that his sacrifice will be for nothing. The cycle of violence continues, and creates a new truth every day, a partial truth which is therefore a lie, and which creates a new violence – an endless cycle.

We could stop here, but we should not. Although these three stories have a beginning, middle and an end, and although the satisfaction on an intellectual level is enormous when we discover that the first episode happened in terms of chronology after the third episode and the puzzle seems complete, this screenplay and film are ultimately much more. There is a sentence thrown in at different points that declares "[...] time never dies. The circle is not round." What does that mean? Does it only apply to a game of chronology or is there possibly more to it?

Now, let us look at the overall emotional structure first, regardless of the story's division into three parts. To do that we will concentrate on the way we react emotionally while watching the movie. Where are the moments where reason meets emotion and which alert us on an almost visceral level? The first such moment seems to be when Kiril decides for humanity, for love, against betrayal on the cost of everything that defined him before – the moment when he gives a definite answer to his spiritual father and lies. We feel the danger, we are anxious for him and the girl; we know the risks, and we are hooked because we want to find out what will happen next. Is there a dramatic question here, and what would that be? Obviously, there is a question that connects to the concrete story of Kiril, but this does not concern us now. Above that, there is an emotional, almost philosophical, even better existential question, which seems to be: Can one be true to oneself, and what are the consequences? Can love prevail? This moment is at minute 16 of the film, which, were we to follow the rules of movie timing is where, strangely enough, the inciting incident would be. The emotional journey has started – with angst.

Kiril and Zamira are discovered and thrown out of the monastery. They seem to have managed to escape. There is a moment when they embrace and when Kiril declares his protection and she, even if she does not understand his words, understands him – a moment of absolute and perfect happiness. Is such happiness possible for a human being? That could be the dramatic question for the second act, that is, the second dramatic question which, again, is on an emotional, existential level, rather than on the usual plot level. Interestingly enough, this moment happens at the 30-minute mark, where we would normally expect the second important structural point in a classic structure, the first turning point, also called point of no return. (see the section on "Working with Rhythm," about how narration rhythm takes care of itself, when the story flows).

There is a scene in the episode "Words," which we quickly forget. It is a funeral scene, in which we see the men we will soon get to know at the monastery, burying somebody; and we see a foreigner, a woman with dark glasses. We soon forget that scene as the action of the episode catches our attention. It still teases us about the truth and leaves us with some doubt about who is the offender and who the victim. Zamira, it tells us, could have killed that man, for whatever reason. It is all a matter of perspective. There is no truth, or at least none at this moment.

There can be no doubt where the emotional midpoint is located. The shooting at the restaurant has such an impact that we are wide open to the devastation that follows from Nick and the other people's deaths. If we could turn the clock back, if only she had let him go, if she had chosen a different place, if they had not insulted that man, if the first word were not that arrogant, if only ... It is one of these moments in life when coincidences lead to fate – or is it fate that leads to coincidence? Personal guilt is mixed up with collective guilt and, again, there is no way of distinguishing or of taking sides.

The devastation is heightened, because the shooting follows the scene where Anne has made the wrong decision of refusing to follow Aleksandar, and is nuanced by the doubt that the baby may be his baby (and that he will never find out and that she may now have lost it). Because of the strangely inserted scene in the first episode, we assume he will die, and we want to shout at her that life is here and now, that we cannot hesitate and refuse to take what is there to be taken. It is time. Time does not wait, says the monk at the very end of the film. For the moment, we are left with as much human pain as is humanly sufferable, and this pain is visceral. We do not just feel for the character, we feel it ourselves. And it is not just about that scene, or that story, it is about life.

There is a scene in the episode "Faces" we quickly forget. Anne is looking at photographs; among them we see Kiril sitting on his suitcase close to Zamira's dead body. Then the phone rings. Macedonia calling, says the young voice, which we assume is Kiril's voice. This makes sense because we know Zamira is dead and that he wanted to call his uncle in London, but was it the uncle who was being buried, and was Anne the woman at his funeral? The story catches our attention, so we forget our questions for the moment.

Aleksandar writes to Anne about the way his camera killed a man – still, the next morning there is a dead body and the story takes a complete turn. There is now no way he cannot take sides or not participate in the action anymore, but he still resists. Then Hana comes, and she asks him to help her daughter as if she were his daughter too. He destroys the photographs and decides to act. He is partly redeeming himself for what he has done in Bosnia; but it is more than that, it is even more than an act of love for Hana. This happens around the 95-minute mark, where a somewhat delayed second turning point would be in the classic script structure models. Here we get an answer to the question of the second act. Is happiness possible? Is humane behavior possible, or loyalty? Does unconditional love exist? Love and happiness are about taking risks. While at the first structural point Kiril made an instinctive decision to take a risk (which got the emotional journey started), here we see that Aleksandar (now an older, more humane Aleksandar) makes a conscious decision.

Again, in order to understand emotional structure, we have to get back to the visceral level, and that has to do both with cognitive and emotional reactions. We cannot separate one from the other. Rationally we may feel bad or worried about Aleksandar taking sides and risks, but if we add the emotional level, then we get an answer to the existential question about unconditional love – and that answer is uplifting. On the one hand, we feel fate as a weight, on the other hand, we feel the humanity, pride and greatness of Aleksandar's decision, which in fact – as we know – is the only decision possible.

Now we get into a kind of third act in terms of the emotional structure. The climax, when Aleksandar dies, completes the emotional arc and answers the question that was asked at the moment when Kiril made the decision to lie. Can one remain true to oneself without consequences? The answer is yes. Aleksandar is smiling. He is dying but he is dying a man true to himself which, ultimately, is the only truth possible.

Aleksandar's struggle with the world and himself is something we know all too well as human beings. He takes a long time to overcome his ambivalence, but we want to believe in his integrity. It is not a political integrity; it has nothing to do with taking the right side, as there is no right side. It is an emotional integrity. When such an emotional integrity is proven, we take it for a happy end or rather most of us do – emotionally, even if our rational mind tells us that the hero has died.

There is a scene in the episode "Pictures," not even a scene really, more of a moment we barely take in. When Aleksandar visits the family of his childhood love, Zamira stands at the door, trying to see Aleksandar. We have looked at a couple of scenes which felt strange at the moment we saw them and which we then forgot about; now it is time to take a closer look at them.

Their existence is linked to the time question. At the very end of the film, we realize that the end of the film is not the end of the story. The end of the story is when Zamira dies. The beginning of the story is with Anne in London, which means that "Faces" comes first, then "Pictures", then "Words", but the photographs of dead Zamira in the second episode are impossible, because she cannot have died. Similarly, Kiril cannot have called, because he must remain silent and without Zamira. What does it mean that the circle is not round?

Looking at the three stories independently, each one is about three people, each of whom makes a decision (or does not make a decision, in the case of Anne) and fails. They cannot escape the cycle of death. The circle, which is not round, does not close because it is a helix of violence. Whatever they do or not do is irrelevant. The words, the faces, the pictures cannot help them. In that sense, this is a European, realistic film. The circumstances are bigger than the characters. There is none of the moralistic and educational mentality of Hollywood dramas. People cannot take their lives in their own hands, they cannot change their fate by becoming better or by accepting their mistakes – or can they? Because, on another level, that of the emotional structure, that of seeing this as one story, this is just not true. These are not three separate stories and cannot be seen as such. These are three stories put together in a particular way and with inconsistencies that point out at the simultaneity of time. The present also includes the past and the future. It is all now one big story, and as such a true spiritual experience. Together with the writer we go from fear, to happiness, to sorrow, to anger and finally to enlightenment, to truth, to peace.

As in every screenplay and eventually film that has a strong emotional structure, this one challenges the way we think and at the same time the way we feel. Let us remember that emotions carry knowledge, and whatever carries knowledge, whatever includes information, is a form of communication. Most importantly, emotions have something to do with our ability to perceive and the expansion of consciousness; and it is in this area where a powerful film, a film with a powerful emotional structure such as this one, can ultimately reach.

The writer seems to have a sole and single commitment, that of telling the truth about the emotions, of providing emotional insight. He does not even attempt to denote what is good or what is bad, he just gives us the human experience and through this the human condition; and by doing that, in such a powerful way, he is doing nothing less than the Greek tragic poets did (see above, the poets' solution). By way of an emotional journey, he cultivates the civilizing emotions based upon love and pity; and in doing so provides a *paideia* (an education, an upbringing) in pity.

It does seem an obvious idea to set love, care and concern for others against all the emotions that lead us to exploit others. This can surely be done by lecturing. It can be done by way of the so-called message at the end of a film. It can be done through the hero's journey, by showing us how someone tries to achieve a goal and ignores his real need and fails until he realizes what is right and what is wrong. There are many ways, but the most powerful and most effective is clearly the way shown here.

Let us remember that in the Greek concept of pity it is not the disposition to mercy and compassion, but the key is the felt connection to the suffering of others like oneself. The aim is to establish the connection to others, as though to say, no matter how great your sorrow, I shall not let you fall out of the world. The hope is to introduce order into disorderly souls. The vision is not for the pitier being separate from another's agony, but that we as an audience (and as writers) respond to it in the depths of our being "as a harp string responds by sympathetic resonance to a note from another source." Indeed, only the felt connection to others, the one that happens both emotionally and intellectually, can encourage human thoughts, the *sine qua non* of human wisdom. Such is, such could be, the new poets' solution.

The structure of the screenplay: Sixth sequence (the theme)

Schelling wrote that when a work of art portrays just the uncommon and not the infinite as well as the common, then it should not be called a work of art.[52]

Aristotle arrives at a conclusion in his controversial and difficult to interpret ninth chapter of the *Poetics*, which screenwriting theoreticians have ignored right up today. It concerns the thematic element that refers to "the common" or the universal (το καθόλου): "... poetry has in all likelihood as its theme the ordinary,"[53] that is, situations that ...

> return to the unchangeable and fundamental human reactions and emotional conditions: thirst for revenge, the pain of abandonment, injured honor and dignity, devoted love, unbridgeable, insurmountable hate, uncontrollable erotic passion with all its fatal consequences and so on. While history interests itself in concrete events (το καθ΄έκαστον) as well as in the people entangled in them, independently of whether they were active or passive participants, poetry (that is fiction, as opposed to history, that is fact) is freed from concrete space-time limitations and interests itself only for the unchanging and the everlasting."[54]

The writer continues "It is apparent that poetry differentiates itself from history, at least in Aristotle's opinion, because it is characterized by its repetition, while history is characterized by its uniqueness."[55] How strange is this observation, especially if we remember that the success of the American and primarily Hollywood cinema is ascribed to its universality, while others simultaneously reproach it for repeating itself, and italicize the uniqueness of European, Asian and other cinema.[56] The concept of universality as well as of globalization is thought to mean a devaluation and ignorance of the differences among the cultures, that is, of cultural diversity and in this sense, to present a simplification of everything.[57]

In other words, drama focuses on "the common," whereas it takes up "the concrete and uncommon myth to illustrate and to convey the common and to make it accessible to everyone, even if this sometimes happens in stages."[58] The goal of the work of art is to attain the knowledge (not the mimesis) of the common "that is the codified sense in the deep structure of the dramatic text" and the pleasure associated with it.[59] For Aristotle, the fable is, as we know, the soul of tragedy – without the fable, the existence of tragedy is inconceivable. "It does not only constitute the organized storyline of the tragedy but the field for the application of the creative abilities of the poet."[60]

Is the longing for "the common" an illness of western civilization? An interesting component that in this context is perhaps not unimportant, appeared in the argument about Bollywood cinema, that is, popular Indian cinema. In the attempt to show that the influence of Indian ideas has more weight than those of the Western narrative tradition, one arrives at the Rasa theory from the classical Indian philosophy of art. The origins of the Rasa theory can be traced back to the book, *Natyasastra* (Textbook of the Art of Acting) from Bharata, which was written in 200 BC. The Rasa theory may be described as an aesthetic schooling of mental ascertainment that may release a work in an audience. "Rasa" literally means "juice" and designates a kind of generalized feeling. Every Rasa is assigned to a corresponding concrete emotion *(bhava)*: love, frivolity, sorrow, anger, decisiveness, fear, disgust, wonder or peace.[61]

In the classical Indian aesthetic, Rasas are of vital importance. They are fictionalized emotions that may be experienced through poetry and art. Poetry, that is fiction – according to the Rasa theory – raises our experiences to a higher level and gives us a kind of emotional insight. For the Sanskrit connoisseurs, moreover, art is less a medium for the transmission of metaphysical visions as a means of edification – this is not much different from the Aristotelian vision. Understanding film then, is much more than a problem-solving process as described in the established psychological theories of narration, which especially concern the Hollywood cinema.[62]

In existing screenwriting theories, the theme is one of those elements of the screenplay about which there are as many interpretations as theories. Robert McKee is opposed to the notion of theme because he believes it is used much too often in the wrong way. Instead, he prefers to use the term "controlling idea" and by this he means the roots of a story or a central idea, implying its function at the same time. It can be explained in one sentence, and it describes how and why the life of a character has changed from the beginning to the end of a story. Phillip Parker does not arrive at a conclusion regarding the definition of a term, even though he determines that the theme gives an emotional dimension to a cinematic narrative and that it shapes the participation of the audience. At several points in his book he uses the concept of theme but in reality means subject matter; and in other places, he recognizes eight thematic types, for example, the need for justice, the longing for love and so on. Linda Seger does not offer any precise definition for the theme as well, but uses the construct to facilitate concentration on an emotional situation. Christopher Vogler uses the concept infrequently and it has little consequence. Syd Field avoids the concept or uses it in the sense of an object of a motion picture narrative. In addition, he claims it is necessary to know what the theme is before one begins to write.

Since past attempts at interpreting the theme in connection with the creative process and concerning its practical application most commonly go off in the wrong direction, and since both categories of effort have primarily led to serve the spiritual (and ultimately the didactic) notion of the story and of character development – and not to serve the creative process itself – a new interpretation of the concept of theme, as it is used within the framework of the method of creative screenwriting and of the emotional structure theory, should be undertaken at this point.

I will use the term emotional theme here since, as stated, the more general "theme" is often confused with the journalistic use of the word and, at bottom, expresses what the screenplay is about. Some scholars distinguish between the theme and the subject matter[63] by identifying the subject or the subject matter as the "external theme" and the dramatic or emotional theme as the "internal theme" of a story. Since the emotional theme has an external and an internal aspect, that way of categorizing a concept can cause confusion.

Frank Daniel designates the theme as the main component of a story and, in fact, as the main reason a story is told. He recommends seeing the theme as a result effect that springs from the film narrative ("the resulting impact that the audience should feel when the picture is over").[64] David Howard and Edward Mabley agreed with him on this point, and they designated the theme, as "the opinion the scriptwriter has about his material."[65]

The emotional theme, however, is more than that. It represents a general human emotion and it gives the script an inner coherence that transcends the plot structure or the character development structure. It is the sense that lies codified in the deep structure of the dramatic text (in Iakov's, i.e., Aristotle's words) and you respond to it in the depths of your being, as a harp-string responds by sympathetic resonance to a note from another source (in Stanford's words). It is a fictionalized emotion that elevates our human experience to a higher plane, a kind of emotional insight (in the words of Rasa theory). It concerns the classic dramatic structure as well as the non-classic, whether it is designated epic or alternative narrative; where for the alternative narrative forms the emotional theme is even more important to the consistency of the narrative structure, because it contains possibilities for the construction of the story that the weak or perhaps non-existent plot cannot offer.[66]

The concentration on a single theme in a screenplay is important, independently of whether this has a classic or an alternative narrative form. In contrast to the novel or other literary forms, several themes, if they appear to have equal weight, function like electric fields or opposed forces that cancel each other out. If we imagine a pile of metal filings on a table and put a strong magnet under the table, then the metal filings will be attracted to an invisible center that the magnet causes. Like the magnet, the emotional theme becomes invisible, but it focuses and orders all the different parts and elements of a screenplay. It brings order to disorderly souls – of the audience, the characters and ultimately of the writer.

The emotional theme is inextricably tied to the "need" of the lead character. If there is more than one lead character, they usually share the same need and the same theme, which provides the context for the alternative narrative form.

The above-mentioned definition of the theme has logical consequences. The audience often cannot name the theme, but it can feel it. The screenwriter does not seek his theme consciously, but rather unconsciously – his theme "finds" him and is often the same theme that occupies him creatively over and over, at least for a large part of his life. This is why we talk about the thematic identity of the screenwriter, which is not to be equated with the so-called artistic-aesthetic "signature." More than anything else, the emotional theme reveals the screenwriter's attitude to life and his worldview. As Gustav Freytag stresses, the personality of the poet designates the dramatic energy more in drama than in all the other arts, and it has the greatest imaginable power over and maximum influence on the dramatic form. This concerns not just the ethics or the morale of a screenplay, but also its artistic style and the emotions that it both contains and evokes.[67]

In the rule, the screenwriter is and should be the only one who decides how a story ends. Even when this is a so-called open end, it reveals a certain attitude towards the theme. If the theme, for example, is guilt and atonement,[68] the ending will show which of the two the writer ranks higher, guilt or atonement. He cannot avoid revealing his attitude, even if he tries to write an open ending. He cannot pretend another attitude that has been imposed on him for other reasons,[69] which is why it is most important the decision be left to him, whatever the commercial connotations. Any other ending not chosen by the writer will ring untrue and will damage the entire screenplay retroactively.

Although the emotional theme emerges primarily from the unconscious mind during the development of the screenplay, and although it is the actual reason why we have decided to tell a story, it is very hard to begin with the theme at the onset of the story; mainly because it is the direct link between our own story and our sensibility as a writer – it is too close to home. This may cause us to write stories that are constructed and have top-heavy structures. Perhaps the thematic pair, which we will investigate further (see the section on "Working with the theme"), offers the only viable creative approach.[70]

The emotional theme is not necessarily required for a screenplay. There are even films that do not have an emotional theme. A film with an emotional theme has, as mentioned, a structure that transcends and is more important than the plot. It has, moreover, something that elevates the film above the ordinary and makes it unforgettable. It has a soul.

The screenplay for the film *The Celebration*, by Thomas Vinterberg and Mogens Rukov, which we will examine next, provides a very good example of a film with a strong emotional theme.

Excerpt from a screenplay analysis: *The Celebration* (Screenplay by Thomas Vinterberg and Mogens Rukov)

The prize-winning film *The Celebration*, directed by Thomas Vinterberg, was the first film shot in compliance with the Dogma 95 manifesto.

Right up to now, this film has served as a model for this particular kind of film.

The film is about some serious drinking, a victim and of course a dinner held in honor of the 60th birthday of the head of a family, Helge Klingenfeld. The entire story takes place in a 24-hour span. The guests arrive, they greet each other, they appear for dinner, sit down at the festive table; the cook and servants prepare one course after another, which are then served while guests savor and discuss what is being served (Is the soup made with lobster or salmon?). They talk about their news and make comments about each other, give toasts, drink coffee and schnapps, dance, sing, drink – until at the end of the celebration only the young people and perhaps a drunken uncle are left standing. There is a parallel storyline in the kitchen – about a cook who cannot cook unless he is drunk.

From Ingmar Bergman to Jodie Foster, filmmakers have been fascinated by what can happen if family members gather to celebrate – an event that usually culminates in a feast. Dark secrets come to the surface, old jealousies are rekindled, injuries are added to old wounds and appear in the light of day – family gatherings are events that are often exhausting and that leave behind some scars. It is certainly not an accident that the two favorite movies of the director, Thomas Vinterberg, are *Fanny and Alexander* and Coppola's *The Godfather*, and that in both of them a family gathering in the form of a celebratory feast is the midpoint of the story.

The main reason for the success of *The Celebration* is most certainly the script. The Dogma films frequently rest on especially strong screenplays, since there is no possibility for special effects or music to stop up the holes or to give a scene a different meaning in postproduction. On the other hand, the film's focus is character dominated – the story always begins with and from the characters. It is their inner life that creates the story line and not the other way around. As a manifesto, Dogma aims at avoiding dramaturgical predictability. No one can say with certainty what is going to happen next, yet Vinterberg and the screenwriter and screenwriting teacher Mogens Rukov have written a masterpiece by employing all the techniques and elements of traditional screenplay instruction.

Systematically, the script obeys the classical dramaturgy of a three-act movie. The first act ends and the second begins with the first speech of the youngest son, Christian, who reproaches his father for the first time for molesting his children. This is the point of no return and here Christian's goal is articulated. He wants everybody to know the truth and to accept it as the truth, and he wants the articulation of the truth to lead to consequences. The reaction of the family that behaves as though they have not listened or have not understood anything is, however, an obstacle that cannot be overcome and that leads to the complications in the second act. Even though the truth lands like a bombshell, the intensity of the plot keeps reaching new heights – or rather depths, until the apocalyptic letter from Christian's twin sister is read by his other sister, Helene, and the truth has finally been established.

What remains are the consequences of this revelation that make up the third act. The climax is reached when the elder son beats the father, and the denouement happens the next morning when the family seems to have reorganized and Michael takes over the duties and perks of the head of the family (strangely enough, the father had offered them to him at the beginning of the film by promising him the right of succession as per the Free Masons tradition, to which he adheres). It is worthwhile, perhaps, to note that the screenwriters had tried out 15 different variations for the ending: the father drowns himself; Michael kills him, and so on. Nothing worked. The screenwriters eventually decided on an ending that in all likelihood condemned the father to the worst form of punishment possible.

A perfect structure, then, that originates from the needs of the characters who embody everything necessary in a screenplay: They have goals, their needs are clear, they give us a clear first impression, they exhibit their humanity – even the father has his qualities – and add to that they have completely understandable motivations. After his childhood experience is revealed, Christian does not need any additional reasons for his actions, we completely understand his motivation, but why did he choose this time, why now after all the years of keeping silent? The reason was the suicide of his sister. That is what drives him to act, the inner action that is revealed in the middle of the film, while the midpoint represents the emotional ground zero for the characters. We are talking about the scene where it becomes clear that Christian is plagued by guilt feelings, because he was not there when his twin sister needed him most. Guilt is a strong emotion, and in this case it is so intense that it finally leads him to overcome the fear of his omnipotent father that has been frustrating him for all these years.

One says that the old Greeks gave the same weight to the words μεθύειν/μεθώ (get drunk) and μετά το θύειν/μετά τη θυσία (after the sacrifice) – we encounter the connection in this screenplay. After the sacrifice of his sister, Christian gets drunk and while he is drinking, he gathers his courage and gets ready to lose everything, even his life if necessary. In one of the most harrowing scenes in the movie, we see him at death's door while he utters the famous last words spoken in the last seconds of life, "Shall I come with you?" he asks his dead sister. She embraces him and sends him back to life.

The screenplay of *The Celebration* pulls out all the stops a skilled screenwriter has at his disposal, which makes for an intense experience. In every scene, a conflict advances the story and simultaneously changes the direction of the story, while the story complications define the characters in a characteristic way and clarify their relationships. If conflict is the heart of and even provides the horsepower for the drama, the horsepower of this film is truly powerful. The screenplay is continually toying with what the audience knows and what it does not know. We, the audience, are the only ones who know of the existence of the twin sister's letter, and while the protagonist – in the previously mentioned scene with the father – ignores it; and the father, who also ignores its existence, even provokes him. "Why hasn't your sister written you?" The screenwriters toy with the audience because they want to leave us in doubt for some time about whether Christian is telling the truth. At some stage, when Christian keeps insisting, we realize that we do not want to believe him, that we will only believe him if we get hard evidence. We are put in the position of the guests who close their eyes, because the truth is unbearable. The story the mother tells, the attitude of the sister – everything speaks against Christian. The only thing that leaves us in doubt is the attitude of the servants who surround Christian with so much love, because they know what happened back then. Still, we, the audience, resist. What if he is exaggerating? What if Christian is making a fuss for other reasons?

This screenplay is, then, one of the best examples for having an emotional theme that is not identical to the subject matter of the film – that in turn is also clear. This film is about nothing less than sexual molestation in a family, and yet it is about more.

"Every family has a secret" was the tag line on the film poster. Where there is a secret, there is also a truth, and the truth has to do with human dignity. The emotional theme represents a common human emotion, and it lends the screenplay an inner cohesiveness that transcends the structure. While the goal of the character in relation to the plot defines and comprises the structure, that is, while it is the engine of the story, the emotional theme is responsible for the unconscious part.

The emotional theme of *The Celebration* is dignity and self-love, in other words, what we call self-respect and what is unobtainable without dignity. There is a snippet of conversation that is enormously important. When the truth is exposed, Christian says or better asks his father, "I've never understood why you did it." The father's answer, "You were not worth more than that." Christian is struck dumb; he is breathless. Dignity is the value of a human being.

With that, we are back where we started – back with the characters. The emotional theme is inseparably linked to the lead character, and above all to what in cinema dramaturgy is called the need of the character; that is, to what the character needs, what he is lacking in order to become a whole person. Christian aims at revealing and accepting the truth, but what he needs most is to re-establish his self-respect, the dignity that his father has taken from him with what he did – because if he does not love himself, nobody else will love him.

The screenplay for *The Celebration* is in every respect a good example for the study of the classical dramaturgical tools. It is, for instance, a brilliant example of how can one dramatize the attitude and the emotions of the characters and of how to avoid obvious dialogue. The cook and the other personnel are on Christian's side. Theoretically, we could get this information through dialogue, by having the servants convey their sympathy and assure their support. Instead, we see how they steal the car keys from a guest so they cannot drive away and avoid Christian's next round of accusations at the trial he is conducting, as they indeed attempt to do at some point. The servants' action takes on a special meaning, since they are putting their livelihoods at risk, but it also creates comic relief, something much needed and well used in such a dismal story.

In the final analysis, we endure this difficult story of heightened human ugliness, because the writer offers hope for the human condition: the servants who conspire to help Christian, the siblings who support him even though they doubted him at first – everyone helps him for their own personal reasons. Above all, the emotional theme reveals the screenwriter's attitude and worldview. In this case, such a view of life implicitly delineates an end that may truly be called happy.

Working with our experiences

Everyone is marked by their special experiences – the result is that we are pre-conditioned and react to certain situations with more emotion than to others. The goal of the artist is not so much to practice self-therapy by practicing his or her art, or to write his or her own autobiography, even if both can happen in the course of the artistic process, but that he or she reproduce the human experience by processing their personal experiences and their cognitive and emotional reactions to them.

Exercise #40:

Create a table of information (rational or emotional) in the left column that you want to dramatize, while you note down various alternatives to their dramatic translation in the right column.

Our experiences are especially important, even where they are not the direct source of a story. It is rarely coincidental that we are drawn to one material rather than another, according to Gustav Freytag.[71] Whatever pulls our fantasy in a given direction is nothing more than a mood and an impression that attracts us to a certain subject matter that is then mulled over unconsciously until we have found the hero and his main scenes.

Lee Strasberg stresses that childhood experiences are surely among our strongest.[72] In his preoccupation with childhood memories that have enormous significance for the content and style of his narrative, Tarkovsky has investigated the difference between the emotional atmosphere of a memory and the facts – as these have been sent and received from one person to another.[73] He feels that confrontation with the specific source of the memory usually destroys its poetic character.

The following exercise should contribute to experimenting with ways to preserve the essence of a childhood experience.

Exercise #41:

Write about an event from childhood or from adolescence you have never written about before and is "new territory" in the sense that you have not quite clarified your feelings about it. Change the sex of the protagonist. What is his or her main motivation? Write a scene that stems from his or her central emotion.

Freytag emphasizes the use of autobiographical material and warns about adapting other genres of poetry that he calls bad material. Whoever has self-confidence and knows himself well enough, he tells us, should choose to use original material that has never been used before – and what is better suited than material from one's own life? Whatever we experience, it is all copy.

The next exercise should be helpful in approaching new experiences that one can "gather" through research rather than by using personal experiences – whereas we will approach such experiences not in a journalistic sense but rather as a source of inspiration.

Exercise #42:
For a specified time take up an activity or an occupation that is as far removed from your normal milieu as is humanly possible. Use the material in the same way that you used the subject mater in the *Cinéma Vérité* exercise (Exercise #39). Immediately after the new experience is completed, note down five to ten new elements that you knew nothing about before. To start with, write a scene directly from your new experience by concentrating on the main emotion. While you read the scene, consider if it is dramatic enough – and if it is not, revise it by adding a new element (a new conflict, a new character, a new element and so on), but be careful not to destroy the emotional core of the experience.

The technique of the reversal

The mathematical concept of reversal is especially important as a metaphor for the fantasy game: We reverse something when we move in the opposite direction. In creative screenwriting, we use reversal not only with movement, the reversal of time for example, but also with other narrative elements. We can replace or change the sex of the lead character, just as we did with the lead character in the childhood experience exercise. We can change the perspective or the genre of the narrative and try out different combinations that will help us distance ourselves from the actual story, without abandoning the emotions associated with it.

The technique of the reversal is especially useful when we are working with autobiographical material. It is the most viable way to distance ourselves from what has really happened and in doing so we retain the emotional center in all of its intensity.

Exercise #43:
Write a scene from the above exercise by changing the narrative perspective and by assuming the emotional perspective of the antagonist.

The Game of Genres is immensely suited to the Technique of the Reversal. A genre is nothing more than the possibility of establishing contact with the audience by quickly increasing certain expectations. The audience knows what it is getting into and expects that the limitations of the genre will be observed scrupulously. The simplest possibility of the reversal is to establish an expectation and not realize it. Genres may be used both as a dramaturgical means and as a creative element in general.[74] The access through the genre has been recommended in recent times by the research of emotive film effects, because film genres are frequently associated with strong emotions that are genre specific and can vary from genre to genre. The genre may be seen as a structure of stereotypes of a higher order, which activate a specific sub-program of psychological behavior with the audience, among which are the emotional and completely normative strategies.[75] The emotional tenor and basic pattern that are realized and maintained through the genre have in turn their starting points in the moments of conflict. Comedy masters its conflicts in a different way than tragedy or the melodrama. In the words of the dramatist Friedrich Dürrenmatt, "Tragedy transcends distance ... Comedy creates distance."[76]

Exercise #44:

Write a scene based on what you know about the first time your parents met. Revise it after you are finished and change the genre. If it has come out as an especially romantic scene, for example, change it into a comic one.

Working with first love

The notice "Based on a true story," which we know from many films, means that the inspiration for the screenplay story is taken from reality, and usually means someone else's experience, mostly the experience of someone we do not know. Exotic experiences number among the classic sources of the art of cinema narrative and may be found apart from the direct transcription of a story by researching a procession of existing works, novels,[77] plays, motion pictures as well as news stories.

To be able to write screenplays, says Akira Kurosawa, one should first study and mull over the great novels and plays and discover why they are great. Where do the emotions come from that one feels while reading a story?[78] This is also the question one should ask if one adapts a pre-existing work. The literary adaptation is, according to Linda Seger, one of the most difficult areas of screenwriting and requires in particular great experience by the screenwriter.[79] Despite this, the first thing novice screenwriters try to write is frequently an adaptation, probably because they assume that it is easier to base a story on existing material. The results more often than not confirm Seger's hypothesis.

In this connection, we will just barely descend into the depths of the exotic and complex form of literary adaptation, by showing how one can approach an adaptation using the method of creative screenwriting. The technique is, in the final analysis, closely related to the technique we have already gotten to know from the use of exotic material and from working with our emotions as well together with our dreams. They also have to do with the corresponding theoretical analysis of the concepts "emotional theme" and "need of the character". What interests us most of all is the initial impression and the initial emotion. What moves us to fall in love with a certain novel, or a play or a stranger's story – in whatever form we encounter them?[80]

In his book, *Die Technik des Dramas*, Freytag refers to the following event:

> Stuttgart, the 11th. Yesterday one discovered in the apartment of the musician Kritz his eldest daughter, Luise, and the ducal dragoon-major Blasium von Böller lying dead on the floor. The record from the scene and the coroner's report concluded that both of them had died from the poison they had swallowed. One speaks of a love affair that the father of the major, the noted president von Böller, attempted to thwart. The fate of the generally respected young girl renowned for her modesty excites the sympathy of all feeling souls.[81]

This news could also have excited the sympathy of young Shakespeare, who from the moment "where the stimulus and warmth have come which he needs to create,"[82] would proceed with absolute freedom and turn every useful element into a dramatic moment and ultimately turn it into one of his best-known plays.

A true story based on the film *The Celebration* (whose screenplay was analyzed in the previous section) was heard by the co-writer and director in the form of a newscast on the radio on March 18, 1996:[83]

> A young man infected with AIDS describes how he revealed the molestation he and his twin sister (who had ended her life the previous year) had suffered at the hand of their father, by giving a speech at his birthday party.

It is rare for there to be such a close correspondence between a real story and a fictional one. The real story usually provides an inspiration that the fantasy of the screenwriter lets gallop off in a new direction and customarily blends the alien experience with his own.

Exercise #45:
Find a news article in a newspaper. Think over what attracted your attention, what made you "fall in love" with it in the first place. Who is the protagonist? Which character did you identify with most? What is the central conflict or contrast? Do you think it is the beginning or the end of a story? I will cite as an example an actual media news report and explore its possibilities as the basis for a film story:

An emotional dilemma

A news agency reports the story of a European tourist in Southwest Asia who had to fight with her two children against giant waves during the tsunami catastrophe in December 2004, which claimed more than 100,000 lives. At the critical moment, and in full knowledge that her children did not know how to swim, the mother of a five-year old and a two-year-old has to make the most tragic decision of her life. She can only save one of her two children. A decision taken in the blink of an eye will scar the lives of three people forever – her own, the boy she decides to save and the five-year-old she sacrifices, but who manages to survive. Days later, the five-year-old stares at his mother inconsolably and cries. Unable to comprehend her dilemma, he tries to understand how his mother could let go of his hand when he needed her so much.

The journalistic approach to such events, even if the reporting is truthful and careful, can be more impressive than subtle due to the power of images. This can have both advantages and disadvantages for the adaptation of the story, since images are frequently less horrid than the images of our own fantasy.[84] What is the main point? How does the story read that has awakened our interest? One thing is certain, for each of us a different story lies hidden in this news report.

The pain of the five-year-old is a possible starting point. We can start the film narrative much later in time, for example – so that the news story becomes the backstory and is the hero's wound in the new narrative. We can also focus our interest on the mother's wound, but how? Is it possible to make such a powerfully dramatic story even more dramatic? The answer is – yes. What would happen if the mother's worst fear came true? What if the five-year-old had died? What if the five-year-old survived, as he did, but went on carrying his unbearable pain forever, a pain that stems from the fact that his mother did not choose him even though his younger brother died after the mother had done everything possible to save him? That screenplay would treat the same emotional theme as the movie *Ordinary People* adapted by Robert Redford and Alvin Sargent from the novel written by Judith Guest or *Sophie's Choice* adapted by Alan Pakula from the novel of the same name by William Styron (even if in that case the two children did not survive).

Working with fairy tales

Fairy tales and myths form a special case, since they do not belong to the category of exotic or alien material, but rather (at least in part) to the collective memory.[85] The process of adaptation has famous harbingers such as *Ulysses* by James Joyce: "[...] a net in which the reality of his very own Dublin has become enmeshed, and simultaneously a system of distorted mirrors that reveals dimensions that would not be seen with the naked eye."[86] Just as Homer's "Odysseus" serves the writer only as a complex system of fantastic components.

Fairy tales speak directly to existential angst and to the human dilemmas,[87] and for this reason are an especially important source for creative screenwriting. What we do in the adaptation of a fairy tale or a myth is to focus on the sense and the symbolic value of some of the elements and functions. The magic filter perhaps cannot remain a magic filter, but what would happen if it became a hard drug at a rave party? Would the drug not acquire the same function?

Vladimir Propp has imagined a constant bundle of functions in his *Morphologie des Märchens,* as found in fairy tales. A.J. Greimas defines and codifies the same functions in his narrative model, which is based on Propp's theories. According to his "archetypical criticism," there is in every human story the same grammatical order. There are uncountable characters who, according to Greimas, fill merely six specific roles and appear in pairs: subject-object, sender-receiver and helper-antagonist. These roles always create concrete, solid relationships: desire and longing, the quest, the goal for the subject-object pair, contact and communication for the sender-receiver pair and friendship or competition for the helper-antagonist pair. A character can also be a helper one time and an antagonist another time.

Exercise #46:
Find a fairy tale that made you especially afraid when you were a child, or that fascinated you; and transpose it into your reality. Begin with a summary of the original as close as possible to the way you can recall it (i.e. without looking it up), by turning your attention to the core emotion. Write a new version, also in the form of a summary. The technique of the intentional mistake is a technique that functions especially well when a fairy tale or a myth is our starting point. For example, Little Red Riding Hood can be bad and the wolf good.

Exercise #47:
Rewrite a fairy tale you know well by switching the roles of the protagonist and the antagonist.

Working with themes

The themes that occupy us evolve and change the way our lives evolve and change. The same is obviously true for our attitude towards life.

Exercise #48:
Answer the next six questions "positive" or "negative" without thinking much about the answer. Do you believe you can achieve everything or that the truth will always come out? Do you believe that there is justice in the world, that good triumphs ultimately, that evil is always punished or that love endures?[88]

I have already spoken about the moralistic narrative form whose important precondition implies the following attitude towards life: that good intentions will triumph, that the world is easy, understandable and consequent, that it corresponds to the good and the true that prevails in the world, and that our fate does not only lie in our hands; but also that our deeds will have no further consequences if only we are ready to admit our mistakes. I have also mentioned the skepticism that can prevail in opposition to this worldview and in opposition to the dramaturgical consequences of the notion that the heroes can take their fate into their own hands and change the course of events as well. This skepticism has led to a series of cinema movements, such as Italian neorealism. Between the two philosophies, there are an infinite number of gradations as well as various versions. The previous exercise may provide us only with a vague idea of our own sensibility in terms of that contradiction. It goes without saying, that there is no right or wrong answer or attitude.

To be accepted, a happy end must be in harmony with the prevailing morality. An end that means a victory for the morally challenged does not produce a happy end in this sense, even though it might be a positive outcome for the specific character. Many writers consciously choose an open ending, because they think it offers a stronger tie to real life experience – which does not seem to have much structure but seems instead like an endless strand of separate events without clear endings.[89]

At first, it seems important to me to stress that an open ending that may not lead to a definite solution to the problems presented in the classic narrative sense, can or even needs to be closed in the emotional sense. On the other hand, the ending can be closed in the narrative sense, but on the emotional level achieve a wholly different effect. A good example of this is the film, *The Graduate*, by Mike Nichols, Calder Willingham and Buck Henry. The union of a couple in love occurs even in the face of bitter resistance by their social surrounding, but signs of uncertainty and certain bewilderment are mixed in with the supposed happiness of a successful escape – which becomes an emotionally open ending. This is what makes the movie so timeless and emotionally intelligent. One is reminded of Oscar Wilde, who in *The Importance of Being Ernest* addresses the happy end that is disconnected from reality when he has the character Cecily say, "I don't like novels that end happily. They depress me so much."

The ending of a story is one of the greatest challenges a screenwriter faces, since it is the most important part of a film and evokes emotions, which the audience will eventually take home. Shortly before the end, we have all the elements of the story, and as such realize them in their best possible and final combination. Different components are important in making this decision – fantastic and ethical, primarily in terms of content, but also ideological components that stand in relation to the message and the worldview that, after all is said and done, we convey with the ending. This is why the ending is the only stop sign or taboo that counts where the work of the screenwriter is concerned. The final word is and should be in his hands – otherwise the whole screenplay will feel phony and fake.

Exercise #49:

Continue a story you have started and finish it. Use, for example, one of the stories thought up during a previous exercise. "How does the story of Alex end, who woke up after 15 years only to discover that his beloved had married someone else and had children with him?" Compare different versions of an ending and the resulting worldviews they convey.

We will see that different writers will create different final scenes, that is, different "messages," even if they tell the same story using the same characters. The final message, the attitude, pops up like an involuntary spasm. In contrary situations, when we start with the goal of conveying a certain message, the result is that we often bring about the wrong, if not the contrary, effect. It is indeed extremely likely that we will convey the exact opposite of what we intended.

Exercise #50:
Spend your day living out a worldview of your choice, that is, a certain life attitude. Try to develop a corresponding attitude towards everything around you and live it with passion. Write down everything that happened to you when you are finished. Write a scene based on a circumstance that irritated you.

Exercise #51:
Try to note down all the points of your own culture that seem funny, dramatic, peculiar or at least interesting enough to share with others. Write a scene based on those elements that inspire you the most.

If the message is the most dangerous starting point, then the theme is the most difficult one. Even so, how can we invent a story if we begin with a specific theme? In the section about conflict ("The structure of the screenplay: second sequence"), I mentioned Gianni Rodari's games in the context of the opposing terms,[90] and in particular the concept that every idea or thought is impossible without its opposite and that there are never individual ideas but instead pairs of ideas. Not least, I spoke about the theory of Henri Vallon that thought is formed in pairs.[91] In thought, the fundamental element is the double structure, and not the individual elements. The pair is thus more primal than the individual elements, says Vallon, and in so doing he opens the pathway to the invention of a story based on pairs of contrasting themes, the theme pair.

Exercise #52:
Draw two columns – in the left one note down an emotional theme and in the right one its opposite. Include situations and events that express either the theme or its antithesis, the anti-theme. Using the technique of

"clustering," that we became familiar with in Exercise #22, apply the theme pair as a source of invention for the development of a protagonist and antagonist through their thematic conflict. Write a summary of the story for a film based on these narrative elements.

Working with shadows

The philosophy of art or aesthetics considers fundamental contrast along with the identification of light and shadow, wherein they melt together up to the point where they become one. Aristotle writes that one establishes sympathy for his characters when they show both good and bad qualities. Freytag uses the concept of "mensch:" The characters must be humane, and that means vulnerable, easy to catch and conquer.

"It is dangerous to wrack your brain about the character of someone else," wrote Strindberg.[92] Like Bergman (who often mentioned Strindberg as a source of inspiration), Strindberg was a clinician:

> I know a nun whom I think highly of, because she is straightforward, but I know that she enjoys carnal pleasures and that she drinks a little. When I realized that, I judged her a hypocrite; but after awhile I understood. She is a nun *because* she is carnal. She does not pretend to be pious. Instead, she practices penitence to restrain her fatal inclinations. I did not see any contradiction in that, but I fear that nuns often have to hide a tendency to criminality.[93]

Strindberg is talking here about a causal "because," which is hidden in an "although". The character he is describing is a nun because she is carnal and not a nun *although* she is carnal.[94]

Each character has a dark and a bright side, that is, a good and a bad side. When one does not know both sides, then one remains superficial. The shadow of a character expresses the other side of the character. If it is a positive character, then the shadow is about the dark side; and when it is a dark, negative character, then the shadow is about the positive side. In any case, the shadow is the companion of the character that cannot be wished away – and as screenwriters we have the duty to research this side, to discover, to expose and, according to the necessities of the story we are telling, even to provoke it into emerging. This is the only way we can reach and convey a deep insight; grasp and elaborate the full potential of a character and realize our own potential as writers.

The characters in a story often do not know their dark side. They keep their eyes closed to what concerns them as well as what concerns others. As writers – but also as members of the audience – we long to "open their eyes," as with a friend who, in our opinion, is most obviously committing a mistake or is the victim of a betrayal. As writers, but also as members of the audience, we react just as we do in everyday life: Mostly we judge exactly those character traits we hide in ourselves, since we are only able to recognize them and to understand them, because they are (also) our traits. Naturally, the characters in a story have the same reaction mechanism: The ambitious reproach the others for being ambitious; the lazy reproach the others for laziness. It is an idiosyncrasy that Marcel Proust loved especially and used often in drawing up his characters.[95]

Exercise #53:
Make a list of things that you could not have as a child, by using the Trick of Quantity. Then look for something that you have done despite the prohibition. How did you feel at the moment you violated the rule? Write a scene based on this emotion.

Exercise #54:
Make two columns. In the left column note down five positive and five negative characters (an example for a negative character would be Hannibal Lecter) taken from motion pictures you are familiar with, and in the right column make a list of character traits that you feel is their shadow. Then note how this is expressed in the corresponding films. Do the same exercise with characters you have created yourself. It is important to remember that the other side of a character mostly represents the opposite pole of his or her central character trait.

Working with the look of a film

The "look" of a film is what gives it its special mood and style. The elements that in the rule determine this look – the colors, the locations, the objects, the costumes – can receive their own dramatic life or take part in the story as one of the dramatic elements. The movies of Billy Wilder and Ernst Lubitsch are mentioned as examples that are known for their masterly dramatic and metaphoric but never overwritten use of props.

Exercise #55:
Analyze the dramatic use of props in the motion picture, *Lost Weekend*, from Billy Wilder.

Objects can indicate something, be it through their obvious use, their intrinsic characteristics or in that they reveal something about the backstory.[96] The way the colors, the locations, the objects and the costumes can be deployed can vary a great deal: Our goal is always what we call a visually enriched script, that is, a script that uses optimally the contrast among its narrative elements.

Exercise #56:
Analyze a sequence from a completed script, by concentrating on how the colors, the locations, the props and the costumes are deployed, especially in relation to the contrast that needs to be established between the scenes that follow one another as well as their dramatic effect.

Working with subtext

One of the most important elements of a good screenplay is what we call "subtext," that is, what lies behind or under the writing. It is the not expressly stated, unconscious life that lends our writing stature and weight, declares William Goldman,[97] but how do we put the unconscious emotion and that not expressly stated life of the characters on the pages of a script?

The construct "subtext" is applied primarily in relation to the dialogue, but it involves more than that. *Gone With The Wind* provides a good example: Scarlet, the lead character, sees that Melanie and Ashley are happy together and accepts Charles' marriage proposal. We see that the proposal was accepted out of sheer spite – not because she wants Charles, but because she cannot have Ashley. We "see" this because the screenwriter wants us to see it. He gives us the information in the way he sets up the scene, as much through the timing of the proposal, that he links directly to Scarlet's realization that Ashley is happy. The scene has the marriage of Charles and Scarlet as its subject matter, but in reality, it is a love scene between Scarlet and Ashley. This reality is the "subtext" of the scene that is achieved using purely dramatic means.

A good example of how subtext works dramatically is the film *All About Eve* (Screenplay by Joseph L. Mankiewicz):[98] Bette Davis plays the role of the triumphant actor, Margo Channing, who is going to be forty years old today. She is in love with Merill, who is eight years younger than she is, and extremely jealous of her own secretary, Eve, who seems to be an angel loved by everyone. This evening Margo has invited guests to celebrate the return of Merill from Hollywood, where he has just shot his first movie. A celebrated 25-minute party sequence ensues that begins with a quarrel between Margo and Merill. The reason for the argument is that he came up to her room too late because the angel, Eve, held him up in conversation.

Margo speaks one of the most famous lines in motion picture history, "Fasten your seat belts; it's going to be a bumpy night." Eight scenes follow in which she gets drunk and manages to insult and depress everyone who loves and admires her. In the course of the party sequence, Margo's behavior becomes more and more unbearable, but we cannot judge her. The screenwriter lets us know that it is neither her jealousy of Eve nor her being angry because Merill came too late. It is about her fear of the fact that her career will soon end, while the two others have theirs in front of them, and that the years pass and life goes by. A fear we are all too familiar with – and that is why we identify with the lead character. The dialogue begins to entertain us from the moment we become aware of the subtext.

The following two exercises describe situations where the dialogue is a pretense that carries the subtext.[99]

Exercise #57:
Write a scene about a couple that buys a mattress. Their dialogue revolves solely around the mattress (the size, the color, the kind, etc.), but in reality they talk about their relationship.

Exercise #58:
Write a scene where someone approaches a woman at a reception. While the dialogue between the two takes place in front of a buffet and it revolves around food and the reception, in reality it is about their loneliness. For instance, they will try to find out if the other is single without revealing their curiosity or their tactics.

The structure of the screenplay: Seventh sequence (the answer to the second dramatic question)

The second turning point designates the transition of the screenplay story from the second to the third act. It primarily posits a dead end and frequently represents the largest and hardest obstacle that can appear in the path of our character and his or her dramatic development. Gustav Freytag uses the concept of "the retarding moment" to describe it.[100] Aristotle does not appear to have recognized nor emphatically named this moment or the first turning point. For him, the second turning point is simply the point where the middle ends. Frank Daniel calls this structural point the "second culmination" or "crisis," that is, the second high point or crisis.

The functions of the second turning point are, according to Linda Seger, the same as the functions of the first one (see the section on "The structure of the screenplay: fourth sequence"). The second turning point elevates the feeling of urgency, increases the tension and accelerates the narrative rhythm: The new, faster rhythm dominates the entire third act and leads to the climax. The second turning point represents the last crisis that precedes the climax. In the theory of myth based on Campbell's work, the second turning point is called "road back," as it contains the decision of the hero to return to the "ordinary world" and to apply what he learned in the "special world" he traveled through. The archetypical myth that follows the rigid progression of separation – initiation – return is now complete. In the optimistic and life-affirming concept employed here, the failure of the hero is not envisioned.

In the system of two questions, the second turning point plays an important role. When the first turning point formulates the second dramatic question, that is, the dramatic question of the second act and with that creates a buildup and release of tension in the second act, then the second turning point is the point where the question is answered. *Spring, Summer, Autumn, Winter ... and Spring* by the screenwriter and director Kim Ki-Duk Duk that is analyzed briefly in the section on "The structure of the screenplay: fourth sequence", provides a good example to illustrate the system of two questions and the way it functions, even with screenplays that are not plot driven.

Working with rhythm

Rhythm and timing are among the most important tools available to the scriptwriter. These are musical constructs – like perhaps the most important word in a screenplay, beat, which means the same as meter. The term "beat" incorporates syncopation on the one hand, that is, a pause in the dialogue and in the plot (because a moment of silence, a short pause at the right moment, says more than a thousand words) and on the other hand the rhythmic variety within a scene.

In the rule, the location of the points in time where the structural "knots" should be to serve the needs of the story, has been rather rigidly established in the various screenplay theories, even if most screenplay gurus do not want to provide a page number or minute when they should occur.

There are always at least as many exceptions as there are rules – in general, however, the timing of the classic screenplay structure exists in the alternative narrative forms, since it concerns the time segments needed to retain the attention of the audience.

Do we need to define the right timing? The musician and drummer Martin Fulterman mentions in almost every interview how his collaboration with the Greek composer, Manos Hadjidakis, was an endless source of inspiration. When he was having difficulties with the 5/8 or 7/8 time signatures, he says, Hatsidakis came up to him and whispered into his ear, "Forget the rhythm! Just sing the melody, and the rhythm will take care of itself."

This is true for musicians, as it is true for writers. The rhythm should pass over into flesh and bone. The exact positioning of the structural points as well as the length of the individual scenes are decisions that a screenwriter must be able to make without thinking about them too long. This can only be learned through practice and experience. The lack of a feeling for rhythm is, like the lack of subtext, characteristic of the inexperienced screenwriter.

Exercise #59:

Analyze a finished screenplay using the length of the scenes as the criterion. How do their length and rhythm differ when placed in the first, the second or the third act?

In their second function described earlier, beats represent units of time, that is, contiguous time segments and as such they create a rhythm within a scene. They are the smallest dramatic unit and therefore the smallest structural element of a screenplay.[101]

In themselves, they are breaks in the action, an interchange of action and reaction or emotional variations. They can originate from small phrases or a short dialogue. The variations in the beat are characterized by variations in the balance of power, that is, in the status game among the characters in a scene. The dominant characters set the tempo – the beat belongs to them. The change in beat is determined by the change in the emotional state of the characters. In that sense, the change in the beat within a scene corresponds to a bigger emotional development or reaction inside a screenplay.

Even in the smallest unit of a story, we can recognize its segmentation into three or five parts, writes Gustav Freytag.[102] It is frequently divided into three parts, since the number three is the magic number of screenwriting.[103] In most cases and especially in the major scenes we recognize a subdivision into three segments, which according to the size and degree of significance of the scene can be either three beats or meters or three-meter sequences, that is, the next largest dramatic unit – what Stanislawsky called the "long distance move" or LDM.[104]

The artistic variation in meter can affect the camera movement as well as the editing of the film. The tension within a scene can be achieved either by classical means, such as by using the perspective of the characters and alternating between the subjective and objective perspective, that is, between the perspective of the character and that of the outsider; or by varying the meter. In the course of an intensive scene, whose effect arises through the emotional exchange between the characters, camera movement seems to heighten the emotional condition of the characters. Would such emotional intensity already be written down in the screenplay? I think so. The scene could have determined the escalating rhythm using changes in the beat – the director can then either ignore or support this.

A good example is the love scene in the motion picture *Wind Across the Everglades* written by Bud Schulberg and directed by Nicolas Ray.[105] The heart of the scene is made up of nine camera angles that follow each other in a rapid shot, counter-shot succession that shows two faces alternating in the traditional way and sets the accent (that is, the beat) on one face after another during a series of alternating dialogue exchanges and embraces. The frame is so tight that the specific effect combined with the multiple angles intensifies the movement and the dramatic energy.

This might be the most important difference between the traditional and "alternative" school of film directing, and simultaneously between what we call the American and European school. In the latter, the director is a part of the scene. The way he directs a scene and the camera movement influences our emotional take on what has happened. Theoretically, we could say the European school ingratiates itself more with the audience than the American school,[106] but it often loses the audience on another level.

Exercise #60:
Analyze a scene by concentrating on the change of beat within a scene. Afterwards, rework one of the scenes you have written by trying to apply a three stage or LDM change.

A beat

It is stated in the first part of this book that the most important thing in writing is to feel the rhythm of the story. Improvisation and the game of aporia should be helpful – these are tools and techniques that we have practiced thoroughly in the second part. In the third part, we will now study the application of these techniques to the whole screenplay, while we demonstrate the completion of the system of two questions and two answers at the theoretical level. This last part also contains the climax of the emotional structure theory. We have already seen how the idea of unity and completion of a film story can be retained, even when it is not about a traditional plot driven narrative structure. Now we will look closer at ways to improve the emotional structure of a work in progress.

Through all this, the more and more we go into rules and regulations that govern the rhythm of the screenplay, a rhythm that will eventually determine the story, let us not forget the composer's advice. Forget about the rhythm. Play the melody and the rhythm will take care of itself.

The End

"Take care of the sense," the Duchess said, "and the sounds will take care of themselves."

Lewis Carroll

Application of Creative Screenwriting and Emotional Structure to the Complete Screenplay

Playing with structure: working with the chronological sequence

The limerick is a form of poetry that organizes a small story and lends meaning to it through structure. More precisely, it is a short, as a rule, humorous poem of five lines that has a defined rhyme scheme.[1] With extremely few exceptions limericks follow the same rules that have been analyzed with great exactitude by the soviet semiologists Chivian and Chegal in their book *Die Systeme der Semantik und der sowjetische Strukturalismus*. The first line usually names the acting person and ends with the name of a place or countryside; the second line unmasks his or her identity, while a surprisingly comical punch line follows a brief description of a person's character trait or behavior.[2] By copying this form and using it as a guideline for composition, one can write limericks. In the same way, one could compose stories if one applied that technique to cinema narrative.[3]

Exercise #61:
Start with a character and use the Technique of the Limerick to continue – begin with a routine, interrupt this routine, then continue by making a decision that takes the story in a new direction, etc. – while at the same time using the Trick of Quantity (see the section on "The trick of failure: the courage to fail and the rule of quantity").

The game with the structure and/or with the chronological sequence of events is a peculiarity of the audiovisual narrative. The screenwriter and critic Michel Chion differentiates between the actual story in the screenplay, that is, what happens when one considers the story in a chronological sequence, and a second level where this story will be told. He calls the second level narrative, but also presentation, course of the plot, dramatic setup – while others call it in turn, discourse,[4] dramatic structure and so on.

The stories, according to Chion, among others, are but a few. That which is endlessly open and renewable is the art of storytelling, the way we tell a story, the way that events and elements of the story are brought to the attention of the audience (narrative methods, hidden, later revealed information, use of time, ellipses, stressed elements, etc.), as well as the emotions and thoughts in it. The art of narration can make a story interesting even if it has no surprises. On the other hand, bad or uninteresting storytelling can spoil even the fascinating aspects of a story – an experience we have all had when struggling to make a joke come out right but telling it in the wrong order or with the wrong emphasis.[5]

Jean-Luc Godard's sentence, "Every film has a beginning, middle and an end, but not necessarily in that order," is notorious. But H. Mankiewicz and Orson Welles presented the first alternative structural form in the history of film long before him with their film *Citizen Kane* – a screenplay that functions like a chronological puzzle, and begins with the last word Kane spoke before he died – "Rosebud." This opening scene (that, seen chronologically, is actually the last scene) contains numerous elements that generate questions and expectations that in the course of the narrative are answered and met.

Exercise #62:
Write the ending of a story as a scene. How did the characters get to this point? What can have happened beforehand?

As we have seen in other places, the ending of a screenplay, primarily the climax, is filled with answers to questions that were presented earlier (see the section on "The structure of the screenplay: third sequence"). Robert McKee sees the climax as the most difficult scene to write and even calls it the soul of the story.[6] This exercise suggests taking the final climax as the starting point and writing "from back to front." When we begin at the end without knowing what has happened previously, the answers most likely will lead us to the questions by themselves. No other scene can generate as many questions as the climax.

The following scene was presented in a workshop as the climax. The group went over the scene again and again using the familiar game of aporia.

Every ending tells a story

MICHAI (11) inserts the key and turns it hard the way he's seen it done so many times. The engine starts and before he can grasp what's happening, the bus lurches forwards. Michai is terrified – he fishes for the hand brake – suddenly "he" jumps in front of the bus; "he" waves his arms like a crazy man and curses: his torso is naked, but at least "he" is not in the house any more. As soon as he sees him, Michai takes his hand off the brake and steps on the gas. His mother's scream – "he" jumps aside. The mechanical monster sputters because of Michai's inexperience in driving, but instead of stopping it picks up speed. The bus is heading for a cliff; Michai tries to step on the brake but can't reach it – the bus accelerates and swerves. He has to get out; he has to get out. He yanks at the door with all his might, opens it and jumps. As he falls he hears the spine-chilling sound of worn metal giving way as the bus goes over the edge. ■

What causes the eleven-year-old Michai to steal a bus of all things, and who is the man who jumps in front of it that he would have killed if his mother hadn't screamed? Where does the man who is naked from the waist up come from, why is he naked and whom had Michai watched starting the bus so many times? The story of little Michai develops slowly through the answers to the group's questions: his childhood with his divorced mother is anything but ordinary, his mother being a woman who has more capacity for love and love of life than this small town can bear. Without her knowing it, Michai defends her honor with his fists as well as he can and where he can – for sure every morning on the school bus. But since the bus has been parking in front of his house more often lately, and since Michai has to spend hours staring at the locked front door, his life has become a living hell. Everybody in the small town knows the school bus driver is married. One day, after his mother had heard the throaty honk of the bus horn and hurried him away, Michai starts to execute his secretly laid plan. The first step: He is going to steal the bus. And then ... (and so on).

The writer wrote the scene starting with a variation of Exercise #16, by combining a character (Michael, an eleven-year-old boy who does not have any friends and draws attention to himself by creating havoc all the time), an object (an old bus that is a junk heap), a place (an abandoned street in a town where every noise is an event), and an activity (someone jumps in front of a car and tries to stop it). Michael has become Michai and the town was transposed to Rumania, the homeland of the writer whose creative fantasy has connected the elements in a most unique way. Michai is locked out of the house regularly because of his mother's affair. He dreams of "saving" his mother. The writer saw and wrote this scene like a climax. The story that is being told, that is, what has led up to this climax is the result of an analysis of the conflict that is revealed during our dialectic encounter with that very scene. That means she has not thought of Michai's story before she wrote that scene. But having to answer our questions leads her to the story. When she turned the bus into the means that Michai finally used in order to get the attention of his mother, the writer, for example, did not "know" that the secret lover was a bus driver or that it was about a school bus. All of these – and even more – are elements of the story that previously existed and "emerged" with the method we are using.

It is the principle of causal coherence, in this case the search for what can or is required to happen before or after an event, which can lead us from the ending to the beginning of a story. This is based on the Aristotelian "το εικός ή αναγκαίον," that is, "the probable or the necessary," a construct duality that is of great importance to the Aristotelian theory. The events must happen in such a way "so that what follows should be the necessary or probable result of the preceding action,"[7] and:

> the structural union of the parts being such that, if any one of them is displaced or removed, the whole will be disjointed and disturbed. For a thing whose presence or absence makes no visible difference, is not an organic part of the whole.[8]

The screenwriter, then, should define what he thinks is essential so that he does not dissipate his efforts with unclear, irrelevant concerns. He should likewise know what serves a better realization of his idea and what he could do without if necessary, that is, sometimes he cannot have it all and needs to decide between different things, for instance, between psychological subtlety, dramatic intensity, the likelihood of an event, how true the story is, that is, the precision of the historical facts.[9] Of course, it is also true that there is a big risk that a screenplay turns out to be too centered, too linear and based too much on a single idea, while everything is explainable and explained. This is what we then call "constructed" or "predictable."

We find the so-called causality principle mentioned in most screenplay theories, because all classic structural models are based on the logical coherence of events. The causality principle leads to structural rigor, which is why many writers avoid it in different ways or intentionally violate it – the results then being alternative narratives. Sometimes situations arise that will even remind us of the Deus ex Machina concept – as does, for instance, the rain of frogs in *Magnolia* – or surprises and (apparent) baseless twists and turns occur, as, for instance, in *Dogville* (Lars von Trier) or in *Lilya 4ever* (Lukas Moodysson).

The dramatic narrative form that is based on the causality principle frequently draws the interest of the reader and the audience into the past and its consequences. One says that *King Oedipus* (*Oedipus Tyrannos*), Sophocle's adaptation (436–433 BC) of the Oedipus myth, the only version of it that has survived, is the original model of the closed form and that it was the first whodunit ever written. If we began with its ending, logical consistency would lead us systematically back to its beginning. In a similar way, classic narrative solves a problem that exists in the present by uncovering its roots in the past, that is, in a certain way by "analyzing" the conflict and the story, while alternative narrative "analyzes" the characters.[10] This means that the center of interest shifts from the analysis of the conflict to the analysis of the characters and that the attention of the audience is thus drawn to the present.

At this point, it may be recalled that the concept of an alternative or epic[11] narrative is normally used for every area that eludes Aristotle's strict narrative rules. Goethe and Schiller defined the substance of the epic as "the independence of its elements," while Döblin defined the difference between the dramatic and the epic as follows. In contrast to the dramatic narrative one could cut the epic narrative with a pair of scissors into its several parts, each one of which, however, would maintain their own lives. In the epic, that is what we call the alternative narrative; the goal is the quest, while in the dramatic narrative the quest is determined by the goal.

Exercise #63:

Use the limerick technique to tell a story that goes backward in time using reverse chronology. Begin with an event that functions like a climax and write the preceding events in the reverse order.

The application of Creative Screenwriting to the alternative narrative can be extremely fascinating and the method can reach its climax there, not only in what affects the relative relationships of time and chronology. A good example of this are the modern offsprings of *film noir*, which eagerly experiment with time by using the medium of audiovisual narrative to create stories about deception and thus play with the theme of trust, the traditional theme in *film noir* narratives, and the counter theme of betrayal. The "lying camera" from the script and motion picture *Usual Suspects* and the parallel narration moving in two different directions in *Memento* are two familiar examples.

The experiments with time and chronology have produced more and more interesting screenplays and films in recent years. While experimenting, though, one should keep in mind what David Lynch, who also loves to play with time, once said, "Secrets are good, but confusion is bad; and there is a big difference between the two."[12]

Analysis of a screenplay: *Slumdog Millionaire* (screenplay by Simon Beaufoy)

This is the story of Jamal Malik, an 18-year-old orphan from the slums of Mumbai, who participates in India's "Who Wants To Be A Millionaire?" and who, with the whole nation watching, wins a staggering 20 million rupees – and gets the girl he loves. Adapted from the novel *Q and A* by Vikas Swarup, the story had much success already as a radio play and as an audio book, before it became the runaway winner at the Academy Awards 2009, going home with eight Oscars, including the Oscar for Best Adapted Screenplay. The film, although it turned out to be a commercial crowd-pleaser, has also received a lot of criticism – Salman Rushdie among others, who complained that the movie "piles impossibility on impossibility" and that book and movie are nothing more than "feel-good."

Interestingly enough, the log line above seems to demonstrate all the problematic narrative issues. The main conflict seems to be between the fact that the boy comes from the slums and that he manages to participate and even win at a game of knowledge. His goal is to win. He does. He also gets the girl. It is like saying: Someone is thirsty in the desert. Ok, this is a conflict, and we would quickly realize it. So we watch him walking through the desert, probably watch him having the same experience again and again. He thinks he sees water, then realizes it is not water; and goes on his merry way. Again, it is like saying: Someone is thirsty in the desert, finds water – and gets the water fairy, too. So what is the story? For one thing, where is the middle? If he achieves his goal, what happens to his need? Does he have a need? Is Jamal's need the girl? We know pretty early on that he wants the girl more than anything else. He knows it, too. So, surely, this is another goal and not a need. What is his character development, what does he learn that he has not known all along? But, more importantly: what do we, the audience, experience, intellectually and emotionally?

The screenplay is structured on three parallel levels. One is the game situation, another an interrogation situation at the police station and the third is the story of his life. All three levels run in strict chronological order. The existence of the two latter levels is explained at the end of the second act: When the show breaks for the night, police arrest him on suspicion of cheating – how could a street kid know so much? So Jamal tells the story of his life in the slum where he and his brother Salim grew up and were orphaned at an early age; of their adventures together on the road, of their encounters with local gangs, and of Latika, the girl he loved and lost. Each chapter of his story reveals the key to the answer to one of the game show's questions. At the same time, a mechanism from the old Persian tale *One Thousand and One Nights* is borrowed, as Jamal, like Scheherazade, tells a series of stories to avoid being punished. It is never implied, though, that these stories might have their source in his imagination or that they might be anything other than the truth. Jamal is telling his own life story. The final question will be answered last: What is this young man with no apparent desire for riches really doing on the game show?

If we take a closer look at the screenplay, using the classic tools of narrative structure, it does not seem to work – moreover, it looks like the screenwriter is mocking classic narrative structure (as if he were telling us: plot is not what this story is about). The marks are all there, but they seem imposed and not organic. The story seems to begin when Jamal is orphaned and meets Latika. This is a classic end of setup, on the 15-minute mark. On the 30-minute mark, they run away from the gang, which has caught them and forced them to become beggars. This is a first turning point, and Latika is left behind – because his brother lets her hand go when she is about to jump on their train. Later Jamal finds her again and tells her that it is their destiny to be together. Still, he loses her once more, again because of his brother. He tries to survive alone while looking for Latika and his brother (or is he not looking for them?). When he finds his brother (in the telephone book!), he follows him to find Latika. He does. He tries to persuade her, she resists, and the next moment we see her, she has changed her mind – again, for no apparent reason. He persuades her to leave with him, but the gang catches her again, and again his brother is the one who does this to him. Now we seem to get to the potential second turning point, and we realize that Latika is watching the show – and that was the reason he auditioned for the show: "I went on the show because I thought she would watch it." No big surprises there, since the third level of his life story had telegraphed long ago that his one and only goal in this life is to be with Latika. And, for no apparent reason, the brother Salim now decides to help her escape so the two lovers can be together. *Ergo*: Super Happy End.

The principle of causality seems to be ignored constantly. Also, as discussed above, the hero has no need. In that sense he is a complete person right from the beginning. There is no character development he must go through with this story, as he does not need to learn anything that he has not known all along. In other words, he does not go through a hero's journey – and therefore, if we take a closer look at the screenplay, using the tools of the hero's journey theory, it does not seem to work either. Still, the film worked for many people and it would be blind to assume that this is not also because of a functioning screenplay. So let us look even closer.

Is it mere dumb luck that the game show host has only asked Jamal the questions to which he has the answers? Or was it meant to be? Is it luck or destiny? Moreover, is the love story with Latika, which seems to define his whole life, luck or destiny? This seems to be a central question in this story. The question is meant to be as obvious as the (rhetorical) answer: It is destiny. In fact this is the answer to the first dramatic question, which is marked clearly when the two meet for the first time – in fact it has an almost dreamlike quality, as if their encounter was always meant to be. In a way, the question includes the answer. We are told this right from the beginning, and then we are told this again and again until the very end. We do not really understand why Latika loves him or why he loves her – she is beautiful, but there are other beautiful women. Love does not need a reason and not everything needs to be explained. Emotional insight, though, is important. And emotional insight is not emotional manipulation, which occurs when we know exactly when we are supposed to feel what. Unanswered emotional questions also arise in relation to the character of the brother. Why does Salim change? Why does he help Latika – and through her his brother – after he has acted in the exactly opposite way on so many occasions? The brothers' storyline and the love story both lack a middle, especially on the plot level. Most importantly, we lose interest in what happens next, not only because we already know what that will be, but also because there is no emotional insight. In fact we see it happen repeatedly, and we remain curiously unmoved. Still, the philosophical, and even more the spiritual questions, even if stated and answered in a rather simple and self-evident way, are there; and they do offer a structure. We can thus analyze the screenplay with the tools we have discussed here, even if, admittedly, this is a rather simple emotional structure.

This movie has found an audience because it asks and answers these spiritual questions and because it has touched a nerve. Certainly one of the reasons is that it was a break from the ordinary to watch a main character suffer grave injustices yet keep on moving forward while staying focused on his objective. He is never distracted by revenge, violence, self-victimization or any other uncivilized emotions. Taking into account that the film was released in the year 2008, the fact that the main character is not focused on money plays an important role. Americans have come to resent people who are living high off a corrupt system, as have people all over the world. When Jamal gets a chance to cheat and does not, and he turns out to have the right answer anyway (which happens to coincide with the answer to the second dramatic question), the satisfaction is great – you do not need to cheat in order to win! You do not need to be evil in order to be successful! The emotional structure of the screenplay (which, again, in this case is based on a system of rather simplistic philosophical/spiritual questions and answers) is unquestionably one of the reasons why *Slumdog Millionaire,* which pits a hard-working young man in Mumbai against a corrupt nexus of money and privilege, has become America's movie of the year.

In his own way the writer chose to go against storytelling conventions. Instead of telling the predictable story of how a boy from the slums gets this once in a lifetime chance to become a millionaire and how he loses that chance as he discovers that all he needs is love, the writer makes the protagonist want exactly what he needs – the girl. He only uses the show to get in touch with her. That makes his ambition more powerful – and his victory more moving and acceptable when he succeeds. The million is not just icing on the cake, it might be even the reward for not wanting it. The writer presents a character who has transcended the desire to get rich. He is not interested in money, he is only interested in love – he is unwavering in his love for her. Indeed, he seems sure about her love, as we see no moment of doubt or emotional insecurity. He does not need to be insecure – the girl does love him back. This, despite the slums and the prostitution, is not a world of damaged people and emotional cripples.

In today's world, as stated above, this film has touched a nerve. It answers the people's prayers and gives them something to dream about. Fair enough. Still, one should point out that, regrettably, even its spiritual attitude and emotional structure at times feel more like a filmmaker's calculation than an honest story from the heart about the human condition.

It is an interesting insight that, like simple and complicated narrative structures, there are also simple and complicated emotional structures. These simpler emotional structures can often be found in films that do not have strong narrative structures and are nevertheless big crowd pleasers. *Star Wars* is a great and much beloved example of the emotional structure at work – it is an emotional journey, not a narrative journey (despite the many plot twists), and its success is based on that. *The Titanic*, another film with a deficient narrative structure, obviously also worked for a lot of people. Like *Slumdog Millionaire* (its screenwriter, Simon Beaufoy, did the same trick with *The Full Monty*), these are simpler emotional structures, which a more sophisticated audience may sometimes not go with, as the emotional impact is at such a basic level that it is easier for the sophisticated logical mind to take over – and thus perhaps lose out on something.

Working with the psychology of the audience

Since the beginning of the history of storytelling, the goal of the storyteller has been to fan the interest of the listener. Scheherazade fascinated the sultan every night with her stories while she kept silent during the day. Is there a better metaphor for the goal of the storyteller and simultaneously (why not?), for a reason to exist as a narrator? From the ancient Chinese to Horaz and from Aristotle to Boileau – in one thing they are all united: The dramatic narrator must awaken the interest of the listener, the reader, the audience, and keep it awake by telling his story with a pleasant rhythm, avoiding unnecessary pauses, surprising at selected points and keeping the story within certain bounds of probability or logic. Edward Morgan Forster has described the nature of the story as follows: "It has only one good thing – to cause the audience to want to know what happens next."[13] "Never bore," was Frank Daniel's motto, who considered the loss of the reader's interest and accordingly the interest of the audience as the only sin a screenwriter can commit. Elementary physiological and psychological conditions such as excitation and relaxation, attention and fatigue, expectation and disappointment, confirmation and surprise were always the focus of attention in procedural arts such as theater, music, dance and, of course, film.[14]

In his well-known interview by François Truffaut, Alfred Hitchcock[15] tells of a hypothetical situation ("while we are talking there is a bomb under our table") and two different possible approaches to writing about it in a script. In the first case the audience would not know anything, the bomb would explode, the audience would jump up and the surprise would last 15 seconds. In the second approach the audience would know about the existence of the bomb and that the bomb will go off in, let us say, five minutes. The same conversation between the characters sitting at that table, which in the first case would have bored the audience to death, is now transformed into something fascinating, and will keep it in suspense for the entire five minutes. The director concludes that the audience should know as much as possible. Since the audience knows more than the characters, Hitchcock's famous bomb engenders a kind of affect that is quite different from the affect that generates sympathy for the characters. It is the Aristotelian οικεία ηδονή (the familiar, appropriate pleasure) that in the case of tragedy signifies the excitement of pity (*Eleos*) and fear (*Phobos*).[16] The laconic sentence, "δι΄ ελέου και φόβου περαίνουσα την των τοιούτων παθημάτων κάθαρσιν" (through pity and fear effecting the proper purgation of these emotions), which introduced the concept of catharsis, has done nothing to make it less puzzling. One interpretation says that the audience senses negative emotions, becomes afraid that the painful event could threaten them and has pity for the hero since he suffers unjustly. The audience knows that what it experiences is not happening in reality. This safety zone puts it in the position of being able to think about the human condition, to accept that pain and misfortune are inseparable components of human life and to reject every feeling of arrogance.[17] Aristotle takes the impact of tragedy on the audience very seriously and for this reason, "we have the right to declare that the *Poetics*, apart from being a work about genre, is also a work about effect",[18] that is, about its reception.

In his attempt to analyze the psychology of art as well as analyzing its reception by the receiver and last but not least in his attempt to explain the term catharsis, the Russian psychologist Lew S. Wygotski utilized two different affect categories,[19] which the German psychologist Richard Müller-Freienfels defined as "co-affects" and "self-affects." Hitchcock's example perfectly describes these two kinds of affects and their different effects on the audience. The surprise of the unsuspecting audience when the bomb goes off belongs to the category of "co-affect," because what the audience feels is the same as the emotion the characters on screen feel. In opposition to this is the suspense of the audience that knows the bomb is under the table – this feeling belongs to the category of "self-affects."[20] Here is an analysis of the process of association that Bernard Beckermann proposed that is relevant, since he specified the dimensions that constitute the reactions of the audience to the dramatic work:[21] these are the descriptive dimension that concerns the text presented on stage; the participational that refers to the emotional charge; the referential that combines celluloid creation and the surrounding reality; and the conceptional that is related to abstract appreciation, that is, to the theoretical considerations presented by the piece.[22] In contrast, Ed Tan differentiates between the purported witness emotions or the emotions of giving testimony (we cannot participate directly in an action, but rather we only observe it from the outside) and the empathetic emotions (we share the emotions as spectators of the character's emotions).[23]

The correct utilization of the two-affect types is extremely important to screenwriting. In Aristotle's *Poetics*, in chapter 11, the terms "*Peripeteia*" (or Reversal of the Situation) and "Recognition" are defined as follows:

> Reversal of the Situation is a change by which the action veers round to its opposite, subject always to our rule of probability or necessity. Recognition, as the name indicates, is a change from ignorance to knowledge, producing love or hate between the persons destined by the poet for good or bad fortune. The best form of recognition is coincident with a Reversal of the Situation, as in *Oedipus*.[24]

The "*Peripeteia*" principally causes co-affects, since the audience is induced primarily to project itself into the acting character, while they also cause a self-affect when the audience's realization takes place even seconds before that of the character's realization. We can conclude that Aristotle almost certainly meant these two affect types when he spoke of fear and compassion: Fear can result from the fact that the audience knows about the bomb, while the characters are unaware of its existence. Compassion, in turn, sympathy, can be designated a co-affect, since the audience has the same emotions as the characters. Suffering with others is identical to sharing their emotions.[25]

The Aristotelian expression "pity and fear" refers to an ideological difference between the supporters of the classic narrative and the supporters of the alternative or epic narrative, because of the fact that with the alternative narrative the audience "feels" the presence of the writer more – sometimes due to the epic element of the voice-over, but also where such is absent – in fact, more than in the classic narrative. This can also result in the audience developing a greater emotional distance to the occurrences and mulling over what it has seen. This was, after all, the goal of the Brechtian Theater, since Brecht opposed "this curious Aristotelian empathy" more than anything else.[26] Nevertheless, the emotions in the Brechtian Theater by no means are missing, and certainly not in the cinematic alternative narrative forms. In the latter case, we have shown how the emotional structure replaces the plot or dramatic structure in a way that makes alienation impossible while epic and dramatic elements are artfully combined.

Today the constructs epic/alternative and dramatic have more or less successfully prevailed as two separate narrative forms, at least in the field of cinema, even though in reality they exhibit only one fundamental difference: Dramatic narrative displays a central storyline, a main plot and a series of sub-plots, while in the alternative narrative a series of plots of equal weight parallel each other and often unfold concurrently.

Jean Claude Carrière, who worked as a screenwriter with directors such as Luis Bunuel, Jean Luc Godard, Milos Forman, Peter Brook and Andrzej Wajda, names three kinds of stories based on the relationship between the writer and the audience. While doing so, he refers specifically to the Aristotelian realization that each story is a game between the known and the unknown:[27]

1) Someone tells the others a story that he knows and they have heard before. This kind refers primarily to stories concerning historical or real events that everybody knows or thinks he knows, like biopics and so on. The interest focuses on the new way of telling them and the quirks of the narrative.
2) Someone tells the others a story that he knows, and they do not know. This kind could refer for instance to thrillers and detective stories. The storyteller knows whodunit and his motive, but the audience only learns these things towards the end of the story.
3) Someone tells the others a story that he does not know and that they do not know either. Carrière calls this kind of story "improvisation," because it leaves room for innovation and for discovery. This is exactly the kind of ground we are cultivating with the creative screenwriting method.[28]

The concepts tension, anticipation, intrigue, mystery, foreshadowing, conflict and momentum are closely related to the Hitchcockian terms suspense and surprise. Suspense means mainly uncertainty and the possibility that something can happen, which will not leave us indifferent. This uncertainty expresses both hope and fear. Suspense must be present before we are led to a climax, just as tension must be present before we are led up to a release.

In order to create tension, the screenwriter generally uses three different tools: the plants and pointers, which should not lead to unnecessary repetition; the complications for which the audience should be prepared in advance; and the crises when the character nears his goal but has it snatched away at the last moment.

In any case, as Hitchcock says: "Emotion is an indispensable component of suspense."[29] Especially in the genres of crime fiction, action and horror, the game with the two types of affect is, perhaps, the most important factor of the plot structure. Tension and surprise, however, are surely not to be assigned exclusively to these genres, but are also dramaturgical tools that can be used in the comedy genre, which is generally considered as one of the most difficult ones. The system of emotional reactions functions in comedy, however, differently from tragedy.

For Bertolt Brecht humor is the emotion of alienation and estrangement.[30] Anton Chekhov describes his plays "The Seagull" and "The Cherry Orchard" as comedies exactly for this reason – because he manages to block the audience from feeling any pity for his character, that is, pity and the co-affect. Brecht sees the technique of estrangement as a technique of comedy, even in the Aristotelian theater of sensuality, and defines in the 42nd article of the Small Instrument of the Theater, "The estranged image is what enables us to recognize the object, which simultaneously lends it an alienating effect."[31]

Exercise #64:
Analyze a sequence of a finished script and note down what the audience knows at each point in time and what the key characters know.

The sequential analysis helps the screenwriter gain an overview of the entire architecture of his screenplay. A sequence can have an independent title, and this title can take the form of a question. The question at the beginning of the sequence poses a connecting tension, which unifies the scenes of a sequence and lends them structure. The answer to that question will be found in the course of the sequence.

The screenplay of the motion picture *The Apartment*, one of the preferred examples analyzed by Frank Daniel, is wonderfully suited for the method of sequential analysis, since it is made up of the traditional eight sequences: two in the first act, four in the second act – so this is about the largest act – and two in the third act. Every sequence here has between five and seven major scenes.

Excerpt from a screenplay analysis: *The Apartment* (written by Billy Wilder and I.A.L. Diamond)

Bud Baxter, a small-time office worker, lets his boss have the key to his apartment to use as a love nest, because he wants to get on in the world. What Baxter does not realize is that the woman he loves is also going in and out of the apartment. Confronted with the cynical scheming of his boss, Baxter makes a momentous decision.

Act One
Sequence 1: Will Baxter finally be able to sleep in his own apartment?
Sequence 2: Will Baxter be able to get a promotion by doing everything he can for his bosses?

Act Two
Sequence 3: Will Fran Kubelick be able to take Baxter seriously?
Sequence 4: Will Baxter continue to let his boss Sheldrake see Fran in his apartment, now that he has learned that she is his lover?
Sequence 5: Will Baxter save Fran?
Sequence 6: Will Baxter continue to deny everything about himself?

Act Three
Sequence 7: Will Baxter choose Fran or his career?
Sequence 8: Will Fran accept Baxter?

In the rule, the sequences should be described from the point of view of the protagonist, even if there are sometimes sequences that do not include the lead character.

The structure of the screenplay: Eighth sequence (the answer to the first dramatic question)

In the third act, the protagonists advance to the final conflict – the final, most difficult obstacle in the way of reaching their goal – and at the same time, the key question, that is, the first dramatic question, will be answered. In the classic structure, it is the point where we experience the completion of the character development arc that in the rule has already happened at the end of the second act. In spite of this, we still require proof of the character's change. We will only believe that the protagonist has definitively changed when we witness his reaction to an event that is similar to the event we experienced at the beginning of his quest in the first act.

This refers, however, primarily to the philosophy of the development and metamorphosis of the lead character in classic narrative, which, as we initially mentioned (see the section on "The structure of the screenplay: first sequence"), presupposes a strong conflict between the goal and the need of the character. It also means a certain philosophical attitude of the writer and a desire to send a message, as clearly expressed as possible. But drama is not life as we experience it. It is rather a distillate of life and systematic conflict. Life rarely presents such clean, satisfying solutions as some classically structured motion pictures, and people rarely change in such a dramatic way. In alternative narratives, the pedagogical approach that the change of a lead character implies is lacking. The structural element we call the climax is still there, but it receives another semantic meaning. It is often the point where the emotional reaction of the audience reaches its peak.

The last structural point, the last conflict, is what most screenplay theoreticians call a "climax" or a "final climax," that is, the highest point. Gustav Freytag calls it the "catastrophe." The highest point is related to the Aristotelian catharsis, while the screenplay theory based on Joseph Campbell's myth theory follows the quest of the hero up to the completed transformation and characteristically calls this point of resurrection. Here the screenwriter shows that his hero has surmounted the difficult passage and been resurrected as a new person.[32]

Independent of what we call the last structural point, one thing is certain – it is about the moment of truth. We will finally get the answers that have to do with the transformation of the hero and with the denouement of the story. This is where both the audience and the writer should have the feeling that the story is over. Since some screenwriters do not take this feeling seriously enough, and continue the narrative unnecessarily, Linda Seger stresses that it should be about one to five pages from the end of the script.

The only thing that can happen next is a brief resolution that finally brings together all the elements that are still floating around in the air.

The climax is considered the point of highest energy, an explosive moment. Yet depending on the style and tone of a story, there is certainly something that may be called a "quiet climax." It does not necessarily have to be action oriented, not any more than indicated by the dramatic questions. Let us look at an example in the film *Spring, Summer, Fall, Winter … and Spring* by the Korean writer and director Kim Ki-Duk: An old monk and his pupil are living together in a small temple at a mountain lake. While the seasons pass them by, the two monks also pass through different stages of their lives that finally merge in a tragedy that seems fated. The tragedy is quasi prophesized by the old monk during the setup. Under the watchful eyes of the old monk, the young monk has the painful experience of the loss of innocence. He playfully ties some heavy rocks to small animals whose freedom of movement is then severely restricted. The old monk does the same to him – when the boy shows regret, he immediately allows him to remove the rocks. If one of the animals has died in the meantime, he will bear this rock in his heart forever. When the young monk finds two or three dead animals, be breaks out in tears. Will he really have to bear a rock in his heart forever? Is the old monk right? Is there no atonement?

The theme is the pain of murderous intentions, says Kim Ki-Duk. The answer to the philosophical-religious question about atonement (that is posed in place of a plot oriented, dramatic question) is provided when the young monk ties a heavy rock to his leg and then climbs a towering mountain to place a statue of Buddha at its peak. That is the climax of the story. In case we have not understood that this is the answer to the question whether he will have to bear the burden of the rock of lethal intentions, the filmmaker intercuts this with the small animals from the beginning of the film. At the first turning point, the young man had left his teacher and taken the Buddha statue with him. Will he come back? Can you find peace in the outside world? That question creates the second act tension. The answer is no. The young monk will not find his fortune out in the world. At the second turning point, he returns for good and takes the place of his teacher, who has died in the meantime. Now he must pass on the wisdom of his teacher to another young monk – however painful this might be. The circle closes here.

The climax is in reality the end of the story. After the climax the party is over and it is time to go home, says Linda Seger,[33] or in the words of Aristotle, "An end ... is that which itself naturally follows some other thing, either by necessity, or as a rule, but has nothing following it."[34]

Working with emotional structure

Our most important task is to create emotion, said Hitchcock. And the second most important one is sustaining that emotion. Such is the extreme importance of the emotional level.[35]

The theory of emotional structure is the pendant of the method of creative screenwriting at the level of analysis. The emotional structure should illuminate the nature of the creative process for both the writer and the audience and show how the screenplay represents consciousness and emotion. As in the concept of "emotional tonality" Michel Haar uses in painting (by which he means the fountains from which a creative work flows from different sources),[36] emotional structure is in the end nothing more than a hypothesis – a hypothesis helpful in avoiding empiricism, deterministic analysis as well as the narrow, pragmatic cataloging of special features.

Gustav Freytag describes in his book, *The Technique of the Drama*, how people who have observed the effects of tragedy on themselves must note with astonishment how feeling and distress (that is caused by the agitation of the characters) in conjunction with the powerful tension (that promotes the coherence of the plot) captures their emotional life. Feeling and distress, however, are also registered with great satisfaction, because the audience, while empathizing with the thoughts, the suffering and the fate of the hero as though they were the audience's own, experiences an unlimited freedom in the midst of the most acute agitation that simultaneously transports it far beyond the events.[37] Now, as pointed out at another place, that could be interpreted either as the audience feeling superior to the characters or as the description of the audience experiencing emotional insight achieved through drama by means of its emotional structure.

The connection of emotional agitation to the forcefulness of fantasy and not least to mental stimulation is an absolute characteristic of the art of drama. Although controversial, I will dare to assert that music can rock our souls even more than the theater. But the feeling it evokes affects emotions directly and leads perhaps less to the simultaneous stimulation of thought. Due to the effect of the images (often in interplay with sound and music) and their direct influence on the unconscious, cinema hones dramatic energy even more than the theater. Cinema, more than anything else, creates sense. By combining the cognitive and the emotional level (with a successful work), the miracle of meaning results. Existence means bickering over the search for meaning and over the injustice of random events – or fate, according to how one looks at it. One is reminded of the childish cry of despair. This is not fair, which means as much as "it has no meaning, it makes no sense". The magic of cinema consists of making meaning, creating sense and enabling emotional insight. Happiness in cinema is the happiness of recognition, awareness and knowledge.

If our most important assignment is creating and sustaining

emotion, and if the "general, that is, the theme or the key emotion," means the codified meaning in the deep structure of the dramatic text,[38] and if in addition the emotional life in the course of a movie has a structure that we can lay out and define, then we can reason out that the structure of a screenplay cannot be the architecture of the plot or the arc of the hero's quest, but rather it must be precisely this emotional structure.

In a very inspirational way, Freytag drew the conclusion that dramatic art has a great influence, not because the audience likes to be tormented, but because it feels a longing for creative endeavor. The dramatic writer to a certain extent forces the audience to create – because it is the audience that must let the whole world of the characters come alive, and all the pain and fate that comes with it. While it is on the receiving end of all this, the audience finds itself participating in a turbulent creative process. The post-creative audience now feels a warmth and delight similar to what the poet felt during the course of his own creative phase. This is ultimately why the feeling and shock, and the pain that is alive in it, mean a satisfaction that transports the audience far beyond the events. So, if we were in doubt, here comes the answer to how Freytag sees things: the audience does not feel superior to the characters; it is rather the emotional insight that is achieved through drama that determines the audience's satisfaction.

Friedrich Nietzsche called this satisfaction "tragic joy," with which the post-creative audience becomes the "audience-artist." The dramatic work permits us to feel a joy that transcends the merely sensuous. The emotional theme and the emotional structure provide us with the joy of meaning, that is, the joy of finding out that everything in life makes sense,[39] a joy that can sweep aside every pain from the outset. The work of art is understood as a medium of initiation to metaphysical joy, whose expression it remains. The whole of art is an act of strengthening, says Nietzsche, who saw the tragedies of antiquity as a way to strengthening – and thus reminds us of the concept of *paideia* in pity, as discussed earlier. According to Nietzsche, the ancient Greeks, the artists and the audience proved they were able to face up to the worst conditions of human existence, to accept them and by doing so change them (see also the remarks on the Indian Rasa theory in the section on "The structure of the screenplay: sixth sequence").

This could mean that the screenwriter must seek out the emotional structure, in contrast to most of the other structural models, either in the emotional reaction of the audience or in the creation of this reaction. The individual structural knots connect to the emotional reactions created with the audience and with the writer, since every dramatic work is an inseparable unit of meaning and perception.[40] It seems important to me to stress here that the widespread view that in cinema emotions are confined to plot-oriented, conscious emotions, is reductive if not fundamentally wrong. It is more the case that an interaction takes place among emotions on various levels, where one must understand emotions as multi-dimensional phenomena in which biological and psychological components are bound up with social impressions and individual experience.[41]

The structural points, the structural knots of emotional structure are frequently created instinctively rather than by careful planning. In the chapter about the emotional theme, it has been mentioned that the screenwriter does not necessarily seek out his theme and that the theme is liable for the unconscious part of the story. In addition, we have already demonstrated in the first exercise of this book that each of us has a functioning narrative instinct and how structurally complete the stories are that arise through an apparently random process. The narrative instinct is something that we already possess as children, and that we can summon at any time when we tell a child a story and observe his or her reactions. In the course of the narrative, we accelerate or decelerate our narrative rhythm as soon as we perceive that our little listener has stopped following us – because he is bored, because we are telling our story too fast or even because we are providing him with more intellectual or emotional information than he can digest. We use the same process when we edit a text – the analysis of the emotional structure of our screenplay may help us adjust the rhythm where it seems necessary – something we cannot or may not do in the first draft, since we would disrupt the creative process if we did.

In dramatic stories that at first glance do not fit in the classic narrative mold, the structural points remain even though they correspond to other functions. The motion picture *Vera Drake* (2004), written and directed by Mike Leigh, provides a good example. The first station in our emotional journey as an audience member is the moment we expect the introductory event or the hook, about in the middle of the first act, 15 minutes into the film. In a film characterized by an especially mild tone that awakens the feeling we are simply watching every day life unfold, we are suddenly forced to watch the rape of a young woman on her first date. A bit later, where we would expect the first turning point in the classic narrative model, we see how Vera Drake performs an abortion on another young woman. We are able to endure this morally and emotionally, because we have seen a possible appalling reason for this unwanted pregnancy. Whatever our ideological attitude, we must feel that Vera Drake is helping the girl. The emotional "cold shower" that we have gotten by watching the rape scene, prepares us for the emotional experience of the abortion and helps us tie it to the first emotional experience, even if the two young women are not the same person. In the classic narrative model, the young woman in the rape scene would probably be the same woman in the abortion scene (causal chain of events). Here the two events have a thematic connection and by their positioning in relation to the special narrative style and mild tone of the movie function as structural knots.

Do emotion and moralizing work well together? Yes and no. The moral in films is fixed on two levels – a global one that encompasses the whole text (the moral of the story) and a particular one, which concerns individual elements of the text (i.e. evaluation of characters and the conflicts).[42] In *Vera Drake* Mike Leigh works on the second, more subtle level. The audience constantly monitors what happens on screen – the emotions and the moralizing interact, which in the end is nothing more than part of the receptive activity, and consequently part of audience reception.

The Aristotelian concept of catharsis was interpreted variously in the past. Aristotle treated tragedy like a coin with two sides – on one side there was the production. There the poet's task is to create a plausible coherence of plot. On the other side is the level of effectiveness, the reception, where the audience is in the center of interest. "For the poet is guided in what he writes by the wishes of his audience," he said.[43] In other words, Aristotle pleads for a poetic of effectiveness.[44] He considers the construction of the plot the highest task of the poet and determines in relation to the reception of the drama the enjoyment of the work, pleasure as the most important and determining characteristic.[45] For him, however, pleasure is twofold and inseparable, rational and emotional – in this connection; we may not forget his thoughts in relation to the general, which we have interpreted as the emotional theme, as the foundation and center of the story.

When the construction of the plot is seen as the most important task of the writer, it often leads to dramaturgical predictability – especially if this requirement is seen as the point of departure for writing the script. This presupposes in turn a completed, closed whole with an inseparable unit and a preconceived architectural plan like mainstream Hollywood took on and promoted.

Still, Aristotelian enjoyment does not mean superficial entertainment in the sense of escapism, revitalization, cheap thrills or diversion.

At the same time, it cannot mean an exclusive, rational satisfaction, since it is the enjoyment of the art of poetry and not poetic expression or the search for truth that is deemed the autonomous creative reason for poetry.

Enjoyment means satisfaction, intellectual and emotional; and presupposes stories, which are provoking and inspiring, which rip us out of our everyday life and shake us to the core. They broaden the scope of our experiences and are themselves inherent experiences, the reason being that successful stories possess the strongest emotional structures.

This in no way means that classic mainstream movies do not have emotional structure. The analysis of emotional structure is merely another instrument of analysis that covers a broader spectrum of screenwriting than traditional screenplay theories. In addition, the classic screenplay narrative adds through its emotional structure another dimension that we can analyze in addition to plot structure and the hero's journey. The director is the first receiver of the emotional structure of a screenplay – with his artistic contribution he can make more or less of its original dramatic energy.

How broad is the spectrum we can cover with the analysis of the emotional structure? One of the greatest screenplay theoreticians of all times is, at the same time, very far removed from what we today rightly or wrongly call the Aristotelian "rules." We are talking about one of the greatest theoreticians of Italian *Neorealismo*,[46] Cesare Zavattini, the screenwriter of 54 films from 1940 to 1992 (among others, he wrote *The Bicycle Thief*).[47] There is certainly no other phenomenon in the history of cinema that has had such an impact on cinema dramaturgy in the entire world as Italian *Neorealismo*. For many, neo-realism meant the liberation from the strict Aristotelian narrative, while for others it created a very significant distance from commercial cinema; the latter believing this was the beginning of the loss of audience for European films.

For Zavattini the goal was not to make up circumstances and transform them into virtual reality by giving them the sheen of truth, but rather to portray things the way they are, so that they reflect their meaning on their own. The true goal of cinema is not to tell stories or myths, he writes – and in doing so provides the theoretical underpinning for an alternative narrative school based on that main difference from the dramatic and which (following the example of the early Brecht) will be designated by many theoreticians as "epic."[48] In alternative narrative, the causal interconnectedness of the story no longer has a central meaning.

Despite this, all the Italian neo-realism films, and those that have followed in their tradition, tell stories. The only thing that sets them apart is how these stories are being told. One plot point, as we have seen, must not necessarily arise from another one; events can bind them together through the emotional theme. In spite of what we might think, the heart of drama keeps on beating. This time the conflict does not reside between the characters, it resides between the circumstances. In specific films, the situation appears where the plot was. The structural points continue to exist – only now they serve other functions. As Hegel wrote:

> Everything leads by way of the plot to the internal character, to duty, to conviction, to intention. Yet through the situation, the exterior of things receives the role it is entitled to, since the objective reality is what shapes the form but which also determines a lion's share of the content[49] and naturally the characters, too, because the circumstances are as active as the heroes and often even more active.[50]

This is precisely the credo of neo-realism.[51]

Many "*auteurs*" of modern times have adopted this conviction, such as Mike Leigh and Ken Loach, who have transposed the theory of neo-realism to the creative process of their films; Mike Leigh has even transposed them to screenwriting.[52] The same is true for some *Nouvelle Vague* filmmakers. Eric Rohmer has developed his own method for writing scripts, to enable him to achieve the closest approximation to reality, especially in the dialogues (in his opinion the truth of the characters emerges this way). Rohmer improvises the scenes he has thought through with the actors who will take over these roles later, and films the improvisation. Excerpts from the improvisation are then written in a new draft of the script, which is then shot literally without improvisation. A unique psychological realism arises in this way from this scenic "micro-dramaturgy."[53] Yet:

> the ticket for admittance to the holy temple of the avant guard or merely proof of cinematic innovation, the touchstone for the true cineaste is the renunciation of the classic narrative cinema, of traditional dramaturgical patterns and narrative structures.[54]

This is very true. But what most forget is that this resentment was born almost simultaneously with the birth of motion pictures. The Russian pioneers did not admire anyone as much as the American director,

Griffith, the inventor of the introverted montage, who shocked his audiences with his motion picture *Intolerance* (written by Anita Loos, Hettie Barker, Mary O'Conner, D.W. Griffith, among others).[55]

Griffith's ambition was to do exactly what many have tried to do after him – tell a story that makes no sense. His intention was to focus the attention to the eternal conflict between repression and justice and to call for more tolerance. The metaphor, which can pack a wallop in lyric writing,[56] will more likely be a sign of impotence in audiovisual narrative. The power of the image provokes certain associations that are often not comprehensible and subjective, meaning that an image can never lose its significance and become a mere form or symbol.[57]

Eisenstein and Dovzhenko, who sacrificed narrative elements in favor of numerous metaphorical images and symbolic montages, followed Griffith's example. The Ukrainian director Alexander Dovzhenko began a line of lyric tradition that can be traced to the present.[58] Waiving the cinematographic narrative in favor of lyric pathos is the most important attribute. Poetic hyperbole collides with the clear proximity to reality, which derives from the power of the authenticity of the image (or what we perceive as such). The importance of the characters is trumped by the importance of the director – the filmmaker's intentions and thoughts are treated as more interesting than the motivations of the characters. The result is a markedly cerebral type of narrative. The Russian school of poetry that Dziga Vertov represents so well in documentary film would be more highly regarded by cineastes than by movie audiences. Inasmuch as it focuses on the ego of the "*auteur*", cinema lyricism does not offer the required safe distance necessary for the construction, positioning and reproduction of a story. The egocentric lyrical cinematographic narrative often only functions on a personal level. It is the narrative of the self-portrait and the ideology of personality.

The big screen is the most attractive mirror of modern times and for the self-centered storyteller it exerts a powerful attraction. At the same time, it disappoints him since he has to admit that the films that move audiences and unite generations are not, in the rule, the ones that only have personal avowals as their subject matter.[59]

The uncontested winner of the popularity contest in cinematographic art is the dramatic cinema, the so-called narrative cinema that includes the classic mainstream movies. The narrative cinema has always prevailed against all attempts to elevate radical personal discourse to the podium (for which a screenplay is not necessarily required, because how personal can someone else's script be?) and to define it as the only one that is exalted, worthy, the only artistic and moral one. Plato's echo is not far away – fiction is of less value than truth, so narrative occupies a lower rank and the person who creates the narrative is a second-rate artist at best and in the worst case a damned liar and a pied piper. The word "fable" in its original sense meant "something unimportant," "chit chat," or "balderdash."[60]

There are, of course, numerous mixed forms.[61] The school of lyrical film narrative is especially suitable for simple or in any case apparently simple subject matters as symbols and metaphors demonstrate a certain focus on the essential. Characters and events with a complex and contradictory nature often elude an adequate treatment in this kind of narrative.[62]

Jean Cocteau, however, wrote, "The poetry of film comes through unusual connections between things and images."[63] A filmmaker, who seems to share this view, is Andrei Tarkovsky. He names these relationships the "Logic of the Poetic."[64] For Tarkovsky the "representation" of the logic of human thinking is of the highest importance, as well as what best corresponds to the possibilities of film as the most truthful and poetic of all the arts. This logic will determine the order of events in the planning phase as well as in the montage that creates the final whole. According to Tarkovsky, the poetic logic of the laws of the development of thought are closer to life than the logic of the classic dramatic structure, whereas he is predominantly against the causal coherence of classic dramaturgy, which for him is very far removed from real life, which is much more complex than classic dramaturgy can show, even though classic drama is considered the only way to express dramatic conflicts.

The rejection of every formalistic order and logic has lead very early on in the history of cinema to narrative experiments that are patently as far removed from classic drama as humanly possible – as, for example, the film *Entr' Acte* by René Clair written by the painter Francis Picabia and *Un Chien Andalou* written by Luis Bunuel and Salvador Dali. Here the narrative is neither the result of utilizing psychological methods nor the result of metaphorical encoding of messages; it is about avoiding all meaning.

The goal of cinema art perhaps cannot be limited to telling a story. There are, one says, other narrative forms of simple storytelling. Yet even if this thought were true, the story would be, as in theater, one of the most important elements possible in the emotional reaction of the audience. The story serves the emotion: This insight does not only result from understanding, from delving into a story, but rather it springs from everything a film can awaken emotionally that would not be revealed to us by any other medium but film.[65] This is the foundation shoring up the theory of emotional structure by means of a theme.

One thing is certain. For the analysis, as for the synthesis of each alternative narrative form, the rules of many screenplay theories appear to be useless. The great advantage of emotional structure is that every successful work of cinema, independently of whether it is constructed in the classic so-called Aristotelian manner or as an alternative narrative, evinces an emotional structure. The concept of success refers, as said, not to the commercial or artistic success of a film, but rather to its ability to communicate with its audience. Even if the audience does not have a key that allows it to enter the intellectual subject matter of the film, the narrative can function out of emotional reasons. As we have seen, the theory of emotional structure offers an opportunity to analyze even artistically successful films that are not created according to the schema of classic plot construction, that is, films that are mostly considered the exception and yet become more and more the rule.

What is particularly interesting in the following example is that it demonstrates the possibilities of the defused, de-dramatized fable at the highest level. Antonioni (who co-wrote and directed the famous script analyzed below) joined as a writer playwrights such as Ibsen, Strindberg and Chekhov, who altered the canon of classic drama forms at the end of the nineteenth century as interest in psychological conflicts started to grow.[66] The new thing was that the conflict did not necessarily step outside based on a plot of colliding characters, but could remain as an inner conflict that may be recognized through events with no dramatic consequences.

Analysis of a screenplay: *La Notte* (screenplay by Michelangelo Antonioni, Ennio Flaiano and Tonino Guerra)

Giovanni and Lydia are a married couple who, after all these years, have very little in common. The camera accompanies them for 24 hours as they travel through Milan and shows how they have become visibly estranged. The news of the death of Tommaso, a mutual friend, at last becomes the key experience, and a dispute ensues.

Lydia and Giovanni visit Tommaso, a seriously ill schoolfriend, in a hospital. The visit upsets Lydia, most of all, when her schoolfriend makes it clear he still loves her, which she cannot bear and leaves. She breaks out in tears in front of the hospital. The beginning, the introductory event, "the hook:" Whatever we want to call it, the pending death of her friend and the love that will die or not die with him, introduces the emotional theme (happiness, the meaning of life), and changes the way Lydia deals with her life. Will it also change her life? We are 15 minutes into the film. In the car, Giovanni tells her about an unpleasant meeting with a beautiful and psychologically disturbed young woman, who we saw when Lydia left the hospital in a dither. Lydia knows which woman he is talking about – the only thing she says now is: "Maybe she's happy." And that means as much as – because I am not. "Why?" Giovanni asks, surprised, and Lydia answers: "Because she doesn't have any responsibility." The scenes of the reading follow, at which Giovanni, who is a successful writer now, will present his new book. We are 30 minutes into the film, and Lydia breaks out of her former life. She leaves without a word – and begins to saunter through the chaotic streets of the large city. Is this the first turning point?

At the beginning, she accidentally and then intentionally comes to a place she had not seen since childhood. When Giovanni comes home, she is gone. He falls asleep, and then she calls. She asks him to pick her up. They soon find themselves in a place where they have been before and shared memories. "Nothing's changed," Giovanni observes – and Lydia answers, "Something is going to change soon."

Giovanni and Lydia decide to go to the party of a tycoon who has invited them, "because the rich like to decorate themselves with intellectuals," as Lydia remarks cynically. Three things happen: Giovanni gets to know the daughter of the tycoon, who hides her melancholy and desperation about her meaningless life and her unhappiness (the theme again) behind childish games; the tycoon offers Giovanni a lot of money and a secure job (and in so doing independence from Lydia, who is rich), if he will write the history of his successful company, and Lydia meets a man who takes her with him for a ride in the rain.

In the middle of the film, the emotional midpoint, Lydia phones the hospital and learns that her friend died ten minutes ago. Ten minutes ago, Lydia had seen Giovanni kiss the daughter of the tycoon.

Nothing happens – neither between Giovanni and the young woman nor between Lydia and the strange man. When the two couples meet accidentally, again nothing happens. The suspicion, the jealousy, the consequences of what they do is not a part of this story. What we expect to happen does not happen. There is evidently no lack of narrative art, but the narrative works towards de-dramatizing the story rather than heightening the conflicts. Expectations are raised, but they are not met. The two women like and understand each other. The audience knows more than the characters – but not enough. We see through the windshield of the car that Lydia is behaving quite differently from before. She is having fun and takes an interest in the discussion (and we hear the echo of Giovanni's question in the bar before the party, "Is it impossible for you to just have fun for once in your life?" Evidently, it is not impossible …). We will never learn why Lydia has changed so much, or what she talked about with the strange man. As the audience, we just hear the rain and the sound of the windshield wipers – we are not allowed into the car. We hear Giovanni who confesses his love to the young woman. Yes, he would love to do his life over, but only if it was with her. When the two women meet, Lydia confides to her that she is not jealous of her – and that this is the problem.

After a while, Lydia and Giovanni leave the party. The night sky brightens; the music of a weary band plays in the background. They walk across a park. Lydia tells Giovanni that her schoolfriend died during the course of the evening, and that she wants to die too, because he, Giovanni, does not love her anymore. The climax. Lydia reads him a love letter and when he cannot tell her who wrote it, she tells him he did, a long time ago. Giovanni hugs her; she stiffens but finally relents – an embrace of despair, not of passion.

The conflict is buried inside the situation: A long process of alienation that the participants find impossible to decipher – and this goes on until the very end. The things that happen that night reveal the fragility of the relationship. Nothing more and nothing less. With few exceptions, the audience does not observe actions, just attitudes. The information is in the details – in the gestures, the reactions or even in the lack of reactions. Maybe the structural points are not related to the plot. unless we see a character breaking down as part of the plot or the starting point of the story, but they connect implicitly to the reactions and the changes in attitudes – and therefore to the emotions of the characters and the audience. A structural net forms – the emotional structure.

In analyzing the screenplay further, we realize that it is put together in eight sequences, and that it uses traditional techniques to connect them, for example, the plant and the pay-off.[67]

1) The hospital – the sequence takes about 15 minutes and begins with the arrival of the couple in the hospital and ends with them leaving. It contains or ends with the hook, the beginning of the story, that is, with Lydia's emotional breakdown.
2) The book reading – it lasts another 15 minutes and begins with the car scene on the way to the reading. It ends with Lydia's sudden departure, the first turning point.

3) Lydia crashing about in the streets of the big city. The sequence ends when Giovanni comes to pick her up. The following dialogue takes place there. Nothing has changed – something will change very soon.
4) In a bar. We are 40 minutes into the film when the couple enter a bar where their inability to have a good time, to talk, to be together – which was obsessively the reason to go there and not to the tycoon's reception – is obvious. The sequence ends with a decision to go to the reception.
5) The game. The sequence begins with the arrival of Lydia and Giovanni at the party, 50 minutes into the film and ends when Giovanni falls for the other woman and leaves Lydia to go look for her. This sequence functions to introduce places and things – Lydia is the first one to notice the other woman and not Giovanni – and contains some exciting allusions to the art of writing: A woman tells Giovanni a story that she would love to "see" herself that strongly resembles the one we are watching as she talks. She assures us that a woman should sacrifice herself for a man. Giovanni asks her why. "Just because," she says, "it makes me cry." The sequence contains the midpoint, which is the death of her schoolfriend in conjunction with the kiss.
6) The drive. Eighty minutes into the film. Lydia is driving in the rain with a stranger who was hitting on her all during the reception. "Don't play games," he says to her and tries to get her to escape with him. While Lydia is enjoying herself visibly, we see that it is impossible for her to be with someone else. "Excuse me, but I can't," she finally says. The sequence ends with a return to the party. We may consider Lydia's reaction and her decision not to "play games," as a second turning point, even if the interpretation is obscure. What is clear is that we are disappointed, almost irritated, by her behavior.
7) The encounter. We are now 90 minutes into the film. We are witnesses to a betrayal or to the despair of Giovanni (that is also a matter of interpretation), as well as the despair of the narrator (I know what I want to write, but I do not know how). The climax is as quiet as the rest of the film. The men collide, if only intellectually – the women are united. "I am not jealous, that is the problem," Lydia confides in the unknown person, and when the couple finally leaves, the

unknown person goes with the words, "You wore me out, you two."

8) In the park. The sequence about the break-up. Lydia tells Giovanni that their mutual friend has died. That this fact as well as the memory that goes with it, and the way he loved her (he always talked about me, and you talk about yourself), has led her to the decision not to love Giovanni any more – the "payoff" of the "thinking" from the bar sequence. Giovanni says he now realizes that what we give out comes back, and how he in the end has given away his life because he never gave anything (resolution of the theme and the attitude of the writer). He insists that he loves her, but then Lydia reads him a love letter, in which indifference is said to be the only true threat. "And who wrote this letter," asks Giovanni, and when she tells him "You, yourself did," he embraces and kisses her – in despair, as though he wants to bring back the emotions he once felt, as though he could deny and erase what was just proven. Yet his last sentence is, "I won't say it" [that I love you].

An open end? It is rather a closed emotional experience that raises the human adventure to a higher plane and enables a kind of emotional insight (see the section on the emotional theme "The structure of the screenplay, sixth sequence").

The technique of de-dramatization is often used in European films – sometimes with great success. In that sense the following example of an analysis could be seen as a modern version of *La Notte*: We will see how de-dramatization works best where expectations are built up that subsequently remain unmet.

Analysis of a screenplay: *4 Months, 3 Weeks and 2 Days* (screenplay by Cristian Mungiu)

Winner of the 2007 Palme d'Or in Cannes this is a drama about a woman who helps her friend have an abortion in 1980s Romania. Using the technique of de-dramatization, there is an uneasy feeling throughout that something terrible is going to happen, and terrible things do happen, even if not what we might expect.

The structure is very clear – and subsequently the story too. The protagonist is Otilia who is arranging for her roommate Gabita's abortion. We are never told why Gabita so desperately needs to have that abortion. The title tells us the exact time she is "gone," meaning the exact time she became pregnant, and indeed that protracted period plays an important role in the development of the story.

Again, this is not a film that is structured by the plot. And yet there is tension, drama, and a story with a beginning, middle and end. What are they? The story seems to begin when Otilia fights with her boyfriend. Up until then we had seen her preparing for something (preparing to travel, we think) with her roommate, but we had also seen her trying to cope with everyday life in communist Romania: everything is complicated and requires extra effort – getting cigarettes, a room reservation, powdered milk, sugar. The black market and the inflexibility of that system are part of reality. We follow every detail, but we only have the feeling that something starts to happen when they have a fight; and we realize Otilia has a secret. This happens at the 15-minute mark.

At the 30-minute mark, we discover that Gabita is pregnant and about to have an abortion. It looks like this structure functions by distributing knowledge to the audience. The characters have that knowledge, so the question revolves around when the audience will receive it. At the 45-minute mark a really strong midpoint carries the emotional theme – trust and its opposite, betrayal, which leads to the loss of innocence. Still, what we feel most is what the characters feel: the utter humiliation and the absurdity of having to pay for death with love and for love with death (of the soul).

At the 90-minute mark, Otilia leaves her boyfriend and two minutes later, she is confronted with the fetus on the floor of the bathroom – surely one of the most devastating images ever seen in cinema. Now, we get the answer to the question of the second act, the second dramatic question. Gabita has managed to have her abortion.

The third act is about getting rid of the fetus. After an agonizing sequence in the dark city where she tried to find the right place, an attempt that functions as the climax, she dumps it and then returns to the hotel. The last scene is in the hotel restaurant where the girls are offered "marrow, liver, brains." The uneasy feeling maintained throughout the film has to do with the fact that we are expecting even worse to happen. We expect nothing less than death, the death of Gabita. But death does not happen. Not in reality. What does occur is death of the soul. The last line we hear is, "We're never going to talk about it, okay?" This will not work, of course. They will remember the things they have gone through forever just as we, the audience, will do as well.

The technique of rewriting

One of the masterpieces of the art of screenwriting in the twentieth century is surely *Amadeus* by Peter Shaffer, directed by Milos Forman. Legend tells us that it was rewritten 47 times before it was green-lit.

Hollywood is known for engaging an army of screenwriters to "develop" the same screenplay, each of them rewriting it at least once. The analysis of narrative problems or the challenge of a specific story does not lead everyone to the same solution, even if one can agree about the location and the type of problem.

The technique of rewriting differs from the technique of writing the first draft – the screenwriter "should sense the charm of a story quickly and happily and yet have the stamina to develop it to its full potential."[68] This is not only the case for screenplays. For historical and economic reasons the screenplay is a literary genre that is habitually rewritten quite a lot, even in the first phase of its development.[69]

In order to revise a screenplay, we must be in a position to analyze it. One of the most useful tools of analysis is Linda Seger's color graph – a colorized step outline that consists of a list of the steps within a story. Every step describes the most important elements that ultimately make up the audiovisual narrative, including the emotional theme. These are then colored differently, so that one can observe their different weight and location within the story.

In this manner, a visual net of signs is established. A good example that shows the range of elements we will record on a color graph is the motion picture *Citizen Kane* by Herman Mankiewics and Orson Welles. A crystal ball that contains a snowy landscape falls out of Kane's hand. In another scene – the scene where the ten-year-old Kane is about to leave his home and his mother to live with a guardian who can guarantee him a secure future – we watch him play in a snowy landscape through a window. The scene where he is to be handed over to his guardian also takes place in the snow. Kane reacts instinctively and attacks his guardian with his sled. During the sequence with the fake news at the beginning of the motion picture, a reporter asks the former guardian of Kane if it is true Kane had attacked him with his sled. The guardian does not respond. When the elderly Kane's second wife leaves him, he breaks the furniture in her room in his fury. He pauses only when he finds the crystal – and puts it in his pocket. The dramaturgical net is composed in such a way that the psychological explanation of his outburst and the core emotion of his life, that is, the loss of his mother's love, are made clear – and this is told solely by use of the crystal ball.[70] The continuity in the narrative that is caused by use of the crystal ball, and the explanatory relationships that arise using this element, will be shown in a color graph using an assigned color and optimized as needed.

Exercise #65:
Analyze a completed screenplay by creating a step outline and color the different elements with different colors.

Exercise #66:
Analyze a completed screenplay by identifying the structural points in both the main story, the subplots and the emotional structure using a step outline, a color graph and a character development arc, if there is one. Note down any proposals for further development.

The future of screenwriting

In previous chapters I have shown how we can analyze screenplays with alternative narrative structures that consequently can be developed further, even if these evince some peculiarities and require their own technique or a special craft, because they do not have a dramatic structure so much as a dramatic system. Such a system can be a game played with the organization of time as well as the free and not necessarily logical, rather associative and emotional, organization of the material. Not least, it can experiment with the possibilities of the changing narrative perspective. The possibilities are infinite and the game played using the means available to the audiovisual narrative art has only just begun. In audiovisual narratives, one is no longer chained to narrative techniques common to the nineteen-century novel – the breakthrough occurred in 1994 with *Pulp Fiction* and *Short Cuts*, and since then there are no limits either in cinema or in television.

The long-term trend seems to be towards increased complexity and the exercise of emotional intelligence: fiendishly complex plots that demand intense audience focus and analysis just to figure out what is happening on the screen; and mind-benders – films designed specifically to disorient you, to mess with your head, some that challenge the mind by creating a thick network of intersecting plotlines, some that withhold crucial information from the audience or that invent new temporal schemes to invert traditional relationships of cause and effect, some that deliberately blur the line between fact and fiction – indeed through use of all the classic techniques of the old cinematic avant-garde.[71] Perhaps because of the complexity involved, one could safely make two observations: most of the alternative narratives are "screenwriter films", that is, are the ideas of a professional screenwriter at work, and the great explosion of cinematic complexity seems to be concentrated more in TV series (most notably, HBO) and to a much lesser degree in movies – possibly, among other reasons, because there are only so many threads and subtleties you can introduce into a two-hour film, but also because TV is traditionally more of a writer's medium.

Charlie Kaufman once described his writing philosophy in the following way:[72]

> I guess my mindset about movies is that I feel like film is a dead medium. With theater, you have accidents that can happen, performances that can change. But film is a recording. So what I try to do is infuse my screenplays with enough information that upon repeated viewings you can have a different experience. Rather than the movie going linearly to one thing, and at the end telling you what the movie's about – I try to create a conversation with the audience. I guess that's what I try to do – have a conversation with each individual member of the audience.

Conversations are two-way affairs, and participatory by nature. But how do you create a conversation using a dead medium? You do it by engaging the minds and the hearts of the audience. You do it by making the audience post-creative in the Nietzschean sense, through tragic joy, emotional structure, call it what you may.

The motion picture industry has had a great tradition of appropriating the narrative structures and the means of expression of the avant-garde and using them in commercial movies. D.W. Griffith's experiments, once belittled by the Hollywood motion picture industry, found their way back into mainstream Hollywood movies by a rather paradoxical migration through the revolutionary Russian cinema narrative school and the Italian and French avant-garde.

It is certainly not an accident that both *Pulp Fiction* and a film like *Memento* were among the ten best films chosen by members of the Writer's Guild, in second and seventh place respectively, while *Citizen Kane* occupies first place. The art of the narrative seems more important here than the story itself, that in turn must be strong and simple enough to carry a complex narrative. These films often have a more rigid structure than the classic dramatic narrative. The reason for this is simple. The audience turns into a detective who is out to discover the truth of the story. If what he discovers does not make any sense or is emotionally unsatisfying, the film will not function as an experience. In this respect, inasmuch as the idea of unity and tight construction of the narrative is retained, it is not correct to say that the alternative narrative does not follow the Aristotelian approach or is even in conflict with it.

Some of the films that could be listed as alternative narrative structures are *Night on Earth, Amores Perros* and *Lola Runs* (episodic narrative structure), *Forrest Gump, Pele the Conqueror, Gilbert Grape, My Life as a Dog* (passive hero with episodic narrative), *Short Cuts, Ice Storm, Code Inconnu, Smoke, The Big Chill, Wonderland, Happiness, Magnolia, The Hours* and *Lantana* (several protagonists with episodic narrative structure and a strong connecting thematic core) *Rashomon* and *Who Shot Liberty Valance* (various narrative perspectives), as well as films employing innovative narrative structures using flashbacks such as *Fight Club* and *The Sixth Sense*, films using different perspectives and associative organization or even the dissolution of time, such as like *Usual Suspects, Memento, Irreversible, Pulp Fiction, Mulholland Drive, Abre Los Ojos, Before the Rain, Toto le Héros, Nachtgestalten, Witnesses, Sweet Hereafter, Lulu on the Bridge, 21 Grams, Elephant* and, of course, *Last Year at Marienbad*, and not least *Lost Highway* (change of protagonists in the middle of the film). The list is long and the possibilities of the medium endless, as much for the emotional structural analysis as well as for what concerns the synthesis, the composition of screenplays.

In place of an epilogue: The era of the screenwriter

The producer, Irwin G. Thalberg,[1] introduced the technique of using several writers or writing teams to work over and revise a single screenplay, sometimes without them knowing other writers had worked or were working on it at the same time. He was also the one that coined the famous saying, "The writer is the most important person in Hollywood, but we must never tell the sons of bitches."

Gustav Freytag, however, had already told writers in 1863 in his book *Technique of the Drama*:

> [...] the technical work of the creative person in drama (is) not quite so easy and effortless [...] this poetic category requires more of the writer than any other: A peculiar, infrequent ability to represent the mental processes of men of action; a moderate temperament combining passion and clarity, education and certainly poetic talent, add a knowledge of human nature and what one calls character in real life, and moreover a thorough familiarity with the stage and its requirements.

Replace the word "stage" with the word "film medium," and the text could have been written with the screenwriter in mind.

The parallel to the playwright is painful for the screenwriter for one reason. Everyone talks about the plays of Sophocles, Shakespeare, Ibsen, Botho Strauß and Sarah Kane the same way they talk about the compositions of Mozart, Beethoven or Schönberg. In film, however, one speaks of the motion pictures of Hitchcock, Welles, Truffaut, Fellini, Polanski or Forman. Who has ever heard of Ernest Lehman (*North by Northwest*), Herman Mankiewicz (*Citizen Kane*), Suzanne Schiffman (*La nuit américaine*), Tonino Guerra (*Amarcord*), Robert Towne (*Chinatown*) or Peter Schaffer (*Amadeus*)?

Permit me a quote from the *New York Times*, concerning the Oscar nominations of 2009: "Each of the films selected for a best-picture nomination – *Slumdog Millionaire, The Curious Case of Benjamin Button, Frost/Nixon, Milk* and *The Reader* – represents the *auteur* ideal, in which a director is bankrolled and left pretty much alone. It is no coincidence that these five films were created by directors who also received best-director nominations".[2] Never mind that *Slumdog Millionaire* was written by Simon Beaufoy who also wrote *The Full Monty*, or that *The Curious Case of Benjamin Button* was written by Eric Roth, who also wrote *Forrest Gump, Munich* and *The Good Shepherd*, just to name a few; or that *Frost/Nixon* was written by Peter Morgan who also wrote *The Queen* and *The Last King of Scotland*, that *Milk* was written by TV writer Dustin Lance Black and *The Reader* by David Hare who wrote *The Hours* and is one of the most celebrated playwrights of our time. Five films and not one of them was written or even co-written by its director. How can the writer and his writing be ignored in such a way?

They say that what a screenwriter writes is something half-baked and that the director "writes" the film when filming. But even theater plays (like compositions) change, are interpreted, re-created – still, other people do not claim they wrote them. They say that the screenplay only comes alive when it is filmed. Before then it is a package of paper to be put in a drawer or 300 KB on a hard drive. But the same applies to manuscripts of novels before they are published or theater plays before they are produced. They say that the screenplay is a product that is not yet in its final form, like the drawings of an architect. Even if it is a masterpiece, nobody will exhibit it in this form, because everybody wants to see the building and not the architectural drawings.[3] But this overlooks an unpleasant fact – even the buildings are known as works of an architect and not of an engineer or contractor.

A play is made for the stage. Even if one reads it in the form of a book, its main reason for existence is its performance and it only achieves its full effect on stage – yet nobody claims that the play is an incomplete creation. The primary reason is certainly that a play can be performed many times in many theaters with different directors. Shooting a screenplay several times has been impossible up to now, mainly because it would be too expensive. The advent of digital technology and the widespread roll back of prices may contribute to a change in this situation. It is no longer unimaginable that in the near future screenplays will be treated like plays and filmed several times.[4]

The second reason is the most important one – and at the same time, it is the one that seems to smash every hope for improvement – the *auteur* theory. In his book *Adventures in the Screen Trade,* the noted screenwriter, William Goldman, wrote in 1983, that the *auteur* theory came out of France where a group of young guys just starting out on their directing careers – Truffaut, Jean-Luc Godard and so on – spread the theory that the director is the *auteur* of the film.[5] Goldman mentioned further how Godard said in an interview several years later that the whole thing was obviously bullshit, just a provocation to grab more attention. For better or worse, a kind of dogma was established. Just imagine, for instance, that since the Dogma Manifesto (which was also penned and presented as a provocation) was proclaimed, all movies would be filmed with a hand-held camera, no artificial light and no music – for ever and ever and with almost no exceptions to the rule. The idea that the *auteur* theory would rewrite the history of the cinema retrospectively and would deride the work of the screenwriter is in a way just as absurd.

The word *auteur* actually designates the person who invents something new and manages to make something from nothing. In the meantime, however, the word *auteur* means director, as least in the movie world.

Why is this the case? Goldman offers the following explanations:

1) It is comfortable (to name a single name and to have to celebrate just that one name).
2) Whoever writes about a motion picture does not really know how a motion picture is made.
3) It is impossible to say who is responsible for what.
4) The *auteur* theory sticks around mostly because of the insistence of the media on making use of it.

There are possibly a few such all-round filmmakers who have mastered screenwriting, camera work, editing, sound and production design, who can only work alone. But the great majority still needs a screenwriter, a producer, a cinematographer, an editor, a production designer, a composer and actors. If a film is the sum of all these parts, why is the director the only one who creates something new? Why is it his film?

Robert McKee says:

> One of the most important factors playing a role in the decline and fall of quality in European films in the past thirty years is the *auteur* theory. From 1945 to 1970 European films dominated the world.

> From 1970 onwards, it has all been downhill. What happened from 1968 to 1970? It was the moment of the elevation of the director to author and the subordination of the screenwriter.[6]

Whatever one thinks of McKee's thesis, the fact is that only one artist begins with a blank page – to create the meaning, the emotion and the vision of a work of art – and that artist is the writer. How did anyone come up with the idea of converting the director into an *auteur*? The transformation of what began as the "politics of the *auteur*" into the almighty prevailing *auteur* theory is one of the curiosities that pop up from time to time in the history of ideas. The "politics of the *auteur*" was not a theory, rather, as the name implies, it was a polemic. The young French filmmakers wanted to delineate their views from orthodox French film criticism. In doing so, they started discovering and pronouncing parts of a theory, but it happened incoherently and non-scientifically.[7]

The American film critic, Andrew Sarris, who brought it to America in 1963, was also the one who first popularized the *auteur* theory – that never became a real theory, because every attempt to support it systematically and scientifically failed.[8] There it finally led to obscure ways of judging movies. A bad movie from an *auteur* was suddenly considered better than a good movie by a director who was not an *auteur*, because according to the *auteur* theory, not every director is an *auteur*: Indeed, a small, but important detail that has been completely forgotten over the course of time. The most famous example is, perhaps, John Huston – who directed his masterpiece, *The Dead*, at an advanced age – and who allegedly was not an *auteur*, because every one of his pictures was different. Just as according to the same theory not every director can be an *auteur*, furthermore a director cannot be an *auteur* who has only made one or two movies – because how can his artistic identity become evident from just a couple of movies?

The critics at the *Cahiers du Cinéma* have indirectly managed to heighten the understanding of film as an art form; but at the same time, they did not overlook the fact that behind the *auteur* theory lay a "cult of the personality."[9] The *auteur* theory goes back to none less than the romantic ideal of the genius. With this the special and modern in the art of cinema was destroyed, that is to say, its collaborative character.[10]

The main opponents of Sarris were the American critics, Pauline Kael[11] and Richard Corliss.[12] Corliss questions the premise that the director creates something from nothing. He calls the director an interpretive and not a creative artist. But then the directors began to write their own scripts – definitely not as a direct response to Corliss, but rather because they could as a result make the film their exclusive product.[13] The *auteur* theory was promoted as an attitude and ideology that took on a life of its own, until Hollywood took it up for promotional reasons in the 1970s. It was simpler to make Martin Scorsese a star and to celebrate *Taxi Driver* as though it were his instead of promoting it as a movie by Martin Scorsese and Paul Schrader,[14] the screenwriter.

In the last ten years, the construct of *auteur* has even gained in importance – perhaps due to a general growing emphasis on the individual in western culture. The claim to individual authorship has become harder to uphold, since film studies have also started to reveal the significance and the function of the other contributions to film, even those of the screenwriter. The most recent theoretical discourse, however, takes place inside a small circle of insiders; and the only opinion that matters to mainstream filmgoers and critics continues to be the opinion of the critics of the *Cahiers du Cinéma*.[15]

The time seems ripe for a change in awareness. As David Kipen, the film critic and director of literature at the National Endowment for the Arts, writes provocatively in his book, *The Schreiber Theory – A Radical Rewrite of American Film History,* in the first 50 years film history belonged to the producers – who has never heard of Louis B. Mayer, Irving G. Thalberg, Jack Warner, Darryl Zanuck, Sam Goldwyn, Hal B. Wallis and David O. Selznick, just to name a few? Because of the *auteur* theory, the next 50 years of film history belonged to the directors. Now at long last, it is the turn of the artists who create something from nothing, the screenwriters.

In his book, Kipen presents a theory of writing that he named after the Yiddish word, *Schreiber*. In doing this, he does not intend to replace the dogmatic *auteur* theory with a new dogma, but rather to show how absurd it all is. He again points to the main problem of this approach – the multiple credits. Hollywood is famous for using an army of writers, who "develop" a screenplay in "development hell." Many of them are not even mentioned in the titles. Where does one recognize the signature of the writer between all the source material credits, shared credits, adaptation credits, story credits, unaccredited rewrites and on-set improvisations?

Does this mean that screenwriting is so much harder than directing or being a director of photography that one person cannot manage it alone? Sometimes, more than one person might direct a movie. The Director's Guild of America, however, interestingly enough, prohibits sharing the credit and insists on sole directorial credits. The director

Robert Rodriguez had to drop out of the DGA in 2005, because it was the only way he could share the director's credit with the writer, Frank Miller. In Europe, the director will claim co-writing credit for fiddling with parts of the dialogue or because he worked on the shooting script, or simply because he directed it – and made changes while directing. I have not heard a single time that a director took credit for the work done by a director of photography, because he discussed with him or even told him how to film a scene. Is writing a screenplay so much more glamorous than directing a movie or supervising camera operators, grips and gaffers that they all want writing credit?

And can meddling with the script be such a good thing? Development is the holy cow of the film industry. A screenplay is never ready, we hear. And everybody has an opinion about it. Indeed, another definition for development could be "the elimination of different-ness process." There is no other art and no other form of writing that is so open to criticism and meddling, or where a writer is more expected to do what he is told, sometimes even against his instincts as an artist. Could such treatment lead to excellent or even merely unpredictable results? Not really.

One should point out that according to European law, at least in most European countries, the hire-and-fire logic of the rewrite system is legally questionable. European law protects the copyright holder's (that is the author's) moral rights, that means his right to first publication, the naming of his copyright, protection from distortion of the text, or to any portion of his work of art and protects his right to re-acquire the rights to his work of art. Such copyright law was first recognized in France and in Germany;[16] before it was then anchored in the Berne Convention for the Protection of Literary and Artistic Works of 1928. Although the USA signed the Berne Convention in 1988, it did not accept the moral rights clause as part of the copyright law, but rather as a part of another body of law called defamation, or unfair competition law. An idiosyncrasy of American copyright law means that the personal relationship of the creator to his work of art recedes into the background and that the commercial aspects come to the foreground and become more important. The investment of a contracting or commissioning body, for example, is more important than the person who created the work of art and it is that investment that is protected, rather than the artist or the work of art. In contrast, the nations that have included the moral rights clause are known as "*droit d'auteur* states."

Moral rights do not have anything to do with the economic rights to a work of art. Even if an artist has transferred his rights of exploitation to a third party, the moral rights remain with the artist in perpetuity. Some legal systems permit a waiver of moral rights. Those legal systems find themselves mentally between mainland Europe and America, and naturally include the United Kingdom and Ireland. The essence of moral rights may not be transferred in any other European country. The moral rights include, as previously stated, the right to maintain the integrity of the work of art created by the author and therefore include the right to protect it from any distortion. The moral rights tradition in Europe theoretically implies that the writer has the final word (the equivalent to the final cut) where his work of art is concerned, that nobody has the right to change his text without the writer's consent. This right is irrevocable and may not be transferred, waived or surrendered.

Even Gustav Freytag writes that the writer of a piece:

> […] may not leave the editing of his text to strangers – even in the cases when it is hard to accomplish without outside help because he does not have much theater experience. The final decision must be his despite everything, and he should not normally let a theater edit [his play] without his permission.

A screenwriter who can have the final say, the last word? A screenwriter who should not let a stranger edit his play? It sure sounds like science fiction. But, surely, there is another especially important reason why someone should be called *auteur* or writer, or whatever terminology one decides to use, because of the right to decide what may be changed in a work of art, that is, to have the right to undertake these changes.

However. in some European countries there are certain legal limitations. In Germany, for instance, one can transfer the right to revisions, but German copyright law sets a clear limit to protect the author, as he still retains in any case the right to prohibit the distortion or any other adverse effect that is apt to endanger his legitimate spiritual or personal interest in his work of art. The German copyright law (UrhG) clearly differentiates between a core area of the moral rights (his right to first publication, the copyright, protection from distortion of the text) and norms with a moral rights bent (his right to access to his work of art, his right to be named when cited, etc.). The same is true for the credit right: the author of the work can waive the right to be credited as author for a certain period of time (i.e. as a ghostwriter); he still retains the right, however, to take credit as author of the work at a later point in time. A conclusive assignment of right to credit by the author is not possible, limitations of the exercise of moral rights arising from contract or tort may not lead to a devaluation of content.[17]

The reality is completely different, however. The rewrite by other writers or even by directors or producers (that writers from other literary forms do not encounter) has become a fixture in Europe, as it was introduced in the belief that this was the secret of success in Hollywood. Europe's screenwriters responded. In 2006, we penned a declaration, the European Screenwriters Manifesto. To quote from the *Los Angeles Times* "it is about as direct, succinct and no-nonsense as they come. Its first three planks are like sharp gunshots across the bow of the filmmaking industry:

- The screenwriter is an author of the film, a primary creator of the audiovisual work.
- The indiscriminate use of the possessory credit is unacceptable.
- The moral rights of the screenwriter, especially the right to maintain the integrity of a work and to protect it from any distortion or misuse, should be inalienable and should be fully honored in practice."[18]

Screenwriters hold these truths to be self-evident. But not everybody does – so we are pushing for a reform. Of thought. Of approach. The manifesto challenged the international film community and began a discussion about what has gone wrong and how it could be set right. And this discussion is still going on, as a step towards acknowledging the rightful place of the screenwriter, as in the theater and, indeed, in any other form of writing. Screenplays are starting to get published as the writers wrote them, European national funds are funding the writers directly and putting more money into script development, fair payment for every form of exploitation and moral rights are not foreign words anymore; film students are getting educated in creative writing and not just writing by numbers, liberating themselves from the stifling one-size-fits-all model, and are more open to and more knowledgeable about different traditions of storytelling. Critics and scholars will follow, perhaps starting to differentiate and honor the differences between writing and direction. Critics and scholars are vital to the reform, as they inform the public and perpetuate bad (or good) habits.

One should measure the *auteur* theory, whether consistent inwardly or practical outwardly, but this must be done in the world that created it, as Kipen says. In all three points, the *auteur* theory has failed. It is a fable that is now regarded as truth and films suffer from it; underwritten screenplays that go into production are the result, scripts that are rewritten so many times by so many different writers that there is no inner consistency and no originality. The opposite of these are screenplays that were written incontestably by one writer who had enough power to insist on the "final word." These are the screenplays of a new generation of screenwriters – Charlie Kaufman (*Being John Malkovitch, Eternal Sunshine of a Spotless Mind, Adaptation*), Guillermo Arriaga (*Amores Perros, 21 Grams, Three Burials of Melquiades Estrada, Babel*), Andres Tomas Jensen (*Mifune, Wilbur wants to kill himself, Open Hearts, Brothers*), Razvan Radulescu (*The Paper Will be Blue, The Death of Mr. Lazarescu*) to name a few – who are and remain first and foremost writers, even if most of them have directed a movie or two. Charlie Kaufman today is mentioned along with literary stars of his generation – David Foster Wallace, Mona Simpson, Michael Chabon, Aimee Bender, Colson Whitehead and Jonathan Safran Foer. For many he is even the new Kurt Vonnegut, and he uses the allegorical methodology of a Calvino, Borges or Pirandello. The Kurt Vonnegut of the twenty-first century writes screenplays? It is possible. Pasolini saw the screenplay as an independent art, a work of art complete in itself. As the Greek-American literary scholar Alexandros Nehamas says,[19] the popular art of one era is often the high art of the next one.

It can only be hoped that the literary side of the screenplay in the future will find greater acceptance – also among screenwriters. After all, drama was only first elevated to being read, that is, publicized, during the romantic period – earlier, only professional readers read it, the way screenplays are read today. Surely, the time for a new evaluation has arrived that allows for the artistic and the resulting copyright significance of screenwriters, and enables the public recognition they are due.

Interestingly enough, the screenplay is in some countries categorized (both in legal literature as in case law) as a form that pre-exists and is independent of motion pictures, a literary work merely adapted by making it into a film.[20] This creates problems in the sense that the creator of a story being adapted cannot be the co-author of the adaptation, that is, the film, at the same time. The film combines elements of the performing arts, the fine arts and music to form a new artistic unity, a cinematographic work. The script, however, already contains the basic elements of the film and its form in all of its essential expressions; and it only requires a creative completion of the filled in framework with the specific means of filmmaking. "Contrary to conventional wisdom, it is important to remember that the film is not to be understood as the adaptation of the screenplay,"[21] but that without a screenplay there is no film.

In terms of its importance to a film, the screenplay is comparable to the combined libretto and score, that is, both together, for an opera or a musical. It cannot be limited in any way to a work of literature as a mere preparation or a stage prior to a film. It is, moreover, the indispensable foundation necessary to making the movie and a constitutive part of it, without which the film would be unthinkable. It is obvious that it also remains a literary work of art, which can be enjoyed as such, even if such an opportunity rarely arises and in the rare event that editions of screenplays distributed by way of the book trade correspond to the writer's version.[22]

In his *Poetics*, his unintended foundation for all screenplay theories, Aristotle expounds the opinion that a drama can also be effective off stage when it is read:

> the Spectacle has, indeed, an emotional attraction of its own, but, of all the parts, it is the least artistic, and it is least connected to the art of poetry. For the power of Tragedy, we may be sure, is felt even apart from representation and actors.[23]

That is why he occupied himself so little with the aspect of appearance, *the* όψις, and why this aspect is not listed among the tasks of the poet. This does not mean he ignores the element of stage performance or belittles it. He sees it merely as a means to complete a work.[24] He further advises the poet to imagine with the eyes of his soul how his creation can be performed onstage.

The screenwriter is, then, the creator of an independent literary work of art and at the same time a co-author of a film. As soon as a film is created, the script – according to current practice – becomes, in this function, an integral, inseparable component of the film and can no longer be exploited apart from the film. In this regard, a double injustice is inflicted on the screenwriter. If a screenplay is not filmed, that proves it is a failure (why else do we never list the scripts that have not yet been filmed in our filmographies?), and is certainly not seen as a work of literature, even if, legally, it is one. If a screenplay is filmed, it becomes someone else's work – so why write a screenplay? One possible legal determination could be that a screenplay, following its updating (and not its adaptation) within the bounds of making a movie is, as an integral element of the movie, no longer identical to its original form of appearance as an independently existing literary work. Accordingly, the screenwriter could be recognized as the author of an independent literary work (also after being filmed) similar to the novel or the theatre play; and at the same time, as stated previously, as a co-author of the film.

The director, certainly, plays an important role. Even Freytag writes, "It is only through the work of a careful director that the beautiful forms in the plays of Shakespeare or Schiller appear onstage in their proper proportions." He added that not every stage enjoys a technical staff that executes its work with a fine touch or true understanding for the play. The writer, moreover, "may or may not write down his intentions. Altogether, there is not much to give." Extensive, written presentations of the theme would make intentions clear, but they also easily immobilize the imagination and, moreover, make the continual transformation and necessary reshaping more difficult.[25]

Today, nothing differentiates Freytag's playwright from the screenwriter – or any other writer, for that matter. He also needs to bring many and diverse talents to his handicraft. He has to quickly and happily feel the charm of the material and nevertheless have the time to bring it to fruition. Even so, a play that fails, warns Freytag, will have meant on average a year lost. A writer, moreover, will have to wriggle his way through uncertainty and inner cramps at the first sign of a well-meaning critic intruding into his soul – to great advantage for his decision-making. The first cloud that appears in the blue skies of a writer's mind, who is happy for having accomplished the task of completing his work, is perhaps painful for a tender soul, but it is also as refreshing as a summer breeze blowing through a sultry summer evening. Last:

> if the young playwright sends the child of his dreams into the world, he will have sufficient opportunity to develop something else in his repertoire of stagecraft. It will be his duty to bear a glittering success without becoming arrogant or pretentious, and to leave behind the dreary failures yet not lose his courage.

For that reason, Freytag wishes for the writer, who is armed with dramatic skill, above all a sturdy and patient heart.

There is nothing to be tampered with here. Drama in general and the screenplay in particular is a difficult art form. This art form has been badly injured by the *auteur* theory. Much damage has resulted, and it is necessary to make this good again for the sake of the screenwriters but also for the entire art form of film. Let us reverse the words of Irvin G. Thalberg, The screenwriters are damn important and we need to tell them so. Does this mean the credit will read – *Taxi Driver* by Paul Schrader and Martin Scorsese? A beginning has been made with the book you are holding in your hands. Not just formally, but rather because it has hopefully made clear that films do not spring from a vacuum. They come from writers who are willing to explore darkness, rough roads and confrontations. The method and the theory I have presented here hopefully will make it easier to explore – and despite everything keep the magic going.

Bibliography

Adorno, Theodor W., *Ästhetische Theorie* (Frankfurt am Main, 1973).

Archer, William, *Playmaking* (London, 1938).

Aristotle. *Poetics*. Translated by S.H. Butcher (London, 2009).

Beckermann, Bernard. *Dynamics of Drama. Theory and Method of Analysis* (New York, 1970).

Benjamin, Walter, Das *Kunstwerk im Zeitalter seiner technischen Reproduzierbarkeit* (Frankfurt am Main, 1963).

Benjamin, Walter, *Ursprung des deutschen Trauerspiels* (Frankfurt am Main, 2000).

Benke, Dagmar, *Freistil* (Bergisch Gladbach, 2002).

Bergman, Ingmar, *The Magic Lantern* (London, 1988).

Bernays, Anne and Pamela Painter, *What if? Writing Exercises for Fiction Writers* (New York, 1990).

Bettelheim, Bruno, *The Uses of Enchantment: The Meaning and Importance of Fairy Tales* (New York, 1989).

Birkenstock, Arne, *Autoren- und Drehbuchförderung in Deutschland. Eine Studie des Kunst* (Salon e.V. im Auftrag der Staatskanzlei NRW: Köln, 2002).

Biro, Yvette, *To Dress a Nude. Exercises in Imagination* (Iowa, 1998).

Biskind, Peter, *Easy Riders, Raging Bull* (New York, 1998).

Blondell, Ruby, *The Play of Character in Plato's Dialogues* (Cambridge, 2002).

Bordwell, David, *Narration in the Fiction Film* (London, 1985).

Brady, John, *The Craft of the Screenwriter* (London, 1981).

Belfiore, Elizabeth S., *Tragic Pleasures. Aristotle on Plot and Emotion* (Princeton, 1992).

Boys-Stones, George R., *Metaphor, Allegory and the Classical Tradition. Ancient Thought and Modern Revisions* (Oxford, 2003).

Brecht, Bertolt, *Schriften zur Literatur und Kunst* (Bd. I. Frankfurt am Main, 1967).

Brecht, Bertolt, *Schriften zum Theater* (Bd. VII. Frankfurt am Main, 2000).

Bresson, Robert, *Notes on Cinematography* (New York, 1977).

Breton, André, *Die Manifeste des Surrealismus* (Reinbek, 1986).

Brooks, Peter, *Reading for the Plot* (New York, 1984).

Brütsch, Matthias, Vinzenz Hediger, Ursula von Keitz, Alexandra Schneider and Margrit Tröhler (Hg.), *Kinogefühle. Emotionalität und Film* (Zürcher Filmstudien 12. Marburg, 2005).

Bunuel, Luis, *Mein letzter Seufzer* (Königstein, 1983).
Buzan, Tony, *The Power of Creative Intelligence* (London, 2001).
Carrière, Jean-Claude, *Über das Geschichtenerzählen* (Berlin, 1999).
Carrière, Jean-Claude and Pascal Bonitzer, *Praxis des Drehbuchschreibens* (Berlin, 1999).
Carroll, Noel, *The Philosophy of Horror or Paradoxes of the Heart* (New York, 1988).
Chion, Michel, *Techniken des Drehbuchschreibens* (Berlin, 2001).
Christen, Thomas, *Das Ende im Spielfilm. Vom klassischen Hollywood zu Antonionis offenen Formen* (Marburg, 2002).
Damasio, Antonio, *Descartes' Error* (New York, 1994).
Damasio, Antonio, *The Feeling of What Happens. Body and Emotion in the Making of Consciousness* (New York, 1999).
Damasio, Antonio, *Looking for Spinoza. Joy, Sorrow, and the Feeling Brain* (New York, 2003).
Dancyger, Ken and Jeff Rush, *Alternative Scriptwriting: Writing Beyond the Rules* (New York, 1995).
Dancyger, Ken, *Global Scriptwriting* (New York, 2001).
De Sousa, Ronald, *The Rationality of Emotion* (Boston, 1987).
Dürrenmatt, Friedrich, *Theaterprobleme* (Zürich, 1955).
Ekman, Paul, *Emotion in the Human Face* (Cambridge, 1982).
Elsaesser, Thomas and Warren Buckland, *American Film Analysis. A Guide to Movie Analysis* (London, 2002).
Egri, Lajos, *The Art of Dramatic Writing* (London, 1960).
Eick, Dennis, *Drehbuchtheorien. Eine vergleichende Analyse* (Konstanz, 2006).
Federman, Raymond, *Surfiction. Der Weg der Literatur* (Hamburger Poetik-Lektionen. Frankfurt am Main, 1992).
Field, Syd, *The Screenwriter's Workbook: A Workshop Approach* (New York, 1988).
Forster, Edward Morgan, *Aspects of the Novel* (New York, 1990).
Freud, Sigmund, *Der Witz und seine Beziehung zum Unbewussten* (Frankfurt am Main, 1971).
Freytag, Gustav, *Die Technik des Dramas. Bearbeitete Neuausgabe* (Berlin, 2003).
Freytag, Gustav, *Technique of the Drama* (Berlin, 2003).
Frijda, Nico, *The Emotions* (Cambridge, 1986).
Froug, William, *The New Screenwriter looks at the New Screenwriter* (Los Angeles, 1992).
Goldberg, Bonni, *Room to Write. Daily Invitations to a Writer's Life* (New York, 1996).
Goldman, William, *Adventures in the Screen Trade* (London, 1983).
Goldman, William, *What Lie Did I Tell? More Adventures in the Screen Trade* (New York, 2000).
Greimas, Algirdas. *Structural Semantics. An Attempt at a Method* (Lincoln, 1983).
Günther, Hans-Christian und Antonios Rengakos (Hg.), *Beiträge zur antiken Philosophie: Festschrift für Wolfgang Kullmann* (Stuttgart, 1997).
Haar, Michel: L'oeuvre d'art, *Essai sur l'ontologie des oeuvres* (Paris, 1998).

Hallberg, Jana und Alexander Wewerka (Hg.), *Dogma 95. Zwischen Kontrolle und Chaos* (Berlin, 2001).
Hegel, Georg Wilhelm Friedrich, *Esthétique* (Paris, 1979).
Hiltunen, Ari, *Aristoteles in Hollywood* (Bergisch-Galdbach, 2001).
Horton, Andrew, *Writing the Character-Centered Screenplay* (Berkeley, 1994).
Horton, Andrew, *Screenwriting for a Global Market* (Berkeley, 2004).
Houston, Jean, *The Possible Human* (New York, 1982).
Howard, David, *How to Build a Great Screenplay. A Master Class in Storytelling for Film* (New York, 2004).
Howard, David and Edward Mabley, *The Tools of Screenwriting. A Writer's Guide to the Craft and Elements of a Screenplay* (London, 1995).
Hunter, Lew, *Lew Hunter's Screenwriting 434* (New York, 1993).
Iakov, Daniel I., (Ιακώβ, Δανιήλ *I.*) Ζητήματα Λογοτεχνικής Θεωρίας στην Ποιητική του Αριστοτέλη (Athens, 2004).
Irving, John, *My Movie Business* (London, 2000).
Johnstone, Keith, *Impro: Improvisation and the Theatre* (London, 1987).
Johnstone, Keith, *Impro for Storytellers* (London, 1999).
Josefsberg, Milt, *Comedy Writing* (New York, 1987).
Jung, Carl Gustav, *Der Mensch und seine Symbole* (Solothurn, Düsseldorf, 1968).
Kallas, Christina, *Europäische Film und Fernsehkoproduktionen* (Baden-Baden, 1992).
Kallas, Christina, Σενάριο. Η τέχνη της επινόησης και της αφήγησης στον κινηματογράφο (Athens, 2006).
Kallas, Christina, *Kreatives Drehbuchschreiben* (Konstanz, 2007).
Kallas, Christina, Bio/Pic ή Οι Ζωές των Λίγων (Athens, 2009).
Kappelhoff, Hermann, *Matrix der Gefühle. Das Kino, das Melodrama und das Theater der Empfindsamkeit* (Berlin, 2004).
Karton, Joshua (Hg.), *Film Scenes for Actors, Vol. I & II* (Toronto, 1983).
Kipen, David, *The Schreiber Theory. A Radical Rewrite of American Film History* (Hoboken, New Jersey, 2006).
Klotz, Volker, *Geschlossene und offene Form im Drama* (München, 1972).
Koster, Severin, *Antike Épostheorien* (Stuttgart, 1970).
Krakauer, Siegfried, *Theorie des Films: Die Errettung der äußeren Wirklichkeit* (Frankfurt am Main, 1985).
Krevolin, Richard, *Screenwriting from the Soul* (Los Angeles, 1998).
Kurosawa, Akira, *Something like an Autobiography* (New York, 1982).
Lazarus, Richard, *Emotion and Adaptation* (New York, 1994).
Lazarus, Tom, *Secrets of Film Writing* (New York, 2001).
Ledoux, Joseph, *The Emotional Brain. The Mysterious Underspinnings of Emotional Life* (New York, 1996).
Leff, Leonard J., *Film Plots* (Ann Arbor, Michigan, 1983).
Lerch, Jennifer, *500 Ways to Beat the Hollywood Script Reader* (New York, 1999).
Lessing, Gotthold Ephraim, *Hamburgische Dramaturgie* (Hildesheim, 1979).
Lopez, Daniel, *Films by Genre* (Jefferson, NC, 1993).

Ludwig, Arnold, *The Price of Greatness. Resolving the Creativity and Madness Controversy* (New York, 1996).

Mamet, David, *A Whore's Profession* (London, 1994).

McKee, Robert, *Story. Die Prinzipien des Drehbuchschreibens* (Berlin, 2000).

McKilligan, Pat, *Backstory: Interviews with Screenwriters of Hollywood's Golden Age* (Berkeley, 1986).

Mees, Ulrich, *Die Struktur der Emotionen* (Toronto, 1991).

Merleau-Ponty, Maurice, *Das Kino und die neue Psychologie,* in: Filmkritik Nr. 11 (1969).

Morris, Ian and Barry Powell, *New Companion to Homer* (Boston, 1997).

Nails, Debra, *The People of Plato. A Prosopography of Plato and Other Socratics* (Indianapolis, 2002).

Naremore, James, *Acting in the Cinema* (Berkeley, 1988).

Νεχαμάς, Αλέξανδρος: Η τέχνη του βίου, Σωκρατικοί στοχασμοί από τον Πλάτωνα στον Φουκώ (Athens, 2001).

Nightingale, Andrea Wilson, *Genres in Dialogue. Plato and the Construct of Philosophy* (1995).

Parker, Philip, *Kreative Matrix* (Konstanz, 2004).

Pfister, Manfred, *Das Drama* (München, 1988).

Polanyi, Michael, *The Tacit Dimension* (New York, 1966).

Polti, Georges, *Les Trente-Six Situations Dramatiques* (Paris, 1980).

Pope, Thomas, *Good Scripts Bad Scripts* (New York, 1998).

Power, Mick and Tim Dalgleish, *Cognition and Emotion: From Order to Disorder* (Sussex, 1997).

Propp, Vladimir, *Morphologie des Märchens* (Suhrkamp, Frankfurt, 1975).

Pütz, Peter, *Die Zeit im Drama. Zur Technik dramatischer Spannung* (Göttingen, 1977).

Rabenalt, Peter, *Filmdramaturgie* (Berlin, 1999).

Rabiger, Michael, *Developing Story Ideas* (Boston, 2000).

Rico, Gabriele, *Writing the Natural Way* (New York, 2000).

Rodari, Giani, *The Grammar of Fantasy* (London, 1996).

Rothenberg, Albert, *The Emerging Goddess. The Creative Process in Art, Science, and Other Fields* (Chicago, 1979).

Russin, Robin U. and William Missouri Downs, *Screenplay. Writing the Picture* (Los Angeles, 2003).

Ryan, James, *Technique of the Character-Driven Screenplay* (California, 2000).

Sayles, John, *Thinking in Pictures. The Making of the Movie* (Boston, 1987).

Schelling, Friedrich Wilhelm Joseph von, *Textes esthétiques* (Paris, 1978).

Schiller, Friedrich, *Über die ästhetische Erziehung des Menschen* (Stuttgart, 2000).

Seger, Linda, *Advanced Screenwriting. Raising your Script to the Academy Award Level* (Los Angeles, 2003).

Seger, Linda, *Creating Unforgettable Characters* (New York, 1990).

Seger, Linda, *Making a Good Script Great. New York,* 2nd edition, 1994, 3rd edition (2010).

Seger, Linda, *Making a Good Writer Great* (Los Angeles, 1999).
Seger, Linda. *The Art of Adaptation. Turning Fact and Fiction into Film* (New York, 1992).
Skaggs, Calvin (Hg.), *The American Short Story Vol. I & II* (New York, 1979).
Solomon, Robert C. (Hg.), *What is an Emotion? Classic and Contemporary Readings* (Oxford, 2003).
Spolin, Viola, *Improvisation for the Theater. A Handbook of Teaching and Directing Techniques* (Evanston, 1983).
Stanislavski, Konstantin S., *An Actor Prepares* (New York, 1936).
Stanislawski, Konstantin S., *Mein Leben in der Kunst* (Berlin, 1957).
Strasberg, Lee, *Schauspielen und das Training des Schauspielers. Beiträge zur "Methode"* (Berlin, 1988).
Strindberg, August, *Théatre Cruel et Théatre Mystique* (Paris, 1964).
Szlezák, Thomas A., *Platon Lesen* (Stuttgart, 1993).
Szlezák, Thomas A., *Reading Plato* (Stuttgart, 1993).
Szondi, Peter, *Theorie des modernen Dramas* (Frankfurt am Main, 1970).
Tan, Ed, *Emotions and the structure of narrative film. Film as an emotion machine* (New Jersey, 1996).
Thomas, Sam (Hg.), *Best American Screenplays.* First Series (New York, 1986).
Truby, John, *Great movies: Why Do They Work* (Los Angeles, 1990).
Truffaut, François, *Mr. Hitchcock, wie haben Sie das gemacht?* (München, 1973).
Vale, Eugene, *Die Technik des Drehbuchschreibens für Film und Fernsehen* (München, 1944/1982).
Vogler, Christopher, *The Writer's Journey* (Los Angeles, 1992).
Volk, Tyler, *Metapatterns Across Space, Time and Mind* (Los Angeles, 2000).
Vorhaus, John, *Creativity rules! A writer's workbook* (Los Angeles, 2000).
Vorhaus, John, *The Comic Toolbox* (Los Angeles, 1994).
Voss, Christiane, *Narrative Emotionen. Eine Untersuchung über Möglichkeiten und Grenzen philosophischer Emotionstheorien* (Berlin, New York, 2004).
Werder, Lutz von, *Lehrbuch des Kreativen Schreibens* (Berlin, 2001).
Wolff, Jurgen and Kerry Cox, *Successful Scriptwriting. Writer's Digest books* (Ohio, 1988).
Wuss, Peter, *Filmanalyse und Psychologie. Strukturen des Films im Wahrnehmungsprozess* (Berlin, 1993).
Wygotski, Lew S., *Psychologie der Kunst* (Dresden 1976; Berlin/Hamburg, 2005).

Notes

Prologue

1 A term used also at the Cultural Diversity Days that the Commission for Culture and Education organized for the European Parliament in December 2008.

2 Compare the Birkenstock study, *Authors and Screenplay Promotion in Germany* that the author drew up for the *Kunstsalon e.V.,* as well as Kallas, *European Cinema and Television Co-productions*, predominantly in relation to the financial, legal and political dimensions of state funding in Europe.

3 The Writer's Guild of America registers 16,000 screenplays or treatments every year. Only 120 to 130 of them will actually be produced. Approximately 800 films are produced annually throughout Europe at a production ratio of 1:4 and in some countries even 1:2, which means that 1600 to 3200 screenplays enter development each year. For the European the goal is to produce – often at the expense of the development of the screenplay. The volume of feature film production, which results from the system, is recorded by the European Audiovisual Observatory. In tentative figures for 2005, the Observatory records 798 feature films made in the 25 member states of the EU compared with 699 in the United States. See European Audiovisual Observatory – "World Market Trends / *Tendances du marché du film*" – Focus 2006, p. 9. (www.obs.coe.int/online_publication/reports/focus2006.pdf).

4 From class notes taken from a lecture by Frank Daniel. He died in 1996 and left behind neither a textbook nor instructions. Wherever I draw from his method, I use notes taken from his lectures as well as my own notes. I also use notes taken from lectures by Linda Seger.

5 Seger, *Making a Good Writer Great*, p. 177.

6 Freytag, *Technique of the Drama*, p. 269.

7 The same is true in part for theater, where there is exactly this kind of an unbridgeable chasm between the semioticians of the theater as performance and the semioticians of drama as literary text.

8 Compare Goldman, *Adventures in the Screen Trade*, pp. 100–105, for an especially informative and entertaining opinion about the true reason for the existence and paradox of the concept "*cinéma d'auteur.*"

9 Out of the 30 movies that won the Oscar for Best Picture between 1965 and 1995, 23 received Oscars for Best Screenplay. One often means the other.

10 He continued, "From the moment you find yourself on the right path and keep going, you discover that you will be learning your whole life. As far as that goes, there is no end to it. At the moment a script writer or a director think they believe they know everything, they need to stop working, because from there on they will be repeating themselves." From the lecture notes of Frank Daniel.

11 Excerpts from his letter of April 4, 1796, written at a time while he was struggling to sort out the material on the historical figure of Wallenstein. Cf. the exchange of letters between Schiller and Goethe, quoted from *Kultur- und Kunstwissenschaftliche Studientexte*, pp. 156 f., 162.

12 von Werder, *Lehrbuch des Kreativen Schreibens*, p. 54 ff.

13 Among which are the following titles: Ken Macrories *Telling Writing* (1970), John Brown's *Free Writing. A Group Approach* (1977), William Coles' *The Plural I: The Teaching of Writing* (1978) und *Composing: Writing as a Self-Creating Process* (1974), Donald Stewart's *The Authentic Voice: a Pre-Writing Approach to Student Writing* (1971), Peter Elbow's *Writing without Teachers* (1973), James Miller and Stephen Judy's *Writing in Reality* (1978), James Miller's *Word, Self, Reality* (1972), James Adama's *Conceptual Block Busting* (1979); Ken Macrories' *Searching Writing* (1980).

14 Philosophers and, starting in the nineteenth century, literary theoreticians investigated the theory of drama in the context of the theory of literature. Theater studies is a younger branch than the study of literature and only won institutional, academic autonomy in the nineteenth century – initially in the USA and France, and then in Germany. For this reason, theater science still mostly depends today on the rich theoretical results of the above-named theories. Naturally, all this applies even more so to the young field of film studies.

15 Compare with, among others: Alberta Tuner's *To Make a Poem* (1982), Robert Wallace's *Writing Poems* (1982), Jeanette Burroway's *Writing Fiction* (1982), D. Kirby's *Two and Two make more than Four* in*: College* English 46, 1984, 3, S. 248. Compare also the bibliography published by NCTE: Robert Day & Gail C. Weavers *Creative Writing in the Classroom. Annotated Bibliographies* (Urbana, 1978).

16 Compare with von Werder, *Lehrbuch des Kreativen Schreibens*, p. 14.

17 Compare with Rodari, *The Grammar of Fantasy*, p. 204.

18 The goal should be the advancement of the so-called writing fever. Dick Ross from the National Film and Television School of England places so much emphasis on storytelling that his classes resemble a storytelling round.

19 von Werder, *Lehrbuch des kreativen Schreibens*, p. 16.

20 ibid. p. 24.

21 "We constantly are learning how to do things right. We know that one plus one is two, but with creative thinking, it may be eleven. Perhaps it constitutes a pair. We need to learn to see things from different angles and free up our heads, try out things that no one has tried before." From the lecture notes of Frank Daniel.

22 The playwright and director Keith Johnstone, who has written two important books, *Impro* and *Impro for Storytellers,* has incorporated the exercises and techniques of the Writers' Group of the Londoner Royal Court Theatre and developed them further in the Actors' Studio, while he created a theater group, which is known as The Theatre Machine, based on this philosophy.

23 Keith Johnstone, *Impro and the Theatre,* p. 14

24 Rodari, *The Grammar of Fantasy,* p. 199: "The creative function of the discovery ... is of greatest importance for scientific research, as it is for the birth of a work of art. It is, however, at the same time also predominantly an indispensable condition of daily life. And nevertheless, [...] in our schools we treat discovery like a poor relative in comparison to paying attention and to memorizing. Up to this very day, the characteristics of the ideal pupil are the quality of patient listening and meticulous remembering, as though patient listening and memory are the *sine qua non* of the ideal student. This (pupil) is admittedly the most comfortable, the one who is easiest for a teacher to manage."

25 The "mutual enlightenment of the arts" is a concept that the literary critic Oskar Walzel introduced in 1917. In the following century, it was a fixture as a concept in numerous research programs of comparative literature.

26 The concept was introduced in 1936 by Kurt Wais.

27 Striving for the *Gesamtkunstwerk,* in which all existing arts are interconnected, was, for instance, the great artistic idea of Richard Wagner.

28 An old wisdom recommends beginning a scene as late as possible and ending it as soon as possible.

29 Invited by Hans Werner Richter between 1947 and 1967, the participants in the German language Writer's Meeting were given the name Group 47. In 2005, Günter Grass founded a new writer's group that emulated the Group 47 model (this group used the working title, the "Lübeck 05"). At their first public reading, however, they distanced themselves from the re-establishment of Group 47 in its old form.

30 Iakov, Ζητήματα Λογοτεχνικής Θεωρίας οτην Ποιητική του Αριστοτέλη, p. 30.

31 The method of Lee Strasberg, well-known as "The Method," was developed in the 1930s and 1940s, after he had studied Stanislawski's method with Maria Uspenskaja in the American Laboratory Theatre. The Actors' Studio, in which actors are trained according to the method by Strasberg, and that he led himself from 1951 to 1982, was founded by Cheryl Crawford, Elia Kazan and Robert Lewis in 1947. His influence on the study of acting and indirectly on cinema narration is beyond doubt.

32 Not unimportant here is also the work of David Mamet and William H. Macy, and what they came to call "Practical Aesthetics", which is based on the practice of analyzing the scene in: (1) its substance, that is, the basic description of what is happening; (2) the wish, that is, the description of what the character wants in the concrete scene but also of what possibly stops him from getting it; and (3) the action, which may be transcribed into a simple active phrase.

33 Szlezák, *Reading Plato*, p. 120.

34 Strasberg, *Acting and the Training of the Actor*, p. 26. The following exercise of Strasberg demonstrates the fact that tension is badly guided energy that hampers thinking and probing. Try to lift a heavy object, he urges us – a table, a piano, something especially heavy you can lift. At the same time, try to solve a simple mathematics problem: Multiply 162 by 5. You will see that it is absolutely impossible to solve a mental problem while the physical tension persists.

35 William Goldman has already carried out this experiment in his book, *Which Lie Did I Tell?*

36 An indirect result of the dialectic encounter with a text is communication instruction during script development. A goal of the game of aporia is to find ways that facilitate the creative encounter for the screenwriter. The role of the dialogue moderator, provided the dialectic meeting takes place within the group, is to intervene and correct where necessary – a role the creative producer may need to fill in practice and one the students learn to play in time.

37 The pre-credit sequence is the sequence that is shown before the credits and as a rule tells the backstory.

38 Compare Rodari, *The Grammar of Fantasy*, p. 33.

39 Schiller, *Über die ästhetische Erziehung des Menschen* (2000).

Pre-Credit Sequence: Theoretical Roots of Creative Screenwriting

1 The theory of drama was investigated by philosophers and (beginning of the nineteenth century) by literary critics in the context of literary theory. On the critical side of literary theory are theater reviews as well as literary ones for which language plays a rather secondary role, as in a screenplay. Theater Arts is a younger field of study than Literature Arts and has had institutional academic autonomy only since the nineteenth century – first in the USA and France, followed by Germany. Theater Arts continue to be dependent on the abundant theoretical results from the above-mentioned fields of study. This is naturally even more the case with the even younger field of film (and television) studies.

2 For a highly detailed and well-founded analysis of the principle terms in Aristotle's *Poetics* as well as their characteristics concerning the acceptance and the effectiveness of a literary work, especially in the tragedy and the epos, I can highly recommend the following book, unfortunately only to readers of the Greek language: Ζητήματα Λογοτεχνικής Θεωρίας στην Ποιητική του Αριστοτέλη by Daniel I. Iakov. Only parts of the important work by the Greek literature critic and professor of ancient Greek philology at the Aristotle University of Thessaloniki have been translated into German or indeed English. Also of interest is, for instance, *Die Einheit der Zeit in der antiken griechischen Tragödie: die aristotelischen Auffassungen* by Iakov, in Hans-Christian Günther and Antonios Rengako's (eds), *Beiträge zur antiken Philosophie: Festschrift für Wolfgang Kullmann* (1997), pp. 245–253.

3 Syd Field busied himself predominantly with storytelling cinema. In the history of film, however, there are also schools which regard the narration of stories as a sellout of the cinematic art form to literary and theater forms and thus as opposed to the true nature of this art form. Jean Epstein, for instance, wrote in 1921: "There are no stories. There were never stories. There are only situations [...] without beginning, middle or end." Most observers, however, regard the narrative as the most important and most indispensable element of the cinema medium. Cf. Krakauer, *Theory of Film*, p. 284.

4 A similar analytic model, which, however, was never used for screenplay analysis, is the one by Vladimir Propp, the Soviet ethnologist, who discovered 31 functions in the system of the fairy tale in his *Morphology of the Fairy Tale*, beginning with distancing, proscription and contravention; and ending with the marriage of the protagonists. Cf. also Rodari, *The Grammar of Fantasy*, p. 94.

5 Freytag, *Technique of the Drama*, p. 95.

6 In keeping with the terminology of Linda Seger.

7 Freytag, *Technique of the Drama*, p. 244.

8 Carrière/Bonitzer, *Praxis des Drehbuchschreibens*, p. 178.

9 Until 1969, Frank Daniel was the Dean of the famous film school FAMU in Prague, his hometown. He then came to America where he was appointed Director of the Center for Advanced Film Studies at the American Film Institute; beginning in 1978 Dean of the Columbia University Film Division together with Milos Forman. He left Columbia in 1986 for USC. His students included Milos Forman, Ivan Passer, Jiri Menzel, David Lynch, Terence Malick, Matthew Robbins, Jeremy Kagan, Tom Rickman, Paul Schrader, Martin Brest, Matthew Weisman, Jeff Loeb, Marion Hänsel, Dominique Deruddere and Jaco van Dormael among others.

10 The "script consultant" is someone who advises the screenwriter, while the "story editors," "script editors" and "script doctors" as their titles indicate, "fiddle around" directly with the screenplay.

11 Dagmar Benke used to teach at the Binger Filmlab in Amsterdam, *et al*. She studied with Linda Seger.

12 When I speak of epic dimensions, I mean the term "epic" as used by Brecht and not as used in Hollywood. Homer's stories are epics. *The Birth of a Nation* by D W. Griffith, Thomas F. Dixon, Jr. and Fran E. Woods, *Ben Hur* by William Wyler and Karl Tunberg (and Gore Vidal, who did not receive a credit in the titles), *2001: A Space Odyssey* by Stanley Kubrick and Arthur C. Clarke, *Kings of the Road* by Wim Wenders, and *Taste of the Cherry* by Abbas Kiarostami are epic films. *Night on Earth* by Jim Jarmusch; *Before the Rain* by Milcho Manchevski and *Lola Rennt* by Tom Tykwer are not epic films. They could be considered episodic films, but we will use the term alternative narratives, which indeed includes a wide range of film narration.

13 Carrière, *Über das Geschichtenerzählen*, p. 204.

14 Cf. Iakov, Ζητήματα Λογοτεχνικής Θεωρίας, pp. 31, 42, where the author points out that the community of parts, which Aristotle establishes at the end of the fifth chapter of the *Poetics,* as well as the theory of the philosopher about the direct origin of two literary genres in the fourth chapter, shows that there can be no differentiation between epos and tragedy even if the philosopher sees the two literary genres as autonomous units, and also sees tragedy as a more mature form than epos, and ranks tragedy higher than epos. Aristotle himself ascertained, "What is available in the epic is also present in tragedy, but what is available in tragedy is greater than what is present in the epic" (*Poetics* 1449b–1450a). Although the philosopher categorically rejects episodic plotting (*Poetics* 1451b, 33), it is certainly wrong to term alternative narratives "epic" or "non-Aristotelian." Interestingly enough, Plato viewed Homer as the father of tragedy (*Politeia* 598d–599), which means he also did not differentiate between tragedy and epos.

15 Thomas Elsaesser and Warren Buckland are among those who use the concept "post-classical" – whereby they make clear that the concept may be understood as opposite to "classical" or as "exaggerated classical"; and that every post-classical film can finally be analyzed both as post-classical and as classical. Cf. Elsaesser/Buckland, Studying *Contemporary American Film*, pp. 26–79.

16 The Hungarian theater playwright and director Lajos Egri, founder of the Egri School of Writing in New York, may have written the classic book *The Art of Dramatic Writing* as early as 1942, but he is still inspiring screenwriters who have made his terminology their own, above all the idea of the premise (a thesis demonstrated in terms of human behavior) and naturally his assertion that good dramatic writing must be supported by understanding human motivations.

17 The introduction by John Freeman in the volume Carl Gustav Jung, *Der Mensch und seine Symbole*, p. 13.

18 Concerning the influence of art on the collective unconscious and vice versa, see especially the complete works of the student and biographer of Jung, Aniela Jaffé.

19 Adorno, *Ästhetische Theorie*, p. 21 *et seq.*

20 Damasio, *The Feeling of What Happens*, p. 189.

21 Dennett, *Consciousness Explained*, p. 418.

22 Lodge, *Consciousness and the Novel*, p. 15.

23 In the meantime, emotional psychology has developed into an independent scientific discipline, while after 1995 in the particularly important writings *Descartes' Error* by Antonio Damasio, *Emotional Brain* by Joseph Ledoux and with the model SPAARS that Mick Power and Tim Dalgleish presented in their book *Cognition and Emotion: From Order to Disorder*, the position that reason and emotion are not conflicting sides is upheld – a realization that is also shared in the analytic philosophy of Ronald De Sousa in his book *The Rationality of Emotion*.

24 Of interest in this context is the international symposium "Cinema and Emotion", which took place in July 2002 in Monte Verità, Ascona, as well as the lecture series "Film and Emotion" at the University of Zurich in the 2002 summer semester. The lectures of these two academic meetings may be found in the anthology of Brütsch *et al.*, *Kinogefühle. Emotionalität und Film*.

25 Bordwell, *Narration in the Fiction Film*, p. 39 *et seq.*

26 For a theoretical film analysis according to Lacan, see chapter "Oedipal Narratives and the post-Oedipal (Back to the Future)" from the book *Studying Contemporary American Film* by Thomas Elsaesser and Warren Buckland, pp. 220–248.

27 Elsaesser, *Zu spät, zu früh*, in Brütsch *et al.*, *Kinogefühle*, p. 416.

28 Tröhler/Hediger, *Ohne Gefühl ist das Auge der Vernunft blind*, in Brütsch *et al.*, *Kinogefühle*, p. 10.

29 Pascal Bonitzer, Francis Vanoye, Serge Daney, Raymond Bellour and Laura Marks belong to this school.

30 In recent years, numerous reception theories and studies have appeared that treated, in particular, audience reactions to cinematic characters and events in feature films. Dolf Zillmann, Alex Neill, Torben Grodal, Carl Platinga and Hans J. Wulff deserve mention alongside Noel Carroll, Murray Smith and Ed Tan. They all examine different aspects of the complex processes of sympathy and antipathy, participation, perspective assumption, feeling infection, autonomous affect development, affective and somatic empathy, which register during a visit to the cinema. Christine N. Brinckmann, most notably, analyzed the role of empathy in documentary films, among other things, in Brütsch *et al.*, Kinogefühle, pp. 333–360.

31 Foucault, *Dits et écrits*, pp. 243–250, quoted in Bellour, *Das Entfalten der Emotionen*, in Brütsch *et al.*, *Kinogefühl*, p. 63. Bellour dares an additional interesting definition, "Emotion is that crease that fixes the impression

received from the sense organs in the soul in the perceptive gap between the unconscious and the conscious."

32 A relatively new direction, which in recent years has resulted in some interesting films in German and Scandinavian cinema, is, for example, a further development of the writing method of Mike Leigh, a method that presupposes a tight and early-on co-operation between the screenwriter and the actors and which involves both the conscious and unconscious minds.

33 The theater, however, had experienced the "de-dramatizing of myths" at the end of the nineteenth century. Ibsen, Strindberg and, above all, Chekhov offered resistance to the rules of classical drama by being more interested in the internal conflicts of the characters, which does not lead necessarily to classic dramatic results. The narrative renewal of the theater, which also influenced American dramatists from Eugene O'Neill and Thornton Wilder to Tennessee Williams and Arthur Miller, did not have, however, a parallel in screenwriting, which mostly trod a very well beaten path. Cf. Rabenalt, *Filmdramaturgie*, p. 104.

34 Haar, *L'oeuvre d'art*, p. 88.

35 Szlezák, *Reading Plato*, pp. 19, 21. "We are, as humans living in a democratic, pluralistic and anti-authoritarian twenthieth century – whether we know it or not – emotionally so attuned to the ruling ideas of relativism that we confront a decisively superior Socrates or Athenian who dares to call an orientation he represents the only correct one, with skepticism or internal resistance and perceive his game of perplexity as lacking openness, and his allusion to insights that may be gained in the future as avoidance. Instead, we should ask ourselves if Plato does not want to communicate something special with such conceptions of characters or wants to convey to us something no longer immediately understandable, and perhaps whether he repudiates a philosophical concept that substantially deviates from the convictions of the twentieth century, yet for that very reason is able to supplement and enrich it."

36 The new interest in the literary form and dramatic value of Plato's dialogues has led the interpretation of the Platonic texts to new places, especially since it has opened a discourse with the fruitful approach comparative literature offers.

37 Szlezák, *Reading Plato*, p. 19 *et segg*. We owe the insight that the *Infinitismus* of the German Romantic Period really does not correspond to the Platonic understanding of philosophy, to the systematic and historical works of Hans Kreimer and Karl Albert. By *Infinitismus,* they meant the conception that thought for Platonic philosophy was a journey without end, an unending search and effort that never reaches a final goal, that the philosopher does not have anything to show, that he is there to question; so the philosophical truth is always a truth that comes with no guarantee. According to Kreimer and Albert, this conception is wrong. To Plato, humans cannot attain ultimate knowledge, but they can become knowledgeable and

remain that for a limited time. Therefore, Eros embodies the substance of philosophy; Eros conquers that for which it strives; but what it has conquered it loses again afterwards.

38 Iakov, Ζητήματα Λογοτεχνικής Θεωρίας, p. 18.

39 Ibid. p. 17. Based on Platonic philosophy, which deals with ideas, art is on the ontological level "τρίτον από της αληθείας," (*Politeia* 597e 6–8), that is, three times removed from the truth.

40 Cf. Popper, *Die offene Gesellschaft und ihre Feinde*. Popper refers in particular to chapter 10 of the *Politeia* of Plato and concretely to 599A, as well as 595B, where Plato seems to explain that poetry destroys the soul of humans and therefore the poet should be banished from the ideal society. Plato's opinions, which question the value of the art for society, in part are even seen as the beginnings of censorship. Still, in that context, one needs to mention other texts of Plato, such as *Ion* or *Phaidros*, in which he refers to the creative process in a less regimented way than Aristotle does. Plato knows the creative procedure all too well – he was supposedly an unsuccessful dramatist in his youth, which could be the actual reason of his vehement rejection of drama. One also says this about Brecht, the modern skeptic and opponent of Aristotle, who himself was an unsuccessful screenwriter and was therefore supposedly opposed to classical dramaturgy. Naturally, both anecdotes are to be savored with a large dollop of caution.

41 Iakov, Ζητήματα Λογοτεχνικής Θεωρίας, p. 18

42 Ibid. Aristotle extends the sphere of activity of mimesis beyond the immediate world of the senses but does not engender a new metaphysic. For him the kind or the form does not differ by any means from the underlying matter of the sense world: It exists simultaneously with it.

43 Szlezák, *Reading Plato*, p. 132. The reader must view this much-negotiated question against the background of whether in reading Plato the myth is subordinate to the logos or whether it conveys a higher truth that the logos cannot attain, explains Szlezák, as he subsequently points out that the acceptance of the latter goes back to the sensibility of modern irrational currents and cannot rest on Plato's deliberations; while at the same time the subordination of the myth to logos cannot be accepted if that implies that the fable is a more or less expendable ornament.

44 Ibid. p. 77 ff. The dialectic art and/or the support for the logos in the Platonic dialogues is to a certain extent the basis for screenplay analysis using the creative screenwriting method and specifically the game of aporia; the logos is exposed to an attack, and its author must assist him, i.e. support him, so that the logos may achieve more objective power. To that end, the author needs to confront the criticism and argue with the critics.

45 The examples are endless, as in the film *Elephant*, written and directed by Gus van Sant, who impassively tells the story of a bloody attack by two students on their school ground. In being non-judgmental, the filmmaker

was accused of putting dangerous ideas in the minds of potential assassins in the audience.

46 Iakov, Ζητήματα Λογοτεχνικής Θεωρίας, p. 88.

47 Ibid. p. 127 ff; Cf. Haar, *L'oeuvre d'art*, p. 37 ff. As the researcher notices, the romantics Schopenhauer, Schelling, Novalis and Hegel who continued the argument hypothesized that art equals truth (e.g. according to Hegel art can attain absolute truth, but it can only be understood through a direct form of intuition or emotion), and this in turn was continued in Nietzsche's Subjectivism and ends in Heideggerian thought. For Heidegger, the artist obeys a truth that he does not create himself and that has an inherent tendency that leads to an artistic work, i.e. to an embodiment or to an establishment. The old Platonic contradiction between art and truth found no end in the writings of Merleau Ponty, but was resolved in the idea of complicity. "The landscape," said Cézanne, "is a thinking object in me, and I am its consciousness."

48 Plato's attack on dramatic poetry in the fourth century BC can be compared with contemporary criticism of television and other mass media. Alexander Nehamas, professor of philosophy at Princeton University, made this remark in his Greek text *Culture, Art and Poetry in the Politeia of Plato: Why Plato did not banish the Artists*, pp.15–28. For Nehamas "from this point of view ... most of us are still Platonists." He regards the attack of Plato on Homer as worrisome, because he sees in it the characteristics that constituted every attack made against popular culture and entertainment since Plato's time. He was and still is the first attacker. The tragic irony, however, is that those who repeat his attacks do so in the name of good taste, of cultivation and of the refinement of morals without ever realizing they are following him. In summary, Nehamas states that in the rule the low art of a given era will be the high art of the next era.

49 Iakov, Ζητήματα Λογοτεχνικής Θεωρίας, p. 34. According to Iakov, the most extensive current argument on the scientifically controversial theme of catharsis is the analysis of Belfiore, *Tragic Pleasures: Aristotle on Plot and Emotion*, while he also recommends the dissertation by White, *A Sourcebook on the Catharsis Controversy* for an overview of the various theories.

50 Ibid. p. 35.

51 For a very different viewpoint of the same thematic complex, see the chapter concerning the poets' solution and the analysis of *Before the Rain*.

52 Here, however, there is an important difference to the tragedies of antiquity, in which an external, often incomprehensible fate influences the hero while oracles affect their decisions, random accidents cause their death, and sins of the parents determine the fate of their offspring, while gods appear as allies and enemies and change the outcome. Cf. Freytag, *Technique of the Drama*, pp. 76, 214.

53 "Διαφέρει γαρ πολύ το γίγνεσθαι τάδε ή μετά τάδε" (1452a 20–1 και 1454a 33 κ.ε.). Cf. Daniel I. Iakov: ibid. p. 32 ff.

54 Aristotle, *Poetics* (translator and publisher M. Wagoner, 1451a 30); Cf. also Iakov, Ζητήματα Λογοτεχνικής Θεωρίας, p. 22. The terms "closed form drama" and "open form drama" stem from Klotz, *Geschlossene und offene Form im Drama*, and refer ultimately to Woelfflin. The unit of plot is the only unit Aristotle expressly esteems and emphasizes. The other two units of place and time are inventions of Renaissance literary criticism.

55 This is in reference to the classical work of Schleiermacher, *Platons Werke.*

56 Szlezák, *Reading Plato*, p. 117 ff.

57 Ibid. p. 22: "This motive is strange to us, because in Europe the postulate of unrestrained publicity of the results from philosophical and scientific work has been accepted for a long time now and as a consequence nobody would even think of the possibility of deliberately holding back a result worthy of mention." Yet, in Plato's view, to convey something to someone for which he is not suited or sufficiently prepared is meaningless – hence the concept "απρόρρητα" (aprorrheta), which means "things that cannot be conveyed ahead of time," because if conveyed ahead of time (before the recipient is ready for them) they make nothing clear (Nomoi 968e, 4–5)

58 The concept of "premise" is, as stated previously, an essential element in the dramaturgical theory of Lajos Egri.

59 Szlezák, *Reading Plato*, pp. 82, 85. A logos is formulated ("the soul is immortal," "justice is better than injustice"), first arguments are declaimed, and then "the father of the thesis" is subjected to a "test," i.e. he is invited to revisit his logos by use of feedback to indicate his fundamental principles – through use of a procedure Plato calls "βοηθείν τω λόγω." The term βοηθείν τω λόγω designates the structural principle of the Platonic dialogue, explains Szlezák, which consists of a targeted higher displacement of the rational level towards a final argument or proof from the αρχή (principle). The discussion continually leads to more questions that are fundamental and in so doing intensifies the dramaturgical tension of the argumentation.

60 Szlezák, *Reading Plato*, p. 152. Szlezák determines that this opinion was shared by many younger researchers, but in the rule, however, was restricted to a conclusion that did not have any consequences for the interpretation.

61 Haar, *L'oeuvre d'art*, p. 13. Philosophers have raised the question of the proper place of art on the scale of human knowledge throughout the entire history of philosophy. As the writer ascertains, there are two reasons that have accelerated the spiritual search for the essence of art, i.e. the formation of an authentic philosophy of independent art. First, the distrust spread by Plato, independently of how much Aristotle may have tried to disqualify it, created a cleft between philosophy and art. In addition, a contradiction between the two appeared that has proven extremely durable. The introduction of the aesthetic provided the second reason.

62 Homer also inseparably links pleasure and knowledge. In the *Odysseia,* the sirens announce to the heroes that all who hear their song will return to their homeland, happy and all-knowing (Ραψωδία μ 188).

63 534b; also Cf. *Apologia Sokratous* 22b, *Phaidros* 245a.

64 Haar, *L'oeuvre d'art*, p. 89. E.g., Paul Valéry determined, by describing his own creative history that the poet does not follow what he wants to say, but that he transforms a certain rhythmic inspiration into words. This rhythm controls the artist like a "mood."

65 Iakov, Ζητήματα Λογοτεχνικής Θεωρίας, p. 69.

66 Ibid. pp. 76–79. This corresponds to the statements in chapter 9 as well, as other text excerpts from Aristotle's *Poetics*, where familiar pleasure is mentioned as the highest goal of tragedy.

67 "From this view, the art of poetry is a thing of those with the gift of fantasy or with a passionate nature; one being capable of change, the other passionately inspired." (*Poetics* 1455a, 32) From these two types, the first has a creative fantasy and can create heroes, while the second succumbs to ecstasy. Cf. Daniel I. Iakov: Ibid, p. 30. Aristotle scholars agree that Aristotle prefers the technical theory of reasonable poetic invention and yet cannot quite ignore the theory of inspiration and the irrational art of poetry associated with it, since enthusiasm has a real basis. Cf. Koster, *Antike Epostheorien*, p. 79 ff. Even though contradictory in part, this points with greater probability to a natural rather than a metaphysical origin for the art of poetry.

68 von Werder, *Lehrbuch des kreativen Schreibens*, p. 51 ff.; also Cf. Iakov, Ζητήματα Λογοτεχνικής Θεωρίας, p. 31, and Moraitou, *Aristoteles über Dichter und Dichtung*, 83 ff. Moraitou discovers that the reduction of the art of poetry to the intelligent is the personal contribution of the philosopher Plato, and that – in the case of the acknowledgement of the godly nature of the art of poetry – Aristotle admitted, at least in part, that the roll of human physiology is important (gall secretion). As Iakov stresses, the following assumption of Moraitou is not very likely (but in his opinion worth mentioning). The intelligent is brought in connection with tragedy, the manic with epos and the lyric, primarily because Aristotle's text does not permit differences between epos and tragedy.

69 Haar, *L'oeuvre d'art*, p. 58. Nietzsche also shared the Platonic position in his two succeeding treaties about the aesthetic in the *Genesis of Tragedy* (1872), as well as in monographs composed during the 1880s, by maintaining that the artist must transcend himself to create.

70 Von Werder, *Lehrbuch des kreativen Schreibens*, p. 54. On the one hand is Edgar Allan Poe's *Philosophy of Composition*, 1846, in which he compared writing with the exactitude of mathematical formulas – and admits to belonging to the Aristotelian school, which also shaped writers such as Thomas Mann, Robert Musil, Hermann Borch and Gottfried Benn – and on the other side, Arthur Rimbaud, who in his *Letters of the Visionary* of 1873

revived the mythological and Platonic image of the ecstatic poet and opened the way for the expressionists and surrealists of the twentieth century.

71 The birthing method is meant to encourage further thought and to permit self-discovery of an answer to the apparent question; a technique also used in psychotherapy and mathematics (Cf. Grothendieck), since all mathematicians think of themselves in the school of Plato and share his view that mathematical truth pre-exists.

72 Haar, *L'oeuvre d'art*, p. 52 ff.

The Beginning: The Trick of Creative Screenwriting

1 Rodari, *The Grammar of Fantasy*, p. 204.

2 In some strange way, we all seem to know what is original, just as filmmakers seem to know what avant-garde is. Cf. Johnstone, *Improvisation and the Theatre*, p. 87.

3 Ibid. p. 10.

4 I am using the construct "story owner" rather than the original "inventor" here for the following reason. In the first version of the exercise, I maintained that the groups in question would invent the stories themselves. The result was unsatisfying. The storytellers incorporated or took into account their biases against the inventor and the story that he would most likely think up or told most of the time. Therefore, their inclinations caused them to be tangled up instead of liberated. To avoid this, I maintained that the story of the inventor would be given to them, which liberated the storytellers immediately, while they had more respect for what they had to discover. The stories instantly improved dramatically.

5 Aristotle, *Poetics* 18/1450b.

6 So or so, the dramatic types of situations are limited. "Gozzi was of the opinion that there are no more than 36 tragic situations. Schiller tried to discover more, but he was unable to describe as many as Gozzi," mentions Goethe in *Gespraeche mit Eckermann.* At the end of the nineteenth century, Georges Polti wrote in his book *The 36 Dramatic Situations*: XXII. Situations – Sacrifice everything to erotic passion. XXIII. Situation – To have to sacrifice your own people. XXIV. Situation – Crimes of love, and so on. In the last chapter, the writer described nine different types of crimes of passion.

7 It is remarkable that alternative forms of narration are very rarely the result of this exercise.

8 Aristotle, *Poetics* 50a, 1 ff.

9 Ibid. 1450b 8–10.

10 Iakov, Ζητήματα Λογοτεχνικής Θεωρίας, p. 43.

11 Aristotle, *Poetics* 6, 50a, 15. Here and in general, Aristotle continues his argument with Plato by stressing that action is the framework of human

existence, because above all, life is activity. Aristotle believes that action is the highest form of expression of human existence, because the goal of life is not being, rather doing (50a, 17). Aristotle reacts to what Plato says when he posits that the person who does something cannot be alienated from his ego and that in acting he shows the unreasonable aspect of his soul.

12 Aristotle, *Poetics* 1450a–1450b.

13 Freytag, *Technique of the Drama*, p. 76.

14 Ibid. p. 238.

15 Ibid. p. 239. Nevertheless, even there one of the protagonists has a more important significance than the other one does. In *Romeo and Juliet*, for example, Romeo dominates the first half of the play, while the second half concentrates on Juliet. We see this idiosyncrasy of the two protagonists in the cinema too, i.e. in the screwball comedy genre.

16 Plato, too, had a thought-out field of characters based on underlying conflicts.

17 A construct Frank Daniel always enjoyed using, like "the need."

18 Keith Cunningham, *Myths, Dreams and Motives*, article in *The Quest*, spring 1992, p. 36.

19 Dogma was signed by a group of filmmakers in 1995 – led by Lars von Trier and Thomas Vinterberg.

20 Paul Schrader was a student of Frank Daniel.

21 www.awesomefilm.com/script/taxidriver.html

22 Ibid.

23 Keith Cunningham, *Myths, Dreams and Motives*, article in *The Quest*, spring 1992, pp. 30–40.

24 Ibid. p. 35.

25 Compare Freytag, *Technique of the Drama*, p. 17.

26 Ibid. p. 22.

27 Johnstone, *Impro and the Theatre*, p. 41.

28 Johnstone, *Improvisation for Storytellers*, p. 219.

29 Cf. the stand-up comedy genre and such celebrity comics as Woody Allen, Jacques Tati, Charlie Chaplin and so on.

30 Johnstone, *Impro*, p. 138. Frank Daniel also employed the technique of interrupting a routine to begin the story.

31 Aristotle names Aeschylus as the father of tragedy in his *Poetics*, since he increased the number of actors to two and diminished the importance of the choir by making the dialogue of the protagonist the main part of the tragedy (4, 49a, 17).

32 Egri, *The Art of Dramatic Writing*, p. 178.

33 Wuss, *Konflikt und Emotion im Filmleben*, in Brütsch *et al.*, *Kinogefühle*, p. 205.

34 Ibid. p. 213.

35 Hegel, *Ästhetik*, p. 203.

36 Related to conflict as a structural element are the dramaturgical constructs "foreshadowing conflict" and "momentum," which we will discuss elsewhere.

37 The American comedy writer, John Vorhaus, acknowledges three types of comedic conflict: global conflict, local or interpersonal conflict and subjective conflict. Cf. Vorhaus, *The Comic Toolbox*, p. 40.

38 Rodari, *The Grammar of Fantasy*, p. 29.

39 Vallon, *Die Herkunft der Gedanken beim Kind*, p. 20.

40 Freud, *Der Witz und seine Beziehung zum Unbewussten*, p. 155.

41 Federman, *Surfiction: Der Weg der Literatur*, p. 15.

42 Johnstone, *Improvisation and the Theatre*, p. 77.

43 Compare Vorhaus, *The Comic Toolbox*, p. 10.

44 That is nearly impossible – for another reason: Those who try to write something commercial, strictly speaking, write what has proven commercial but which with certainty will not be commercial by the time the film that has been based on the commercial script is finished.

45 Anna Hamilton Phelan is the screenwriter of *Mask, Gorillas in the Mist* and *Girl, Interrupted*. Cf. Froug, *The New Screenwriter looks at the New Screenwriter*, p. 35.

46 Frank Daniel developed a list of questions, which he called a "character questionnaire." Some interesting questions appear, "What does he think about his father? What does he hate and like about him? His brothers, sisters? What does he despise about them? Was he overprotected, did he feel rejection or affection as a child? What does he do for a living? How does he view his profession?" etc. Many screenwriters, on the other hand, write a character biography in order to become better acquainted with their characters.

47 Kappelhoff, *Tränenseligkeit*, in Brütsch, *et al., Kinogefühle*, p. 36. The motion picture theoretician points out that what one attributes to the identification and projection of characters proves to be a complex aesthetic-semiotic activity when viewed more closely.

48 Egri, *The Art of Dramatic Writing*, p. 234f.

49 Seger, *Making a Good Script Great*, p. 21.

50 Vogler, *The Writer's Journey*, p. 101.

51 Aristotle, *Poetics* 7/1450β.

52 Seger, *Making a Good Script Great*, p. 25.

53 Ibid. p. 25.

54 Ibid. p. 27.

55 From the poem Munich Mannequins, in Sylvia Plath's *Collected Poems*, Faber and Faber, 1981.

The Middle: Techniques of Creative Screenwriting

1 Eick, *Drehbuchtheorien*, p. 129.

2 Guillermo Arriaga, the Mexican screenwriter, e.g. of *21 Grams, Amore Perros*, gladly calls himself a novelist for the screen and stresses that there

are no arbitrary words in his screenplays and that he polishes the language of a screenplay the same as in a novel.

3 Carrière/Bonitzer, *Praxis des Drehbuchschreibens*, p. 87.

4 Rodari, *Grammatik der Phantasie*, p. 31.

5 Freytag, *Die Technik des Dramas*, p. 95.

6 Vogler, *The Writer's Journey*, p. 22.

7 Rico, *Writing the Natural Way*, p. 3. For the exercise about the two brain hemispheres working together, see the exercise in the volumn *Left brain/Right brain* by Robert Masters Masters and *Multitracking* by Jean Houston from his book *The Possible Human*, p. 63, 72.

8 Rico, *Writing the Natural Way*, p. 14–39.

9 Mindmapping was invented by the mental trainer Tony Buzan in the 1960s. He became well-known for his concept of mindmapping and the introduction of its methodical application. See Buzan, *Creative Intelligence*, p. 29.

10 Friedrich Schiller (1759–1805) tried to do justice to both types of writing poetry, the rational and the emotional, in his seminal work of the theoretical literary scholarly paper *Über naive und sentimentalische Dichtung*.

11 Johnstone, *Improvisation and the Theatre*, p. 121.

12 Rodari: *Grammatik der Phantasie*, p. 82.

13 The story is based on the short story, *Erfindung einer Sprache*, in: Kohlhaase, *Silvester mit Balzac*.

14 Aristotle, *Poetics* 18/1455b.

15 Freytag, *Die Technik des Dramas*, p. 95.

16 Aristotle, *Poetica* 7/1450b.

17 Vogler, *The Writer's Journey*, p. 185.

18 Carrière/Bonitzer, *Die Praxis des Drehbuchschreibens*, p. 116.

19 Johnstone, *Improvisation and the Theatre*, p. 32.

20 Miramax's marketing campaign was built around the surprising plot twist at the end and it was one of the first movies where journalists and critcs were asked not to reveal the secret of the plot twist, something that became common practice in the years to come.

21 W.B. Stanford, *Greek Tragedy and the Emotions*, p. 24.

22 The focus group screenings that test the reactions of the audience, especially in Hollywood. The results are recorded and used to recut or market the film.

23 Dyer, *Film, Musik und Gefühl – Ironische Anbindung*, in Brütsch, *et al.*, *Kinogefühle*, p. 129.

24 Larry Sider, Head of Post-Production in the English National Film and Television School uses sound in a similar way at the international Symposium School of Sound, which he directs (www.schoolofsound.co.uk).

25 The exercise is based on a John Vorhues exercise.

26 Rothenberg, *The Emerging Goddess*, p. 55.

27 This exercise is a slightly altered version of an exercise in the book by Linda Seger called *Making a Good Writer Great*, p. 155

28 Chandler, *Ich, Fellini*, p. 181 f.

29 Rabenalt, *Filmdramaturgie*, p. 195.

30 The original is the film *Scarlet Street* from the novel and play by Georges de La Fouchardiere and Andre Mauezy-Eon, adapted by Dudley Nichols and directed by Fritz Lang, in which Edward G. Robinson becomes a criminal, is blackmailed and hunted, only to ... wake up.

31 In ten years of working with this technique, I have not experienced a single case where it did not work, even if it sometimes required an entire week.

32 Bunuel, *Mein letzter Seufzer*, p. 139.

33 This dialogue allegedly took place at a party in Paris with Jean Paul Belmondo, but even in Jean-Luc Godard's *Pierrot Le Fou* Fuller, who was playing himself, says, "Cinema is emotion." The film critic Ed Tan comes to the same conclusion in his book, "Emotion and the Structure of Narrative Film", which be ends by saying that in this sense, and more than anything else, the traditional feature film is a genuine emotion machine. (p. 251)

34 Carrière/Bonitzer, *Praxis des Drehbuchschreibens*, p. 88.

35 Ibid. p. 85.

36 Bresson, *Notes on Cinematography*, p. 37.

37 Schneider, *Ein folkloristisches Straßentheater*, in Brütsch *et al.*, *Kinogefühle*, p. 144.

38 Tan, *Gesichtsausdruck und Emotion in Comic und Film*, in Brütsch *et al.*, *Kinogefühle*, p. 266.

39 In his book *La Psychologie des sentiments* (1896) and in *Problèmes de psychologie affective* (1910).

40 Freytag, *Technique of the Drama*, p. 73.

41 Hitchcock, for example, was afraid of birds in an almost paranoid way. This phobia is mirrored in the lead character in his film *The Birds*, adapted by Evan Hunter from the novel of the same name by Daphne du Maurier.

42 As quoted by Carrière/Bonitzer, *Praxis des Drehbuchschreibens*, p. 239.

43 In his 1992 book "The Psychoanalytic Theory of Greek Tragedy", Fred C. Alford shows how the complex tragedies of the Greek poets can illuminate, and be illuminated by the psychoanalytic ideas of Klein, Lacan, Freud and others.

44 See also Alford, "Greek Tragedy and Civilization: The Cultivation of Pity", in *Political Research Quarterly*, Vol. 46, No. 2 (June 1993), pp. 259–280.

45 Ibid. p. 262.

46 See *Saving the Story* (the film version), by Michael Cieply, *NY Times*, Nov 17, 2008.

47 W.B. Stanford, *Greek Tragedy and the Emotions*, p. 24.

48 Alford, *Greek Tragedy and Civilization: The Cultivation of Pity*, p. 273.

49 As in the *Iliad* (19.302), where the captive women in Achilles' tent join in the lamentations over the body of Patroclos and Homer comments, "It was a pretext, for each was bewailing her own personal sorrows."

50 Compare with Alford, *Greek Tragedy and Civilization: The Cultivation of Pity*, p. 274.

51 Again, education, intelligence, *paideia*, etc. do not mean the same today as in the past. They have nothing to do with IQ; they refer to a combination of cognitive and emotional intelligence and to those who think and feel at the same time. It is through thinking and feeling at the same time that we can educate and become educated.

52 Haar, *L'oeuvre d'art*, p. 39. Haar refers in turn to Schelling's *Système de l'idéalisme transcendental*, p. 255.

53 Aristotle, *Poetics* 1451b, 5.

54 Iakov, *Angelegenheiten Literarischer Theorie*, p. 20. "The philosopher defined what he meant by "the common" more precisely in chapter 16 where he defined the main plot point in Ιφιγένεια εν Ταύροις. In other words, Aristotle pointed out what Propp later called "functions" in Russian fairy tales.

55 Ibid. p. 66. For this reason, Aristotle concluded that poetry is something more philosophical and more serious than chronicling history.

56 In the attempt to counter the dominance of the American cinema at the economic level, Europeans have employed the co-production to solve this problem, which has led to the concept of the "Europudding", i.e. a concept that is a pejorative for national waste. Cf. Kallas, *Europäische Koproduktionen im Film und Fernsehen.*

57 Perhaps the term "cosmopolitism," that the Munich sociologist and university professor Ulrich Beck rediscovered in his book, *Power in the Global Age*, is the better concept. In it, Beck describes a "third way" between Huntington and Fukuyama. Cosmopolitism embraces – in contrast to globalism, a linear construct that can only be grasped as an economic process – everything that is excluded by globalization. He challenges us to regard positively the others in the world, especially since the national and international are inextricably interconnected to each other both inside and outside national borders, by disputing every tendency to abolish differences. The concept "cosmopolitism" stems from Greek philosophy and is a word formed by joining cosmos and polis, i.e. on the one hand, we are all a part of humankind and on the other hand, are members of the various nations. In addition, cosmopolitan also means the world is our city.

58 Iakov, *Angelegenheiten Literarischer Theorie*, p. 80. The literary critic tells us that, as Halliwell has accurately determined, the common in this instance represents something that is the fundament of the dramatic text. In this regard, he shares Armstrong's opinion about the subtext. (*Aristotle on the Philosophical Nature of Poetry*, 447–55).

59 Iakov, *Angelegenheiten Literarischer Theorie*, p. 88.

60 Ibid., p. 43.

61 Schneider, *Ein folkloristisches Straßentheater*, in Brütsch, *et al.*, *Kinogefühle*, p. 26.

62 Ibid., p. 27. The film critic concludes from this that it is not the gain in knowledge, rather the game of emotions that is at the heart of the matter.

In doing so, she ignores the information content of the emotional insight that enables poetry.

63 E.g. the film *The Full Monty* is mentioned, whose object is unemployment and whose emotional theme here is self respect. There is no longer a goal and the unemployed's feelings of worthlessness predominate.

64 From class notes taken of lectures by Frank Daniel.

65 Howard/Mabley, *The Tools of Screenwriting*, p. 55.They take two screenplays as examples: *Annie Hall*, written by Woody Allen and Marshall Brickman and *When Harry Meets Sally* written by Nora Ephron. While Harry and Sally succeed in resolving their differences, and fall in love at the end, Annie and Alvy separate. The resolutions of the two stories betray the two different attitudes to the same material.

66 Benke, *Freistil*, p. 43. Perhaps uniquely, Benke is consequent in employing the theme in the narrow sense of the definition or the term.

67 Freytag, *Die Technik des Dramas*, p. 72.

68 Cf., q.v. the film *Magnolia*.

69 In working as a script consultant, Linda Seger has only one taboo: the ending. This means that she never questions the ending. Unfortunately, not everyone applies this ethical principle. Usually, everyone who suggests changes to the script – whether producer, director, editor or dramaturge – tries to impose their own tastes, especially for the denouement.

70 Over the years I have experimented with a wide range of approaches to write a story that originates with a theme. All of them but the one recommended here have not worked, because they became immersed in essays and ideological proclamations of intention.

71 Freytag, *Die Technik des Dramas*, p. 271.

72 Strasberg, *Schauspielen und das Training des Schauspielers*, p. 47.

73 Rabenalt, *Filmdramaturgie*, p. 195.

74 Eick, *Drehbuchtheorien*, p. 111. The genre subject matter in screenwriting literature meets either rejection or misgivings or is rather understood without reflection and pragmatically as a collection of guidelines. In doing so, one forgets all too easily that genre cinema can only succeed if the established and thoroughly repetitive conventions employed are varied continuously by a new narrative process.

75 Wuss, *Filmanalyse und Psychologie*, p. 313–317.

76 Dürrenmatt, *Theaterprobleme*, p. 45.

77 If we analyse the profile of the Oscars from 1965 on, we see that most of the motion pictures that won the Oscar for Best Screenplay, are adaptations of literary works. The majors prefer the adaptation of a literary work of fiction, especially best sellers, for reasons that have to do with an easier and more effective marketing campaign of the resulting motion pictures. Recent examples of this practice are *The Da Vinci Code, The Reader, The Curious Case of Benjamin Button, Slumdog Millionaire*, etc.

78 Kurosawa, *Something like an Autobiography*, p. 193.

79 Linda Seger has taken this as the subject of her best-known book, *The Art of Adaptation*.

80 We ask this question when faced with original ideas. One of the most important pieces of advice that I have received from Frank Daniel is at the same time one of the oldest magic tricks of the scriptwriter, only no one knows who first thought it up. "Write a love letter to your idea. Put the letter in an envelope, close it and hide it in a drawer you do not use very often. When the right moment arrives, when your ideas have stepped out, when your have fallen out of love, when you are stuck and cannot make any headway, open the envelope. The answer to your problem will be in there!"

81 Freytag, *Die Technik des Dramas*, p. 15.

82 Ibid., p. 21.

83 Schepelern, *Film und Dogma*, in volume Dogma 95: *Zwischen Kontrolle und Chaos*, p. 359. In the same text it is mentioned that according to exhaustive research the anonymous man cannot be found, which then leads to many being of the opinion that the story originated in the fantasy of the artist, something Vinterberg personally denied.

84 See the much publicized discussion about the film *Shoah* by Claude Lanzmann.

85 "She was my first love," said Dickens about Little Red Riding Hood. There are many versions of this fairy tale, the most popular being the one by the Brothers Grimm. As is well known, most of the classical fairy tales have very old roots. *Cinderella* stems from the Egypt of the third century AD, but first arrived in China in the ninth century, and after that, the heroine received her European features. The fairy tales of their own people inspired Anderson along with the Brothers Grimm.

86 Rodari, *The Grammar of Fantasy*, p. 87.

87 See especially Bruno Bettelheim's book, *The Uses of Enchantment. The Meaning and Importance of Fairy Tales*.

88 The exercise is a revised version of an exercise from Linda Seger from her *How to Make a Good Writer Great*.

89 Christen, *Happy Endings*, in Brütsch, *et al.*, *Kinogefühle*, p. 191.

90 Rodari, *The Grammar of Fantasy*, p. 29.

91 Vallon, *Die Herkunft der Gedanken beim Kind*, p. 20.

92 Strindberg, *Thêatre Cruel et Thêatre Mystique*, p. 112.

93 Ibid., p. 117.

94 Carrière/Bonitzer, *Praxis des Drehbuchschreibens*, p. 109.

95 Ibid., p. 113.

96 Pütz, *Die Zeit im Drama*, p. 115.

97 Goldman, *Adventures in the Screen Trade*, p. 125.

98 German Title: *Alles Über Eva*.

99 Both are slightly altered versions of exercises from Linda Seger's book, *Making a Good Writer Great*.

100 Freytag, *Die Technik des Dramas*, p. 95.

101 The beat is termed the smallest structural element of the screenplay by both Robert McKee and Linda Seger.

102 Freytag, *Die Technik des Dramas*, p. 156.

103 According to Frank Daniel, an item, a character or another element must appear three times to achieve dramatic energy.

104 See especially Stanislawski's book, *An Actor Prepares*.

105 The story that accompanies this motion picture (USA, 1957) is, however, that the writer-producer Budd Schulberg fired the director Nicholas Ray during the shoot, finished the picture himself and edited it. Cf. Bellour: *Das Entfalten der Emotionen*, in Brütsch, *et al.*, *Kinogefühle*, p. 88 f.

106 The American screenplay professor, Jeff Rush, represented this thesis in his inspirational lecture at the *Holden Scuola per le Techniche Narrative* in Torino.

The End: Application of Creative Screenwriting and Emotional Structure to the Complete Screenplay

1 The first limericks appeared around 1820 in England, but the rigid rhyme pattern existed earlier. The name is either derived from the Irish city of Limerick or from the Irish soldier song, "Will You Come Up to Limerick?"

2 An example of an English Limerick (unknown origin): "She was peeved and called him mister,/not because he came and kissed her,/but because, just before,/when she was out of the door,/this same mister kissed her sister."

3 Cf. Rodari, *The Grammar of Fantasy*, p. 64. Gianni Rodari, for example, has used the technique of limericks to invent stories.

4 A construct of Émile Benveniste from *Problèmes de linguistique générale*. The Russian formalists (Propp, and so on) termed this art of narrative *Sujet*.

5 Cf. Chion, *Techniken des Drehbuchschreibens*, p. 97.

6 Cf. McKee, *Story*, p. 224.

7 Aristoteles, *Poetics* 7/1451a.

8 Ibid., 8/1451a.

9 Chion, *Techniken des Drehbuchschreibens*, p. 100.

10 Rabenalt, *Filmdramaturgie*, p. 85

11 Concerning the accuracy of the term "epic," see the section: "Creative screenwriting in the context of prevailing theories of the drama and screenwriting."

12 Lynch, *Lynch on Lynch*, p. 304.

13 Forster, *Aspects of the Novel*.

14 Rabenalt, *Filmdramaturgie*, p. 24.

15 Truffaut, *Mr. Hitchcock*, p. 241.

16 The word pair "*eleos* and *phobos*" are reproduced in the different languages in different ways. For instance, in the German language they are reproduced

as "compassion and fear" since Lessing. Manfred Fuhrmann discovered that this translation was in error and that the word "*Eleos*" is best translated as "misery" or "emotion" while the word "*phobos*" is more appropriately translated as "shuddering" or "horror." Cf. Aristotle, *Poetics* p. 162 f.

17 Iakov, Ζητήματα Λογοτεχνικής Θεωρίας, p. 34 ff.
18 Ibid., p. 44.
19 Wygotski, *Psychologie der Kunst*, p. 241.
20 Rabenalt, *Filmdramaturgie*, p. 43.
21 Cf. Beckermann, *Dynamics of Drama: Theory and Method of Analysis*
22 Iakov, Ζητήματα Λογοτεχνικής Θεωρίας, p. 85.
23 Schneider, *Ein folkloristisches Straßentheater*, in Brütsch *et al.*, *Kinogefühle*, p. 145.
24 Aristotle, *Poetics* 11/1452a
25 Rabenalt, *Filmdramaturgie*, p. 44.
26 Under the notion of empathy, one understands in general the ability to empathize with another person cumulatively or analogously even if in a mostly weaker form mixed with one's own and other feelings. Cf. Brickmann, *Die Rolle der Empathie im Dokumentarfilm*, in Brütsch, *et al.*, *Kinogefühle*, p. 335.
27 Edward Branigan formulated it this way, "Narration is a process of calibrating states of knowledge." Schneider, *Ein folkloristisches Straßentheater*, in Brütsch *et al.*, *Kinogefühle*, p. 147.
28 Carrière/Bonitzer, *Praxis des Drehbuchschreibens*, p. 92.
29 Truffaut, *Mr. Hitchcock*, p. 245.
30 Brecht, *Schriften zur Literatur und Kunst*, p. 7.
31 Brecht, *Schriften zum Theater*, p. 36.
32 Vogler, *The Writer's Journey*, p. 227.
33 Seger, *Making a Good Script Great*, pg.p. 33.
34 Aristotles, *Poetics* 7/1450b.
35 Truffaut, *Mr. Hitchcock*, p. 245.
36 Haar, *L'oeuvre d'art*, p. 91.
37 Freytag, *The Technique of the Drama*, p. 73.
38 Iakov, Ζητήματα Λογοτεχνικής Θεωρίας, pp. 88.
39 Haar, *L'oeuvre d'art*, p. 61 ff., as well as the presentations of "tragic joy" in Nietzsche, *Geburt der Tragödie*, chapters 16, 17, 21, 22.
40 Haar, *L'oeuvre d'art*, p. 16. The reference points to a work of art in general where the writer represents the thesis that philosophy, especially of Heidegger and Merleau-Ponty, sees in art the paradigm of the divided truth of our existence or our relationship to the world, while already Nietzsche rescinded the old Platonic damnation.
41 Eder, *Die Wege der Gefühle*, in Brütsch, *et al.*, *Kinogefühle*, p. 228. Psychological network models of emotions from the field of cognition science oriented psychology makes it possible to comprehend this specific

connection. Jens Eder and Andreas Keil are currently working on applying these models to the area of film analysis.

42 Wulff, *Moral und Empathie im Kino*, in Brütsch *et al.*, *Band Kinogefühle*, p. 384.

43 Aristoteles, *Poetics* 1453a–1453b.

44 Iakov, Ζητήματα Λογοτεχνικής Θεωρίας, p. 69 ff.

45 Ibid., p. 69.

46 The term neo-realism was coined by Umberto Barbaro, who taught in the Centro Sperimentale di Cinematografia in Rome.

47 Zavattini, *Heute, heute, heute!*

48 Rabenalt, *Filmdramaturgie*, p. 95, 104. Of special interest in connection with neo-realism is the fact that while the opponents of the Aristotelian theory reproach it for formalism and moralism, the final and decisive step from the moral to the aesthetic was taken with Aristotle. Cf. Iakov, Ζητήματα Λογοτεχνικής Θεωρίας. The ethical dimension of film schools, like neo-realism, could also be seen as a step in the opposite direction.

49 Hegel, *Aesthetik*, p. 424.

50 Ibid., p. 429.

51 Rabenalt, *Filmdramaturgie*, p. 87

52 Mike Leigh frequently explained that he wants to show people with all their mistakes in his films and that he enjoys life in all its vulgarity.

53 Rabenalt, *Filmdramaturgie*; p. 95.

54 Ibid. p. 186.

55 Griffith was the first filmmaker who was interested in the thoughts of the characters. He mentioned the novels of Charles Dickens as a source of inspiration for the parallel montage and the close up.

56 Cf. Aristotle's remarks about style in the *Poetics* 1458a,18 ff., 1459a,12 ff., and not least his presentation concerning the metaphor (1459a, 5–13, 1459b, 35). The book of Boys-Stones, *Metaphor, Allegory and the Classical Tradition* is also of interest in this regard.

57 Rabenalt, *Filmdramaturgie*, p. 188 f.

58 Among the few films that have actually managed to approach the lyrical core would be Dovzhenko's film *Earth* (1930).

59 Carrière/Bonitzer, *Die Praxis des Drehbuchschreibens*, p. 144.

60 fabele, favele ([un]true stories, fairy tales, entertainment), borrowed from African fable (loose talk, chit chat, or gossip) or from the Latin fabula.

61 Like, for example, some of the scripts of Kusturicas films, who made *Underground* (screenplay: Dusan Kovacevic and Emir Kusturica's films) in 1995, to shatter the headiness of historic films through the use of alienation and grotesque comedy.

62 Rabenalt, *Filmdramaturgie*, p. 192.

63 Cocteau, *Geheimnisse der Schoenheit*, in: *Prosa*, p. 205.

64 Tarkovsky, *Die versiegelte Zeit*, p. 20 f.

65 Carrière/Bonitzer, *Praxis des Drehbuchschreibens*, p. 175.

66 Rabenalt, *Filmdramaturgie*, p. 104. As Rabenalt explains, Anton Chechkov's plays were a significant influence on the psychologically oriented American playwrights Eugen O'Neill, Thornton Wilder, Tennessee Williams and Arthur Miller with their psychological character portraits and de-dramatized fables.

67 The concept "planting" may be found in screenwriting literature in the 1920s (*Writer's Digest*, p. 97). Frank Daniel defined both concepts as follows: "Planting is an apparently offhand establishment of an idea, character, property, costume, set, etc., to be used more significantly later in the film. A payoff makes significant use of something previously planted, adds to the participation of the viewer and allows for poetic metaphors. If plants don't get paid off, the audience will be frustrated and disappointed." From class notes of a Frank Daniel lecture.

68 Freytag, *The Technique of the Drama*, p. 270.

69 In practice, the screenwriter must tarry for much too long a time in the first stage of development, i.e. the prose stage (exposé, treatment). This procedure is rather damaging for the story. Although prose helps the screenwriter make his intentions clear, these texts have "the disadvantage that they easily immobilize the imagination and that they make the continually necessary revision and editing more difficult." See Freytag, *The Technique of the Drama*, p. 274. Freytag concludes that one page can be completely sufficient for the treatment.

70 Rabenalt, *Filmdramaturgie*, p. 99.

71 Cf. Steven Johnson, *Everything Bad is Good for You*, p. 129.

72 Ibid. From an interview on Charlie Rose. p. 164.

In Place of an Epilogue: The Era of the Screenwriter

1 Thalberg was Head of Production at MGM from 1924 to 1933.

2 With the Film Academy's Evolution, *Quality Emerges Triumphant* at NYTimes.com

3 Birkenstock, *Autoren- und Drehbuchförderung in Deutschland*, p. 26.

4 The first attempts in this direction have already been undertaken. There is talk of simultaneous remakes.

5 The French word *auteur*, of course, also means "author." Since the author in that sense is obviously the screenwriter, which nobody denies, one could say that *auteur* in the case of the director might best be translated as "creator" or "causer."

6 Eick, *Drehbuchtheorien*, p. 240.

7 Ibid., p. 21.

8 The first article from Sarris on this subject appeared in the spring edition of the magazine *Film Culture*. Cf. Kipen, *The Schreiber theory*, p. 26.

9 Eick, *Drehbuchtheorien*, p. 22.

10 Even today, some organizations for directors call the director "the primary creator in a collaborative process," a paradox, actually.

11 Pauline Kael described how Orson Welles stole the credit from Herman Mankiewics in her book *Raising Kane* (1971) – for their collaborative work on *Citizen Kane*.

12 Richard Corliss attempted in his book, *Talking Pictures* (1973), to ferret out the subjects and idiosyncrasies of famous screenwriters, e.g. Ben Hecht, who worked together with Josef von Sternberg, Howard Hawks and Ernst Lubitsch.

13 Even today, most film students think that they are only "real" filmmakers if they direct and write the script, too. In reality, however, what happens is the opposite. Billy Wilder and Preston Sturges became directors to protect their scripts, so were first and foremost screenwriters. The same is true of Francis Ford Coppola, Cameron Crowe, Paul Schrader, Lawrence Kasdan, David Mamet, John Sayles, Kevin Smith, Paul Haggis, *et al.* We know all of them – not as screenwriters who directed pictures, but rather as directors who wrote their own scripts. Not every brilliant writer is a good director, just as not every brilliant director is a good writer.

14 The counter argument that then one must also name the director of photography, the actors and so on, cannot be taken seriously. Not because the writers and directors and maybe the composers are the only ones who create original works, while the others are dependent on their contributions, but rather because a film cannot be made without a script – at least in most cases.

15 Eick, *Drehbuchtheorien*, p. 23 f. Structuralism (de Saussure, Christian Metz) contributed wide-ranging, scientific changes, as did deconstructuralism later in the sense that they countered the romantic ideal of the *auteur* theory as they revealed many other levels of generating meaning. Semiotics in the end makes clear that not just the writer, but also the reader or receiver generates meaning, and Roland Barthes even propagated the "death of the author." His view was that meaning was created by an act of the reader.

16 In this context, it is important to add, however, that our current understanding of artistic creation has its roots in the eighteenth century, the same as our construct of the modern copyright (the Englithenment in France, the cult of genius of Sturm and Drang, romantic art theory). The highly esteemed revision of a work of art in the European Middle Ages recalls the contemporary plagiarism in modern Asian culture. A sense of injustice did not exist there; quite the opposite, the more successful one copied a master, the more praise was expected. At the beginning of the renaissance the idea of the individual took center stage and the author acquired rights that rewarded the creator for his work of art. In the eighteenth century, the rights for mental achievement (and the concept of immaterial ownership) were articulated.

17 Cf. Wandtke/Bullinger, *Urheberrecht*, vor §§ 12 ff. Rz. 8.l

18 Jay A. Fernandez, European writers issue a manifesto, in *Scriptland*, Special to *The Times*, February 21, 2007.

19 Nehamas, *Kultur, Kunst und Poetik in Platons Politeia.*

20 Bohr, *Die urheberrechtliche Rolle des Drehbuchautors*, in: *Entwicklungslinien in Recht und Wissenschaft*, p. 141–162.

21 Ibid., p. 150.

22 Again and again, attempts have been made to print original screenplays. The hope that the screenplay can be considered as analogue to the theater play lurks behind the attempt to start a literary tradition in its own right. Unfortunately, only a very few original screenplays appear in book form. See Dennis Eick: *Drehbuchtheorien*, p. 18 and p. 151. The magazine, *Scenario*, whose editions offered three scripts per edition, is no longer in publication.

23 Aristotle, *Poetics* 1450b, 1453b,3–5, 1462a, 17. Cf. Including Iakov, Ζητήματα Λογοτεχνικής Θεωρίας, p. 44.

24 Ibid., 1455a,22–32, 1459b,24–6, and Halliwell, *Aristotle's Poetics*, S. 337 ff.

25 In the European script development system the writer often works for months on treatments until nothing remains of the original idea.

Index